Redeeming
the Time

Redeeming the Time

A Political Theology
of the Environment

Stephen Bede Scharper

Continuum · New York

1998

The Continuum Publishing Company
370 Lexington Avenue
New York, NY 10017

Printed in the United States of America

Library of Congress Cataloging-in-Publication Data

Scharper, Stephen B.
    Redeeming the time : a political theology of the environment /
Stephen Bede Scharper
            p.   cm.
    Includes bibliographical references and index.
    ISBN 0-8264-1134-7 (paperback : alk. paper)
    Ecology—religious aspects—Christianity.   I. Title.
BT695.5.S27   1998
261.8'.32—dc21   96-53591

An abbreviated version of chapter 2 appeared in *Cross Currents* 42,
no. 2 (summer 1994) and appears here with permission.

To my father,
Philip J. Scharper,
who taught me
to look for
the next horizon

See then that ye walk circumspectly, not as fools, but as wise,
Redeeming the time, because the days are evil.

–Ephesians 5:15–16

Contents

Acknowledgments

Many voices, visions, eyes, and hands have helped shape this study, and many people deserve more thanks than space affords. I wish, nonetheless, to thank Gregory Baum for his supportive, careful, and incisive assistance throughout this project. I am also indebted to Douglas John Hall for his helpful comments on sections of this work, and to Will Friesen for his friendship and guidance through the swelling stream of literature on religion, theology, and the environment.

David Burrell, C.S.C., Mary Jo Leddy, John Mihevc, Rebecca Cunningham, Jay B. McDaniel, George Howard, Andrew Weigert, and Hank Schlau provided helpful, constructive responses to portions of the text, and I remain indebted to all of them for their supportive suggestions. I am also grateful to Justus George Lawler, Evander Lomke, and Martin Rowe of Continuum for their interest in this project and their patience during its "gestation."

The wisdom and generosity of Thomas Berry, C.P., have inspired and informed this work in multiple ways, as have the contributions of Brian Swimme, who, in a conversation several years ago, raised the theological question of the role of the human in light of environmental concerns, a question that infuses this study.

Several institutions and granting agencies have also contributed to this project, including Fonds pour la Formation de Chercheurs et l'Aide à la Researche and the J. M. McConnell and Max Binz Fellowship Committees of McGill University. I am also indebted to Jennifer Warlick and the financial support of the Institute for Scholarship in the Liberal Arts at the University of Notre Dame.

Most importantly, however, I would like to thank my wife, Hilary Cunningham, whose brilliance and creativity as a scholar are matched only by the breadth and graciousness of her person.

Knowing Our Place

Altered Landscapes and Altered Roles

For several years, I have taught an undergraduate course on religion and the environment. We often begin the course with a story, the approximately three-thousand-year-old creation story of Genesis. For some students, this is their first encounter with one of the most powerful stories ever told, a story that in many ways lies at the heart of the contemporary controversy over Western humanity's relationship to the environment. The students are attentive to the language of humans having "dominion . . . over all the earth" and of the divine injunction for humanity to "fill the earth and subdue it" (Gen. 1:28). Yet they also note the sanguine refrain after phases of creation: "God saw that it was good." They note that God discerned goodness in creation "days" before humans even entered the scene, suggesting to some that creation, from God's perspective, had inherent value apart from humanity's appreciation or exploitation of its gifts.

We then fast-forward to another story, a front-page news item from the 8 May 1992 *Montreal Gazette*. The banner headline declares: "Environment Kills 35,000 Children Daily: UN." The story, based on a UN study, *The State of the World's Economy, 1972–1992*, presents a deeply disturbing statistic: thirty-five thousand children die each day owing to environmentally related diseases. These diseases, the story continues, stem largely from polluted water, contaminated land and air, and poor sanitation facilities. The piece notes that these dying children, all under the age of five, reside principally in the Third World or nations of the South, where environmental regulations, when they do exist, often go unenforced. The story underscores the sobering fact that environmental pollution takes a macabre social toll — the lives of tens of thousands of children who die before their time. Highlighting the parallel rise in world poverty and ecological destruction, the UN report intimates that environmental concern, at root, is as much about saving children as it is about saving whales.

This study, like the class, is a journey between these two stories. In this work I consider the relationship of the two narratives and reflect upon the paths and impulses that led the human family from God's original creation to our current environmental and social tragedies. Through this journey, I have come to realize that such devastating statistics merely scratch the surface of our current ecological dilemma.

In the crepuscule of the twentieth century we are experiencing, as a human community, what has been somewhat controvertedly termed a "global ecological crisis." Acid rain, measurable global warming, rain forest destruction, accelerated species extinction, ozone depletion, a proliferation of toxic waste in our soil, seas, and skies are but a handful of the most infamous manifestations of this crisis.[1] The "docents" of the environmental movement have raised the stark possibility that much of this destruction is irreversible and that we of the human family may be rendering planet Earth, our home, incapable of sustaining human life. This has led to a comprehensive ontological, ethical, and religious reexamination of what it means to be human and what our relationship to the nonhuman world should be.

As an educator, I witness students, mainly in their late teens and early twenties, grappling with these perturbing realities and trying to integrate them into their own life trajectories. As I watch this, I experience many emotions — compassion, anger at the sources of this devastation bequeathed to their generation, and self-criticism of my own role in ecological destruction. I have ultimately been left, however, with hope in the persons and struggles charting a different path, one of sustainability and mutuality rather than despoliation and plunder.

This hope centers on both understanding and transforming the human relationship with the environment or, more accurately, the nonhuman world. Theorists from across the board analyzing the human-nonhuman relationship have been compelled to critique not only their own traditions in this regard but also the entire Western conception of the modern self. They are probing notions of the role of the human emerging from the Enlightenment, the Industrial Revolution, and modern technology and science and are critiquing these understandings in a burgeoning environmental literature. The current ecological crisis is calling into question conceptions of modern identity in which humans are characterized as distinct from and masters over the natural world. The result is an emerging paradigm of the self, one that stands in critical dialogue with modernity.

A Growing Christian Chorus

As is sometimes the case, mainline theology and churches can be dilatory in responding to social movements that have achieved prominence in society as a whole. The environmental movement in North America is a vibrant case in point. Though theologian Joseph Sittler had addressed the issues of ecological devastation as early as 1961, he was, as a Christian theologian, flying solo. While a major development in environmental awareness was being fashioned in the early 1960s, this emergence was not immediately reflected in mainstream theology.

The secular environmental movement received a remarkable boost with the publication of Rachel Carson's *Silent Spring* (1962). Indeed, Carson's work is "generally credited with beginning the modern era of environmental concern" (de Steiguer 1997: i). A biologist and former editorial director for the U.S. Fish and Wildlife Service, Carson had already been recognized as a gifted scientist and writer with her best-selling work, *The Sea around Us* (1951). In *Silent Spring,* Carson not only documented the baleful effects of DDT and other pesticides, or "biocides," as she called them, on birds, fish, and humans but also articulated a new paradigm for the dynamic of nature. Unlike Dr. Robert

13

White-Stevens of American Cyanamid, who vociferously assailed Carson's study and claimed that "man" was "at war" with the "enemy" of insects threatening agriculture and human survival, Carson painted a vista of nature whose leitmotif was not "warfare" and competition but interrelationship and cooperation.[2] Though the model of nature as interrelated and cooperative may seem commonplace today, it was virulently attacked by U.S. chemical companies and scientists of Carson's day.[3] As sociologist Riley E. Dunlap (1991) has argued, environmental concern in the United States and Canada developed dramatically in the mid-1960s and reached a peak with the inaugural Earth Day in 1970; while the movement experienced a marked decline through the rest of 1970s, it intensified in the mid-1980s with another high-point reached at Earth Day 1990.

In addition to Rachel Carson's book and the widespread attention it received both in the Kennedy White House and the U.S. Congress, which enacted legislation outlawing the use of DDT as a result of her findings, other factors contributed to the growth of environmental awareness. In the mid- to late 1960s, the Sierra Club and other conservation organizations were appealing to a broader audience for their initiatives, such as saving the Grand Canyon from development. This was paralleled by a marked increase in outdoor recreation and vacations, which was reflected in increased membership in conservation organizations. Moreover, the U.S. Congress began passing legislation meant to preserve wilderness areas and endangered species as well as improve air and water quality, leading to the passage of the National Environmental Policy Act (NEPA) in 1969 (see Dunlap 1991: 287–88).

The modern environmental movement in North America was fueled also by significant publications following *Silent Spring*, such as Paul Ehrlich's *The Population Bomb* (1968), Barry Commoner's *The Closing Circle: Nature, Man, and Technology* (1971), and *The Limits to Growth: A Report for the Club of Rome's Project on the Predicament of Mankind* (1972) (de Steiguer 1997: 1–3). The increasing awareness of ecological destruction helped spawn a growing chorus of Christian voices attempting to respond to the crisis, as well as acknowledge Christianity's role in our current ecological state.[4]

Christian theologians and activists have raised a myriad of questions in light of environmental concerns: What is the proper role of the human, from a Christian vantage, in light of the ecological crisis? How has Christianity colluded with destructive Western approaches to nature? Is Christianity itself antithetical to the environment? Are there aspects of the Christian tradition that nurture a responsible environmental ethic? What is the "vocation" of the Christian in light of ecological despoliation?

The responses to these queries are as wide-ranging and as complex as are the questions themselves. Christian ecological reflections have created a literary stream that has cut through rocky intellectual terrain and splintered into many tributaries. This work attempts to chart a course through this swelling literature.

The Context for the Christian Ecological Debate

Cultural historian Lynn White Jr., in his now famous 1967 *Science* article, "The Historical Roots of Our Ecologic Crisis," prompted immediate and widespread Christian reflection on the environmental crisis. Claiming that the Judeo-Christian tradition was the world's most "anthropocentric" religion, White laid the blame for Western technology's exploitative relationship with nature at the doorstep of the Judeo-Christian heritage. To put it baldly and succinctly, White claimed that there had been a "murder," not homicide but biocide, and that the smoking guns were to be found in Western synagogues and churches.

Though Lynn White's 1967 article in *Science* can be regarded as the "starting gun," if you will, in the race to reevaluate and perhaps refashion Christianity in light of our ecological crisis, the enormity and magnitude of the emergency, it can be suasively argued, would have eventually spawned such a radical questioning in the Christian tradition with or without White's volatile commentary. The proliferation of religious publications, workshops, videos, books, and institutes centered on environmental issues is a testimony to the significance of environmental concern in religious circles. Christians have joined with other faith communities in such organizations as the National Religious Partnership for the Environment (headquartered in New York), the Elliot Allen Institute for Ecology and Theology (Toronto), the Program on Ecology, Justice, and Faith (Princeton, N.J.), the North American Coalition on Religion and Ecology (Washington, D.C.), and the Justice, Peace, and the Integrity of Creation initiative of the World Council of Churches (WCC), to name but a few.

In theological and religious debates, as suggested, a crucial question has been the role of the human in light of humanity's hand in ecological despoliation. Because of the centrality of Christ, truly God and truly human, Christian theology regards the understanding of the human as one of its essential tasks. In the wake of the present environmental crisis, the dominant self-understanding of the human is presently being challenged and rethought by Christians.

Dieter T. Hessel, a prime articulator of the Christian "eco-justice" movement, writes of the prominence of the human role in light of ecological concerns:

> Ever since Francis Bacon asserted the modern ultra-anthropocentric agenda of conquering nature for human convenience, technologists, economists, politicians and theologians have shown confusion about the human vocation. Are we here for creation's sake, or does it exist for us, particularly our kind? What is our responsibility to future generations, as well as everykind now alive? For the sake of both human and otherkind, members of this tool-making species that does ethics must learn to revalue the natural world, to welcome diverse human cultures and animal and plant species, while working for a just and sustainable community. (Hessel 1995: xiii)

This concern for the "vocation" of the human is also underscored by Canadian theologian Douglas John Hall:

16

> Perhaps no question plagues the contemporary spirit so much as the question of the human *telos* — the "chief end of Man," as the catechists of the past phrased it. "What the hell are people *for?*" asks the American novelist Kurt Vonnegut, with characteristic bluntness — and he speaks for the whole epoch. (Hall 1993: 233)

This study is an attempt to contribute to this larger effort of examining the role of the human in Christian theological responses to the ecological "crisis," a question that is surfacing as a paramount concern in this emergent literature.

A prime example of such a rethinking is the work of cultural historian Thomas Berry, a self-designated "geologian." Berry, who represents an important trend among Christian responses to the environmental crisis, offers a novel interpretation of the place of the human in the cosmos. Claiming that the human agent is both the principal cause of the ecological crisis and the principal hope for its salutary resolution, Berry places the human in the driver's seat, as it were, of geological and cosmological evolution.

In this work I examine how the role of the human is an inherent problematic not only in Thomas Berry's work (considered in chapter 4) but in other Christian ecological literature as well. I review some of the principal categories or paradigms of Christian ecological literature, such as the Gaia theory,[5] process theology, new cosmology, ecofeminism, and liberation theology. While an initial investigation suggests that all of these paradigms do, in a sense, view the role of the human as a principal problematic, all of them approach this in distinct and often inchoate but complementary ways.

All these approaches, I contend, make important contributions to a renewed understanding of human interaction with nature. Yet each model, on its own, seems somewhat incomplete in its portrait of the human. On the one hand, a certain segment of this religious and theological literature diminishes or undervalues the role of the human in our ecological destiny. Influenced by deep ecology and the Gaia theory, both of which ascribe a minimalist role for the human in their respective schemas, some of the

17

religious discourse lacks a fully nuanced understanding of and appreciation for the importance of the human agent in both the razing and reclamation of the life-systems of the planet. On the other hand, much of this literature neglects to examine seriously humanity's historical context, which includes economic, political, and social dimensions.

Through a study of these paradigms for approaching the environmental crisis, this work explores the idea that only a theology that views the human agent as a principal actor in both the devastation and reclamation of the life-systems of the planet can be a viable ecological theology. With the reading assistance of liberation theology from Latin America, with its emphasis on solidarity, a preferential option for the destitute and downtrodden, and societal transformation, this work raises the possibility of a political theology of the environment. Such a theology embraces the social, cultural, political, economic, and moral dimensions of the role of the human in light of the ecological crisis. This theological approach, however, strives to be self-critical and, at its best, remains open to the insights of other models, such as those offered by process theologians, new cosmologists, Gaia theorists, and ecofeminists.

This work, then, attempts to systematize and scrutinize the role of the human, the theological anthropology, in selected Christian approaches to environmental concerns. To do this, I have chosen paradigms in environmental literature that I hope shed particular insight into this larger quest to explore the vocation of the human in light of ecological decimation. This selective analysis thus includes paradigms that are often unanalyzed in overviews of the literature or whose individual architects are analyzed apart from the intellectual systems they represent.

This approach is novel, I believe, for at least two additional reasons. First, its focus on theological anthropology, the role of the human, in the selected paradigms considered is unique among sustained treatments of Christian ecological literature. Second, it attempts to review the literature from a vantage based on some enduring insights from Latin American liberation theology, insights that can help shape the contours of a political theology of the environment. The analysis, therefore, does not simply fashion a typology; rather it critiques Christian environmental literature from a particular perspective, a liberationist paradigm, one that takes the preferential option for the poor seriously, emphasizes solidarity and praxis as much as theory, and argues that the call to justice in personal and societal relations is a "constitutive" dimension of being Christian. This perspective, when trained upon environmental issues, leads to a political theology of the environment. Thus, this work strives to represent analysis not for its own sake but for the sake of social transformation — in this case, a transformed way of being human in light of ecological concern.

Itinerary

While this study does not provide an exhaustive map of the sundry directions taken in Christian ecological theology, it does consider the salient tributaries of this literature. Consequently, each chapter corresponds to one of these major paradigms, focusing on its approach to the environmental crisis and delineating, in particular, the role of the human within it.

Chapter 1 surveys the contours of Christian environmental literature — up to the present — engendered in part by the publication of Lynn White's accusatory article (1967). These responses, I suggest, fall within three categories: the "apologetic," the "constructive," and the "listening." While the apologetic approach tends to dismiss White's argument as biblically shallow and historically naive, the constructive approach acknowledges a certain Christian culpability for participation in or insensitivity to environmental destruction. It also suggests a retrieval of ecologically liberating ideas and motifs from the Judeo-Christian legacy. The listening approach extends the debate by transcending White's perspective, leaving Christians with a new openness to the environment and consequently new opportunities for revelation.

Having sketched a broad overview of Christian ecological literature in light of the Lynn White debate, I turn to specific approaches. (Those less interested in the details of this theological debate may wish to skim or skip this section entirely.)

Chapter 2 examines the Gaia theory of atmospheric chemist James Lovelock and microbiologist Lynn Margulis, which suggests that the earth is a living, self-regulating organism. The theory postulates that humanity plays a very modest role in the overall workings of the planet, a position that, I argue, is at odds with both Christian theology and historical evidence.

Chapter 3 considers the process ecological theology of John B. Cobb Jr., Jay B. McDaniel, and Catherine Keller, which builds upon the insights of mathematician and philosopher Alfred North Whitehead (1861–1947). Suggesting that all reality is in a process of becoming, these theologians raise provocative insights concerning humanity's interrelationship with nature, animal rights, and Christian responsibility toward the environment. The prospects and problems of uniting their approach with a political theology are explored.

Chapter 4 surveys the striking terrain uncovered by what has become known as "the new cosmology," whose chief architects are cultural historian Thomas Berry and mathematical cosmologist Brian Swimme. Claiming that the universe is the primary source of revelation and that the human is the locus where the universe becomes aware of itself, Berry and Swimme provide a complex notion of humanity, viewing it as united with all matter by the "big bang" of some fifteen to twenty billion years ago and yet at the center of the universe's contemporary self-consciousness. This multilayered understanding of the human is also scrutinized from a political theological vantage.

Chapter 5 looks at the burgeoning ecofeminist movements as articulated by such theologians as Rosemary Radford Ruether and Sallie McFague and by the physicist Vandana Shiva. As a social ecology, ecofeminism directly links political and ecological analysis, noting a correspondence between the oppression of nature and the oppression of women in both the First and Third Worlds. As a form of political theology, it promotes a notion of transformation and liberation, though its exponents vary widely in their understanding of the human role in light of a domineering patriarchy. These sundry notions of the human, as well as ecofeminist understandings of nature, are highlighted and critiqued.

Chapter 6 investigates novel developments in Latin American liberation theology as it addresses ecological decimation. Brazilian theologian Leonardo Boff has spearheaded this reflection, showing a prominent parallel between oppression of the poor and oppression of the earth. While also critiquing the highly individualistic and domineering modern understanding of the self emerging from the Enlightenment, Boff and other liberation theologians, such as Julio de Santa Ana and Ivone Gebara, have in recent years been paying particular attention to the victims of modernization: indigenous peoples, women, tropical rain forests, and natural biodiversity. Their insights involve the element of praxis and commitment to ecological theology while also incorporating contributions of other approaches.

The conclusion, chapter 7, examines the interface of a liberative, critical theology and emerging ecological theology. Here, I explore how a political theology of the environment — one that takes into account economic, social, cultural, and political concerns — may be a useful, indeed, an essential, addition to Christian ecological literature.

From Science to Spirit

While contemporary science is thankfully highlighting the effects of human pollution and ecological destruction on the planet, the ecological crisis is about more than just ozone depletion, chloroflorocarbon (CFC) emissions, and PCBs in fish. This crisis is not simply a scientific or technical one. To be sure, the installation of industrial smokestack scrubbers, the use of biodegradable cleansers and lubricants, and the advent of recycling are all sanguine and important developments in our social behavior. Yet it is increasingly apparent that our new behavior must be grounded in new values, a new understanding of the self, and a fundamentally altered understanding of our relationship with our environment if we are to have a sustainable future. We are being summoned,

21

in short, to a new ontology, a novel way of being human and relating to the nonhuman world.

The so-called environmental crisis, thus, is ultimately a spiritual crisis, a point made with some trepidation by former U.S. senator and subsequent vice president Al Gore in his work *Earth in the Balance* (1992). While Gore is reluctant to name this as a spiritual dilemma, he cannot avoid the designation given the scope of our distress. Reflecting on the use of the term "spiritual" in this context, he asks: "What other word describes the collection of values and assumptions that determine our basic understanding of how we fit into the universe?" (12). Such a crisis, Gore concludes, demands a spiritual response. This ecological crisis, then, challenges us to find a new way of "knowing our place" as we venture into the next millennium.

As intimated, this work explores political theology as a helpful guidepost in this quest. Such a theology seeks to integrate the insights of environmentally sensitive behavior within the framework of environmentally grounded values. Ultimately, this is a theology that draws from social analysis and critique and builds upon a sense of justice informed by the Judeo-Christian tradition. This approach suggests that this new ontology to which we are called requires not only a new self-understanding but a new way of acting and reflecting on that action, a new praxis, as it were. Our Christian solidarity with the destitute and oppressed, our "action on behalf of justice,...[which] is a constitutive dimension of the preaching of the Gospel" (the words are those of the 1971 World Synod of Catholic Bishops' statement "Justice in the World"), must be expanded to embrace a solidarity with the natural world, a realm of which we are a mysterious and integral part — not as lords and masters but as potent and complex participants.

We are learning that the fate of the earth is our fate; the destiny of the life-systems of the planet is our destiny; and solidarity both with the oppressed and the poor and with nature has more to do with our own spiritual, physical, and ecological well-being — and redemption — than we had ever before imagined.

Chapter 1

Christian Theological Responses to the Ecological Crisis

An Overview

This chapter briefly identifies three branches of Christian ecological discourse that have emerged in Christian environmental
theology since 1967, the year Lynn White Jr. accused the Judeo-
Christian tradition of helping foster environmental destruction.[1]
This overview represents neither an exhaustive survey of the
progress of Christian environmental theology nor even a thorough review of its main practitioners since the publication of
White's polemic. Rather, it is a typology that strives to help situate some of the main currents of this literature. I depict these
approaches as "apologetic," "constructive," and "listening" and
attempt to indicate the overarching theological anthropology, the
role of the human, within each approach.

While a number of surveys of Christian ecological literature
have been assembled during the 1990s, none of them, with the
exception of the brief report of the Episcopal Commission for
Social Affairs of the Canadian Conference of Catholic Bishops
(1993), examines the role of the human in this burgeoning field.
Moreover, none of them adopts a liberationist perspective in
their lens on the literature. Environmentalist and philosopher
Max Oelschlaeger, for example, breaks down the literature according to political attitudes — conservative, moderate, liberal,
radical, and alternative (Oelschlaeger 1994: 118–83). Theologian
John F. Haught, interestingly, divides this unfolding literature into

"apologetic" and "sacred" and then advocates the need for a third approach, which he calls "eschatological" (Haught 1993). Peter W. Bakken, Joan Gibb Engel, and J. Ronald Engel (1995) take a historical and thematic approach to the linking of ecology, faith, and justice concerns into the "ecojustice" movement, as developed principally, but not exclusively, in Protestant and non-Catholic Christianity. The Justice, Peace, and the Integrity of Creation initiative of the WCC is one of the most vivid examples of this nexus.

The first response explored in this typology, the "apologetic" approach, I argue, directly counters Lynn White's argument, suggesting White has in the main misread the Christian tradition. The authors in this camp attempt to refute White's charges largely from within a Christian context, utilizing biblical scholarship and Christian tradition in framing a response. This model sees the role of the human primarily in relationship to the Christian community and church traditions.

The "constructive" approach, which involves the majority of those responding to White's critique, acknowledges traces of validity in White's analysis, accepting some Christian culpability in ecological destruction. In addition, it takes ecological concerns seriously and attempts to adduce an environmentally responsive theology, suggesting images, metaphors, and other motifs in the Judeo-Christian legacy that may be fertile and inspirational for environmental theology. This model sees the role of the human primarily in relationship to the worldwide human community and seeks to respond to a troubled human community in the midst of ecological peril.

The "listening" approach does not concern itself directly with the Lynn White controversy but rather takes much of his critique for granted. Building less upon the Judeo-Christian tradition and Scripture than the other two approaches, this framework strives to nurture a religious consciousness that "listens" to nature and creation itself. Thus, this approach sees the role of the human to be in relationship not primarily with the church or society but with nature and the cosmos itself. Its principal dialogue partners are neither Scripture, church tradition, nor even social science but rather the natural sciences and non-Christian religious and cultural resources, as well as nature itself.

There is, of course, a necessary "artificiality" that accompanies any such categorization of such a swollen and swelling body of literature; certain authors write from several vantages, and there are threads that weave through all three categories. Thus, the creation and delineation of such a schema are often ambiguous and unsatisfying enterprises. Nevertheless, such a typology of the major tangents of ecological literature may be useful in ascertaining how a theological anthropology is being hewn in this vast and diversified intellectual landscape.

While this field of environmental theology had begun to be cultivated several years before White's article, most commentators concur that White's indictment of the Judeo-Christian tradition's hand in ecological destruction significantly shaped the development and tenor of this emergent literature.[2] Each of the works considered in this chapter forms part of a larger reassessment of fundamental Western ethical and religious values engendered by environmental degradation. The typology employed attempts to provide a general outline that indicates that the role or vocation of the human — that is, a theological anthropology — becomes a critical concern in the ecological literature; this more specific locus, the role of the human, will be treated in the subsequent chapters, each of which focuses on a distinctive ecological paradigm.

Reassessing the Christian Tradition: Lynn White Jr.

Much systematic Christian reflection on environmental issues traces its provenance to the aforementioned article written by cultural historian Lynn White Jr.[3] In the article, White attempts to uncover the Western, Christian origins of the ecological crisis. Given the significance of this article in helping shape Christian ecological reflection, an overview of its argument appears warranted.

White begins his critique by exposing what he feels are the presuppositions underlying modern technology and science, illustrating that successful technology emerges from the West, not the East, and it has been gaining steam ever since Copernicus began charting the heavens. Western technology advocated a dominance over and a "ruthlessness toward" nature, he argues, as evinced by the scratch plow of European peasants and the medieval move from a seasonally based to a harvest-based calendar.

What did Christianity contribute to this emerging technological worldview? White contends that Christianity, as the ideological and spiritual engine behind Western culture, enhanced this rapacious regard for nature. The Judeo-Christian tradition proclaimed that all of creation was wrought simply for humanity's benefit. Made in the image of God, humans, in the Judeo-Christian ethos, saw all of creation as set apart and therefore instrumental and human-serving. (Here White's exegesis is somewhat threadbare.)[4] Such a perspective leads to White's scathing claim that "Christianity is the most anthropocentric religion the world has ever seen." This critique forms part of White's overarching claim that the Middle Ages played a determining role in establishing Western technological dominance, aided by the distinctively activist character of Western Christianity.

Christianity, in an attempt to crush animism, White avers, cut down the sacred trees of the pagans. It fueled and fused with the emerging Western science and worked "hand on ax," so to speak, to subjugate the earth. As an antidote to this crisis, White proclaims that we must either fashion a new religion or recast our old ones. His suggestion is that Christians should adopt Saint Francis of Assisi as the patron saint of ecology — a step taken by Pope John Paul II in 1980. Francis, according to White, spoke of humanity's equality with all creation rather than its dominance over it, introducing a refreshing humility of the human species within Christianity.[5]

Interestingly, White, in one sense, attempts on a much more limited scale to do with Christianity and the ecological crisis what sociologist Max Weber had done with Protestantism and capitalism a century before. Whereas Weber, in his *Protestant Ethic and the Spirit of Capitalism*, had attempted to show the congruencies between the rise of the Protestant ethos in Europe

and the emergence of capitalism, White's purpose is more ambitious. He seeks to show the causal connection, not just the
congruencies, between environmental degradation and the Judeo-
Christian heritage. Whether or not he achieved his goal, his
arguments have touched off both defensive responses from Christian theologians concerning the complexity of the Judeo-Christian
message about the environment, as well as the exodus of Christian environmentalists toward other more allegedly "ecologically
friendly" faiths.

It must be observed, however, that White offers a chiefly
cultural or "idealistic" cause of the present crisis, jettisoning an-
tecedent theories, such as that of Karl Polanyi, that stressed a
"materialistic" or social and economic cause. Such materialistic
causes of ecological destruction are of great concern to social
ecologists, as we shall see especially in liberation theology (see
chapter 7). White's claim that Christianity has been a principal
progenitor of those ideas and values that have resulted in the de-
basing of nature formed the vortex of the ensuing controversy
within Christian and ecological movements.[6] One author who
furthered White's critique was John Passmore, whose work *Man's
Responsibility for Nature* (1974) sees Judeo-Christianity, in conjunction with the advent of the Scientific Revolution, producing
a perduring, legitimating ethos for environmental destruction.
Moreover, Passmore sees little environmental support coming
from organized religion, for it has generally condoned, he asserts,
the economic growth model that has fueled Western capitalism
(Passmore 1974: 3–40; Oelschlaeger 1994: 25). White's position
on Christianity's ecological culpability is not shared by most of
those represented in this overview, but some are more interested
in refuting White's claim than are others, as we shall see.

All of the theological and religious authors in this sampling are,
however, somehow involved in the common project of "reinventing tradition," a term coined by British historian Eric Hobsbawm
(see Hobsbawn and Ranger, eds., 1983). That is to say, all are involved in a search for a Christian discourse that has one foot in
the past (tradition) and yet speaks in a fresh and vital way to the
present ecological condition (invention). All are trying to discern,

27

to varying degrees, the elements of the Christian heritage that are germane to our present threatened moment.

An "Apologetic" Approach

As mentioned, the apologetic approach seeks to defend the Judeo-Christian tradition in light of Lynn White's critique, culling from biblical scholarship and church tradition to refute many of White's claims. In other words, it seeks to defend the Judeo-Christian tradition from within the tradition for those who embrace that tradition. Some of the work of Robin Attfield, Thomas Sieger Derr, and H. Paul Santmire is emblematic of this approach and will be treated below.[7]

Robin Attfield

Robin Attfield, professor of philosophy at University College in Cardiff, England, adopts an almost defensive posture in light of Lynn White's critique (see Attfield 1983a). Though useful in showing the limitations and shortcomings of White's analysis, Attfield's early contribution remains confined in some sense to the parameters of the Lynn White/Christian culpability debate. As suggested, according to White, a rapacious Western technology has been loosed upon the environment, and the Christian tradition "bears a huge burden of guilt" for its destructive wake. Attfield is part of the intellectual team defending that tradition.

Aiming to rectify certain claims of Lynn White, as well as commentaries by John Passmore (1974) and William Coleman (1976)[8] concerning the androcentrism of Christianity, Attfield sifts through biblical, patristic, and medieval evidence showing the centrality of stewardship and cooperation with nature in the Christian theological tradition. Attfield contends that there is much evidence that is eschewed or underplayed by these assaults. He thus sets out to reveal more benign approaches to nature within the Judeo-Christian tradition.

Attfield acknowledges that while it is important to underscore what needs to be rejected within the tradition, unnuanced critiques only serve to delegitimate the Christian legacy. This could lead, he argues, to a forgoing of Christian resources that could actually support core — and ecologically beneficial — Christian attitudes (1983a: 369).[9]

Attfield reviews the main premises of Lynn White's argument and then shows how Passmore and Coleman, with slight alterations, essentially support the thrust of White's critique. For Attfield, White overstates Christianity's impact on Western society's attitude toward nature (1983a: 370). Attfield further charges that White fails to prove many of his claims, for example, that the medieval use of the plow was ecologically disastrous or ethically reprehensible.

While acknowledging that Passmore disagrees with White's contention that the Hebrew Scriptures are unequivocally exploitative toward nature, Attfield does assert that Passmore sees Christianity as having "despotic" attitudes toward the created world. Passmore, according to Attfield, does not discern the stewardship notion in the Christian tradition until the work of Sir Matthew Hale (1609–79), revealing Passmore's blindness to earlier Christian strains of the stewardship motif. Attfield contends that Coleman to a certain degree subscribes to Lewis Moncrief's critique of White as articulated in "The Cultural Basis of Our Environmental Crisis" (Moncrief 1970). In this essay, Moncrief notes that many non-Christian civilizations also denigrated the environment and suggests capitalism played a more decisive role in environmental plunder than did Christianity. Moncrief also rejects White's critique concerning the medieval period (Attfield 1983a: 372). Coleman, too, rejects White's analysis of the medieval period but points to the allegedly mechanistic thought of William Derham (1657–1735) and other figures to show that Christianity did indeed contribute to the global ecological crisis by bestowing its blessing on an emerging capitalist system (Attfield 1983a: 371).

Attfield attempts to counter Passmore and Coleman by reviewing biblical, patristic, and medieval evidence. He argues that, *pace* White, the Hebrew Scriptures do not suggest that all the created world exists solely to serve humanity (1983a: 373). Moreover, Attfield notes that, while the Hebrew Scriptures do indeed seem to reject the sanctity of nature, they also include restrictions on the use of forests (Lev. 19:23) and animals (Prov. 12:10), in contradistinction to some of the claims made by White and Passmore. Attfield further argues that the Hebrew notion of dominion, as it relates to kingship, involves accountability and responsibility, and not mere exploitation. Attfield also asserts that the New Testament manifests a similar concern for animals (see Matt. 10:29; Luke 14:5) and creation, in harmony with the Hebraic perspective.

Though White does draw a distinction between the soaring piety of the Orthodox East and the more pragmatic spirituality of the West, Attfield contends that Christian attitudes were much more varied than White and Passmore attest. With allusions to Basil, Chrysostom, and Justin, Attfield attempts to lay bare a deep concern for animals among the church fathers.[10]

Regarding Reformation thought, Attfield contends that, long before Sir Matthew Hale in the 1670s, Calvin expressed forcefully a notion of stewardship. Attfield, in addition, attempts to nuance Passmore's rather harsh reading of Descartes's attitudes toward animals (1983a: 381) and rebuts Coleman's assessment of Derham's insensitivity toward nature. While Attfield concedes that while Derham may have been excessively eager to "bless" capitalism, he also contends that Derham's celebration of human industry does not necessarily mean that he would support extensive deforestation and pollution of the earth (1983a: 384).

Attfield concludes that Christian attitudes toward nature have not, as a rule, been exploitative, despite the claims of White, Passmore, and Coleman. Indeed, he points toward Western civilization's almost sacred belief in the inevitability of progress as having a much more pernicious and powerful effect on the environment than Christianity ever could. The Judeo-Christian tradition, he avers, has never maintained that humanity has the right to treat animals or nature in a careless or selfish manner and concludes that the notion of stewardship is a cornerstone, rather than a sidelight, of the Christian church.

The thrust of Attfield's response, significant for its engagement with not only White but some of White's chief early respondents, suggests that the role of the human fashioned both by Scripture and church tradition was not one of arrogant plunderer of the nonhuman realm, as suggested by White, but rather a much more complex role, defined by sacred texts and church fathers as a role of stewardship.

Thomas Sieger Derr

Thomas Sieger Derr, former professor in the Department of Religion and Biblical Literature at Smith College and an early architect of the WCC's work on the Justice, Peace, and the Integrity of Creation initiative, was among the first theological voices to critique White's thesis. Like Robin Attfield, Derr reviews the work of Clarence J. Glacken (1967) and claims that the genesis of Western technology and science is "multiple, complex, and obscure" and that it is a "false simplification" to isolate one particular religious strand when a myriad of nonreligious elements also were factors, such as geography, climate, population growth, capitalism, philosophy, and democracy. Moreover, he wonders how White explains ecological disaster in non-Christian parts of the globe, such as the overgrazing and deforestation that may have helped erode Egyptian, Assyrian, Roman, and other civilizations (Derr 1975: 42–43; see also Derr 1995).

In addition, like Attfield, Derr indicates that there is impressive evidence of an early and enduring Christian concern for environmental preservation, citing Glacken's treatment of Saint Augustine, Saint Thomas, and others who evoked divine "immanence" or "indwelling" in nature and thus belied characterizations of Christianity's mere instrumental approach to the nonhuman world. For Derr, then, the "orthodox" Christian stance toward nature is not "arrogance" but "respectful stewardship of an earth which belongs only to God" (Derr 1975: 43). As Derr contends:

White, and those who applaud his thesis, feel that the current chorus of celebration for stewardship is a belated response and a disguised confession of prior guilt, and doubtless new ecological awareness has stimulated it. But it remains orthodox doctrine, and has certainly not been submerged for centuries....Nor is stewardship incompatible with anthropocentrism. The Judeo-Christian placement of man at the apex of creation as trustee for the rest of nature certainly does not mean that nature may be manipulated to serve the whims of man. That would contradict the meaning of "trustee" or "steward." But at the same time it puts man prominently into the picture and avoids the dangerous unreality of making nature without man our moral standard. (1975: 43)

In contradistinction to deep ecology, which suggests a diminished value and role for humanity in light of ecological destruction, Derr speaks of a responsible anthropocentrism, intimating that humanity's special role and power are not, according to Christian tradition at least, a "license to kill" but a call to responsible use of power.

Derr, who greatly respects White, a Presbyterian, as a scholar and as a "humane and Christian man," feels that White may have unwittingly given aid to antidemocratic, antihumanist elements that White himself has long countered. He notes a bitter irony that White's "Historical Roots" has been heralded by an environmental movement tinctured by "elitist antidemocratic values," by ecologists who, he polemically charges, accept human starvation as a naturally occurring cycle and endorse totalitarian means to control population, by "romantic" Luddites who wish to abandon the modern era, and by sundry anti-Christian advocates spurred by personal motives to denigrate the Judeo-Christian legacy. "Historical Roots," Derr claims, belies White's Christian humanism and inadvertently promotes "paganism, authoritarianism, and brutality" (1975: 43).[11]

Derr's work is significant for a variety of reasons. Not only does it, like Attfield's critique, claim that White misread the

Judeo-Christian tradition, but it also articulates the possibility for a responsible Christian anthropocentrism and holds up the model of stewardship, so fruitfully taken up and developed by myriad church statements and theologians, most notably Douglas John Hall, as we shall see. In accenting the responsibility inherent in the Christian human vocation, and the importance of the human, Derr anticipates the equating of ecological concerns and justice issues, known as "ecojustice," that has characterized much Christian, especially Protestant, reflection and activism from the 1960s onward (see Bakken, Engel, and Engel 1995).[12]

H. Paul Santmire

H. Paul Santmire's work, in part, can also be viewed as an outgrowth of the Lynn White debate.[13] His comprehensive overview of the Christian ecological legacy, *The Travail of Nature* (1985), is partially engendered by White's assessment that the Western Christian theological heritage is "ecologically bankrupt." His approach is similar to but far more exhaustive than Attfield's: both set out to examine the "great white male" tradition within the classical theological and biblical traditions of Christianity to provide a thorough, "accurate" history of Christian reflections on nature. Though ostensibly directed to both environmentalists and Christians, Santmire's work is primarily written for the latter camp. Rarely does he deviate from the Christian intellectual sojourn in the realm of nature to record how Christian groups responded to the conservationist voices of the nineteenth and early twentieth centuries, for example, or to the hundreds of North American ecological groups that have sprung up in the latter half of this century. This omission, of course, does not detract from Santmire's prodigious achievement in his comprehensive history; it merely suggests that *The Travail of Nature* (1985) remains a valuable resource mainly for *Christians,* as it seeks to set the Christian ecological record straight in the wake of Lynn White's indictment.

Santmire addresses his ambitious, encyclopedia-like work, as mentioned, to two groups: environmentalists (and those concerned about the fate of the earth) and Christians. For the environmentalists, he hopes to clarify the record and rectify the unnuanced, if not downright bad, "press" the Christian tradition has received vis-à-vis nature. For the Christians, he attempts to show that the Christian theological heritage, while promising for those wishing to fashion novel and positive dimensions regarding nature, is also highly ambiguous (1985: xi). His goal is to understand the "travail" of nature in Western Christian thought while simultaneously laying bare the ambivalent ecological promise of Christian theology (1985: 175).

Santmire contends that the critique of Christianity's culpability in the destruction of nature, from Feuerbach to Lynn White, has led theologians and other Christians to look eastward to other religious traditions, to view a Christian theology of nature as a contradiction in terms, or to speak tentatively of their own tradition's ecological heritage. What these voices lack, he argues, is a historical framework, an overarching, careful exploration of the theology of nature in the "biblical-classical Christian tradition." *The Travail of Nature* aspires to fill that void and also to support and assist in the vital quest for a "new theology of nature" in light of the deeply rooted environmental crisis (1985: 197).

Santmire assays to demonstrate that the Western theological tradition is certainly not ecologically bankrupt, nor is it lined with pearls of ecological riches. It is marked by two overarching motifs: one "spiritual" and the other "ecological." To help categorize the tradition, Santmire articulates three major metaphors: the metaphor of ascent, the metaphor of fecundity, and the metaphor of migration to a good land. With the "transparency," as it were, of these motifs and metaphors, Santmire scrutinizes the major thinkers on the "overhead projector" of the Christian legacy, from the Gnostics, Irenaeus, and Origen to Karl Barth and Teilhard de Chardin. He also assesses the biblical legacy as it pertains to nature, which he defines as "the earth."

While it is impossible to delineate Santmire's critiques of this panoply of Christian thinkers in this context, a few highlights are important to mention.

34

The Gnostics, for him, represent the most egregious example of the ascent metaphor in the West. Irenaeus affirms nature as humanity's blessed and God-granted home, in opposition to Gnosticism, and adopts the migration metaphor in his "chiliastic" eschatological vision. Irenaeus, Santmire concludes, exhibits an "administrative" rather than an "ontological" anthropocentrism (1985: 43) and represents the emergence of an ecological motif in Christian theology. Origen, however, as a philosophical theologian, doesn't share Irenaeus's understanding of the divinity's concern for nature. His metaphor is one of ascent rather that migration, and his otherworldly view of salvation leads to a diminishing of the natural world (1985: 53).

The thought of Origen, Santmire claims, reverberates in the work of Augustine, another philosophical theologian, but with a confessional dimension. Yet Augustine moves from a spiritual metaphor to an ecological metaphor with his emphasis on divine goodness, the beauties of nature, and the situation of human salvation history within the grander realm of creation history. Santmire boldly asserts that Augustine represents the "flowering of the ecological promise of classical Christian theology" (1985: 73).

This ecological flowering faded in the twelfth century and in the theology of Thomas Aquinas, according to Santmire. This period saw the rise of the metaphor of ascent and was marked by a deep alienation of humanity from the natural world. Aquinas's views were restrictively anthropocentric, Santmire argues, though ambiguous, affirming and denigrating nature, celebrating God's goodness yet leaving nature out of ultimate completion in God. For Santmire, Aquinas is closer to Origen than many acknowledge, notwithstanding his reliance on Augustine (1985: 90–95).[14]

Despite the ambiguous dimensions of Saint Bonaventure and Dante regarding nature, Saint Francis, emerging out of this period, represents a full-blown embrace of nature and stands as a triumph of the ecological motif in Christian Western theology. For Santmire, "Francis's vision of the descending, universal goodness of God, his obedience to the kenotic Christ, his hope for the consummation of all things, and his childlike love for all the creatures of God commend themselves to us today...as compelling data for our own theological reflection" (1985: 118).

In examining the Reformation and modern secularization, nurtured in part by Kant and the emerging natural sciences, Santmire is again faced with radical ambiguity. On the one hand, the ecological motif did permeate the Reformers' work (especially Luther's) in their reflections on the beauties of God in nature and nature's ultimate resuscitation in the eschaton; on the other hand, this motif was held in unresolved tension with their "soteriological-anthropological" focus (1985: 130–33).

Both Barth and Teilhard, according to Santmire, while trying to incorporate a wider vision of creation than did their contemporaries, wind up in a personalistic framework. By unwittingly giving his benison to modern secularization, Santmire contends, and refusing to elaborate a theology of nature, Barth "by default" leaves us with a view of nature that is assessed in terms of "personal being" (1985: 155). Teilhard, a "synthetic" thinker, building on evolution, developed the notion of a "cosmic Christ," but, unfortunately, this was done from a personalistic perspective. For Santmire, Teilhard's thought reveals the dominance of the spiritual motif rather than the ecological, relying, as he claims, on the metaphor of ascent in the embrace of evolutionary thought that is expressed in the achievement of the "Omega Point." For Santmire, "both Teilhard and Barth reach out to claim the whole of reality....But nature slips from their hands, from Teilhard's finally, from Barth's quickly" (1985: 171).

Moving to the biblical tradition, Santmire proclaims that the Bible has "to do with history, not with nature" (1985: 176). He proffers an approach to biblical theology that develops an ecological reading, centering on the land of promise and the fecundity of God (1985: 189). Santmire also includes sketches of the Hebrew Scriptures and the New Testament, noting their ecological richness but also their spiritual motifs. Santmire believes that his study shows the possibility of a fresh ecological reading of biblical faith, guided by the work of Irenaeus, Augustine, and Francis, that could ultimately bring the travail of nature to a "blessed ending" (1985: 218).

•

As this selective analysis of Attfield, Derr, and Santmire indicates, the apologetic approach speaks from and to the Christian tradition. It sees itself as defending and upholding the Judeo-Christian heritage in light of the charges lodged by Lynn White Jr., aiming to demonstrate that the ecological promise of the tradition is much more complex and potentially useful for contemporary environmentalism than White suggests. In contrast to White, this approach proposes that the role of the human agent depicted in the Judeo-Christian narrative is not that of a domineering overlord who exploits nature only for its instrumental value but rather that of a steward of creation, which always remains under the ownership of God, not humanity. The focus here is less on the culpability of the Christian story in creating our current ecological destruction and more on its positive and potential contributions to a sustainable future. Moreover, this vantage posits as well the role that other factors, such as the growth of capitalism, democracy, nationalism, science, and industrialization, have played in environmental degradation, offering the proposal that religion may not be as determining a force in the cavalcade of history as White and others contend.

A "Constructive" Approach

The constructive approach, as intimated earlier, adopts a self-critical perspective in dealing with the accusations leveled at the Judeo-Christian tradition by Lynn White Jr. On the whole, it concurs with White's assessment that the Judeo-Christian tradition may have indeed at worst encouraged ecological destruction or at the very least expressed an insensitivity to it, though the authors within this approach exhibit a much greater sensitivity to the wide variety of Christian practices, traditions, and expressions than does White.[15] Moreover, it strives actively and explicitly to incorporate ecological concerns within the theological enterprise and has been accompanied, especially in Protestant circles, by concerted activism. In addition, its perspective is as much influenced by the larger human community as by the church, underscoring its concern that theology be responsive to major social movements. In this sense, it sees the role of the human as that of a faithful, engaged, and responsible participant in shaping social, economic, and ecological issues and concerns that confront global society. Among the most important designers of this approach are Douglas John Hall, Jürgen Moltmann, and Walter Brueggemann.

Douglas John Hall

Douglas John Hall's *Imaging God: Dominion as Stewardship* (1986), like Jürgen Moltmann's *God in Creation: A New Theology of Creation and the Spirit of God* (1985), though an explicitly Christian theology of nature, interestingly enough transcends the intellectual dust storm kicked up by Lynn White's critique. Because of this, they both, it could be argued, have much wider applicability and broader appeal than does Santmire's *Travail*, Attfield's "Christian Attitudes," or Derr's work.

One reason, perhaps, for these works' more expansive appeal is their respective starting points. Both Hall and Moltmann begin, not with the legacy of Christianity's role in the ecological crisis, but with the ecological crisis itself. Hall's work cogently commences with the claim that "something is wrong," followed by the disquieting fact that every day, "citizens of the United States of America consume 2,250 head of cattle in the form of McDonald's hamburgers" (1986:1). Hall's initial presupposition is not that something is wrong exclusively with Christianity but rather that "something is fundamentally wrong with our civilization," and it has to do with "the distorted relationship between human and nonhuman nature" (1986: 1). From the outset, then, Hall reveals his work to be in response to a broad cultural problem rather than simply a Christian one.

In *Imaging God* (1986), Hall constructively examines the *imago Dei* and dominion motifs in the Judeo-Christian tradition.[16] Compelled by the ecological crisis, Hall carefully reexamines the Christian tradition in search of "buried treasure" within the legacy of Jerusalem that may offer hope and help concerning the responsible stewardship of nature. Hall is indebted to, though critical of, the tradition, attempting both to fashion a theology of nature in light of the ecological crisis and to reiterate the primacy of God as a counter to the anthropocentrism of the Judeo-Christian heritage. Rather than seeking to deemphasize the human, Hall attempts to recast the human family so that stewardship for the created world can be seen as the goal of the Christian enterprise.

Hall commences his exploration, as noted, with the realization that "something is wrong" in our civilization's distorted and denigrating relationship with the nonhuman world (1986: 1). Scientists in particular have been illustrating the perils we face in the present ecological crisis. The human community is in deep sin, which Hall astutely identifies as an ontological problem, and his response is to plumb the depths of the ontology of Sacred Scripture to see how such an approach might help Christians curb, rather than create, further environmental diminishment.

Hall sets out to (1) fathom the problem with the human conception of the human-nonhuman relationship; (2) examine the nature and extent of Christianity's culpability in this troubled relationship; and (3) offer an alternative Christian conceptualization to this relationship.

Hall's approach is initially contrite, self-critically examining Christianity's role in the ecological crisis, claiming that Christians in this regard must be willing to adopt a stance of *metanoia*. Hall contends that the calling of the human person within creation "is to image God, and that the imaging of the God (*Dominus*) described in the tradition of Jerusalem would mean exercising the dominion of stewardship" (1986: 60). Hall explores the *imago Dei* in the Hebrew Scriptures and New Testament, concluding that this motif is really a spiritual movement, a process and struggle that will entail new interpretations. Turning to historical conceptions of the *imago Dei,* Hall looks at substantionalist and relational conceptions of the symbol, noting that the human person has a special calling through that symbol. He then discusses "the ontology of communion," detailing the tripartite notion of human relatedness: being-with-God, being-with-humankind, and being-with-nature. Hall underscores the fact, however, that these three dimensions are inextricably intertwined; they are in a single relationship and thus cannot be considered to exist in isolation.

Hall claims that the essential character of the person in the Judeo-Christian tradition is bound up in the *imago Dei* symbol. The theological history of this symbol posits the notion of this divine image (1) as a substance or endowment of the human; and (2) as a consequence of the divine-human relationship. The Bible and the Reformers, Hall argues, endorse the relational aspect of this symbol; this view says that the essence of the human is to be in a relationship of love, and we image God through loving. God, other humans, and nonhuman creation are hence the three dimensions of this relatedness, and these are inseparably linked (1986: 133). In short, Hall does a biblical ontology, showing that the ontology of communion is inherent in the Judeo-Christian Scriptures. Hall demonstrates that this relational biblical ontology doesn't deny uniqueness of the human but emphasizes that we must be stewards of creation. Hall explores the distinctiveness of these three dimensions of the interrelation, being-with-God, being-with-humankind, and, most thoroughly, being-with-nature. Hall notes that human attempts to tame, control, and stand above nature have been highly detrimental for the world of creation. He contends that while the biblical record on nature is ambiguous, there is a more intimate relationship with nature depicted in the traditions of Jerusalem than originally suspected, and there does exist an ontology of communion, reciprocity, and mutuality of being (1986: 177). If this ontology had been previously explored, Hall surmises, perhaps our civilization would be experiencing a different destiny. The *imago Dei* leads to a distinctive dominion for the human, but one, Hall argues, that entails stewardship. This analysis points out the need to develop a Christology that takes into account the contemporary reality of the ecological crisis.

Hall points out three areas where we have been deficient in our understanding of the relationship between human and extra-human: the sacrificial element in the stewardship of nature, the preservational dimension, and the recognition of the spiritual element in nature (a major theme of Thomas Berry). Hall presents a cogent and constructive analysis of the ontology of the Bible to help with the Christian conversion necessary to help avert ecological catastrophe.

Jürgen Moltmann

German theologian Jürgen Moltmann is another important author who falls within the constructive schema. Like Hall, Moltmann claims that what we call the environmental crisis is not merely a crisis in the natural environment of human beings. It is nothing less than a crisis in human beings themselves. It is a crisis of life on this planet, a crisis so comprehensive and irreversible that it can justly be described as "apocalyptic." According to Moltmann, it is not a temporary crisis, and as far as we can judge, it is the beginning of a life-and-death struggle for creation on this earth (1985: xi).

Both Hall and Moltmann thus proclaim that underlying their constructive theological enterprises is both a social and an ecological crisis. What motivates their work, then, is not simply a theological problem but a problem of planetary survival jeopardized by humanity's pernicious relationship to the created world. Consequently, they both engage in richly researched systematic theological constructions. For Moltmann, this leads to an ecological doctrine of creation in light of the ecological crisis, exploring the knowledge, time, and space of creation, as well as creation's evolution, its Sabbath "feast," and God's image in creation — the human person — all from a Trinitarian, messianic perspective.

Yet while both Moltmann and Hall adopt self-critical, rather than defensive, postures in examining Christianity's past role in the ecological crisis, both see in the Christian legacy useful and salubrious dimensions that can be recast to deal with current threats to our environment. Moltmann's methodology is eclectic and ecumenical, drawing from Roman Catholic, Protestant, Jewish, and Orthodox theology and situating the ecological crisis within the social-scientific literature of Karl Marx and

Ernst Bloch on alienation from nature and "nature as sub-ject" respectively.

This fundamental, systematic theological examination is pri-marily a treatment of the Holy Spirit; Moltmann explicitly iden-tifies "God in creation" as the Holy Spirit, and his starting point is "the indwelling divine Spirit of creation."[17] Moltmann unpacks the "household" dimension of the word "ecology," leading him to the "inner secret" of the Trinitarian mystery, which is "the in-dwelling of God." This insight leads to his extensive treatment (in chapter 11) of "the Sabbath," whose inner secret he dis-cerns as "God's rest," and which for him constitutes the "feast" of creation, in which God uniquely and surprisingly sanctifies a period of *time* rather than a mountain or a stretch of earth (1985: 283ff.). For Moltmann, the Spirit is the "holistic" prin-ciple of creativity and cooperation in creation, as well as the principle of individuation. Ultimately, the Spirit represents the principle of intentionality, in which all created beings in the Spirit are directed toward their potentialities, their "common future" (1985: 100).

Reflecting his previous work, Moltmann's project is infused with a deep sense of hope in the messianic future promised by the Judeo-Christian God. This openness to the future permeates the study and informs his discussions of the evolution of creation, heaven and earth, God the creator, the messianic calling of human beings, and the Sabbath, among other subjects. (Indeed, this work is merely volume 2 of a larger work entitled *Messianic Theology*.) Moltmann's particular gift is to apply his messianic orientation to an ecological doctrine of creation. In treating the "knowledge of creation" in chapter 3, Moltmann forcefully expresses his mes-sianic thrust. He claims that (1) knowledge of the world as divine creation is the product of revelation, not observation; (2) through an understanding of the world as creation, God's revelation as Lord is universalized; (3) seen as God's creation, the history of the universe is bound up in God's rule, initiated in creation and culminating in God's kingdom; and (4) the time of the Christian apprehension of creation is the time of Jesus the Messiah. "Under the presupposition of faith in Jesus Christ, the world is revealed in the messianic light as a creation that is both in bondage, and open for the future" (1985: 56). This openness to the future is a source of Moltmann's steadfast Christian hope.

Eclectically, Moltmann touches on several key themes examined by other authors both within and without the constructive approach. Like Brueggemann, as we shall see later in this chapter, Moltmann suggests that the notion of "home" fulfills the messianic promises to the poor and alienated (1985: 5). Like Hall, he points to the significance of *imago Dei* for an ecological theology and speaks in terms of the likeness to God, implying a divine-human relationship through which humans are thereby enabled to relate to God (though Moltmann doesn't explore this image in as thorough manner as does Hall) (1985: 216–24). And, like Sallie McFague (treated in chapter 5), Moltmann unpacks certain alternative symbols, not of God, but of the world, such as "Mother Earth," "the World as Dance," and "the Feast of Heaven and Earth" (1985: 297–320). Lastly, as with Thomas Berry (considered in chapter 4), Moltmann's analysis is influenced by recent findings in the natural sciences, particularly nuclear physics and biology, that point toward the interrelationship of all matter (1985: 2–3, passim).

Thus, for Moltmann, the role of humans is to respond to the ecological crisis as responsible agents of history, attuned to the Holy Spirit's presence in creation and guided and girded by God's hope-yielding eschatological promise.

Walter Brueggemann

Walter Brueggemann, also writing from a Protestant perspective, is similarly motivated by a contemporary crisis in preparing his work. Unlike Hall and Moltmann, however, Brueggemann focuses on a crisis that has more to do with human feelings of rootlessness and anomie than with ecological destruction (1977: xv). Brueggemann's *The Land: Place as Gift, Promise, and Challenge in Biblical Faith* (1977), by tracing the story of a faithful community's bond to the earth and to God, and the consequences of abusing that bond, yields many important insights for those wishing to improve the human relationship with the environment. In contradistinction to *God in Creation* and *Imaging God,* Brueggemann's book is an exercise in biblical rather than systematic theology; *The Land* is, nonetheless, a constructive biblical theology, and Brueggemann creates a cogent case for his claim that the land is perhaps "*the central theme* of biblical faith" (1977: 3). *The Land* remains "an excellent and provocative introduction to the extensive literature on the ethics, sociology, and theology of land in the Bible" (Bakken, Engel, and Engel 1995: 52).

Brueggemann's principal project in *The Land,* in addition to addressing questions concerning rootlessness in modern society, is to provide a novel "prism" through which the Bible can be scrutinized, that prism being the narrative-of-the-land motif in the Bible. Consequently, Brueggemann's influential book is fashioned around the threefold history of the land: (1) promise of entry into the land; (2) story of land management and exile; and (3) the renewed story of promise commencing in exile and resulting in a kingdom.

Written shortly before the critical homelessness problem exploded in the United States under the Reagan administration, *The Land* attempts to speak to the pervasive "sense of being lost, displaced, and homeless...in contemporary culture" (1977: 1). Brueggemann uses land to denote both actual turf and the symbolic expression of wholeness and joy marked by social integrity, well-being, and coherence, claiming that land is perhaps the core theme of biblical faith. He also notes that because Christian theologies have focused predominantly on God's intervention in human history, they have created dichotomies of time and place and consequently have paid little attention to the central theme of land in the Bible.

Though not explicitly ecological, Brueggemann's analysis nonetheless holds out enticing tidbits for those wishing to fashion an ecological theology. His reflections on wilderness as both a chaotic and "gifted" place are intriguing in light of contemporary Native American groups who still live off the wilderness — especially groups in Canada such as the Inuit and Cree of northern Quebec — and who indeed see the wildlands as "gifted."

Moreover, the author's insight that when the people of Israel at last attained land, they faced new responsibilities toward it, and when they abandoned these, were cast into exile, can be instructive for ecological theologians. Insightfully, Brueggemann adopts a storytelling approach rather than an academic one to relate the saga of Israel's relationship to the land — a rich history for sociological, ecological, as well as theological reasons. Indeed, if we consider the earth as our home, we too, like the covenant-breaking Israelites, may find ourselves one day homeless, "vomited" into exile owing to our irresponsible use of our gift from God.

In discussing the hermeneutical implications of his study, Brueggemann claims that the biblical notion of land is germane for today's "dispossessed," whom he identifies as blacks, the poor, and women. Those seeking to develop an ecological theology could perhaps add to Brueggemann's list certain species who now face extinction, bereft of their "home" owing to wanton habitat destruction and pollution. Brueggemann thus sees the human agent in the Judeo-Christian legacy as inextricable from the land, suggesting that any theological anthropology that attempts to divest itself from "the soil," as it were, will prove not only unfaithful to the tradition but also extremely dislocating psychologically, culturally, and spiritually.

•

As we have seen with this selective treatment of the work of Douglas John Hall, Jürgen Moltmann, and Walter Brueggemann, the constructive approach attempts to look critically at the Judeo-Christian tradition in light of its teachings concerning nature. On the whole, however, its primary concern is the threat ecological destruction poses for the world community, how Christianity has played a hand in that destruction, and how it can be made a constructive ally rather than adversary in future attempts to create a sustainable society. In this way, it speaks to both those within the tradition and those outside of it. The "vocation" of the human is a central concern here as well, one, as we have discerned, infused with a sense of divine immanence and placed in communal relationship with God, other humans, and nonhuman reality as well. In this sense, the special role of the human is respected — its unique power, its fashioning in the image of God — yet its call to be responsible for the creation and the world community is also emphasized.

The "Listening" Approach

In contrast to both the defensive and apologetic approaches, the listening approach does not deal directly with the charges laid by Lynn White and others. In many ways, it assumes not only Christian but religious complicity in a larger societal dynamic of ecological destruction. Unlike the constructive approach, its principal concern seems not to resurrect images and motifs from the Christian tradition that will foster an environmentally sustainable ethos but rather to pay attention or listen to "nature" itself. It posits a role for the human agent as responsive not merely to religious or societal debates but to the natural world itself and claims that only in such radical openness to the earth's systems can we fashion a truly workable and nonharmful response to the nonhuman world. The listening approach to the environmental crisis is forcefully suggested in the work of John Carmody (1939–96), a former Jesuit; Albert Fritsch, a current Jesuit; and Passionist priest Thomas Berry, an author I deal with in greater detail in chapter 4.[18] Berry, perhaps more stridently than Carmody and Fritsch, advances the process of human listening as "a matter of life and death," but all three authors would agree that the time has come for humans to lower their voices, to cease imposing mechanistic patterns on the biological processes of the earth, and to begin quite humbly to follow the guidance of the larger community on which all life depends. In this paradigm, there is also an openness to non-Christian religious sources, to physical sciences that have been unfurling sobering data on ecological destruction, and to appropriate technologies that are more compatible with the natural life-systems of the planet.

John Carmody

In his small but wide-ranging work *Ecology and Religion: Toward a New Christian Theology of Nature* (1983), Carmody sets out on a self-described "scouting" mission to chart the contours of a new Christian theology of nature in light of our contemporary environmental crisis. Taking a structural cue from Bernard Lonergan, Carmody divides his work into two parts. In part 1, the "listening" phase, he delineates facts and figures regarding the environmental crisis and, in thumbnail fashion, presents the religious, economic, scientific, technological, political, and ethical issues involved in the recent dialogue between ecology and religion.[19]

Part 2 represents the constructive phase of the book, wherein, again following Lonergan's lead, Carmody delineates foundational, doctrinal, systematic, and practical theologies that "a new Christian naturalism" would entail.

To set an appropriately urgent tone, Carmody begins the work with "a dramatic scenario" — Cubatão, Brazil, that nation's petrochemical center, where the air pollution is so noxious that the mayor and many officials refuse to live in the town, and of every one thousand babies born, forty are dead on arrival and another forty perish within a week (most of the babies who die are visibly deformed) (1983: 3). Carmody contends that while some Protestant theologians have done yeoman's work in addressing the ecological crisis, most mainline Protestant churches, along with the Roman Catholic and Eastern Orthodox churches, have paid little attention to ecological concerns. In surveying the sundry issues — religious, scientific, ethical, and so on — in part 1, Carmody reveals his background in Eastern religious thought, arguing that Eastern religious traditions have perhaps been more attentive to nature and that some of their insights, such as the notions of *ahimsa* and *satyagraha,* could assist Western Christians in their attempt to fashion a germane and responsible theology of nature (1977: 63ff.). (Here he echoes sentiments of Lynn White Jr. and Thomas Berry.)

While Carmody covers a vast array of concerns, some highlights include the need for reusable resources, for simpler lifestyles and population control, for a renewed sacramentalism incorporating nature, and for a reverence for life that translates into constraint of our addictive consumerism.

In part 2, Carmody underscores the importance of a conversion to Christ as the bedrock of any sound theology, natural or otherwise. He also delineates his own tremendous sense of grace (influenced by the work of Jesuit theologian Karl Rahner), a naturalist sacramentalism, and the possibility of sins against nature. In reviewing biblical and traditional theological teachings concerning nature, Carmody avers that the Pentateuch, the Prophets, and the Wisdom Literature point to the land as *God's* gift, whereas Paul, the Synoptics, and John attribute this gift, in some way, to Christ. Carmody also contends that there is a much more cosmological dimension to Pauline texts than many have discerned. (Though Teilhard de Chardin explored this, he is considered by many to be, according to Carmody, "eccentric.") After a cursory review of patristic, medieval, Reformation, modern, and contemporary voices, Carmody concludes that while all of them shaped the biblical material using the scientific and spiritual resources of their day, all have borne the unmistakable mark of anthropocentrism, which, for Carmody, "seems to be the mainstream of the Christian tradition" (1983: 166). (Here he is in clear disagreement with Attfield.)

Carmody completes his review with the claim: "God has given nature many titles to reverence." He then explores, through a futuristic story of a child raised in an ecologically sustainable environment, how we might come to love nature as a neighbor or a blood-relative, an affection he deems essential for any workable theology of nature. Like Berry, Carmody writes of the mystery of the created world, the need for silence in the face of creation's awesome mystery, and the presence of sacramental grace in the beauty of nature.

Through his twofold approach, Carmody is able to provide a scathing critique of a corporate and greed-driven consumer society from both an ecological and Christian perspective and to touch on some of the principal social, economic, moral, cultural, historical, and religious issues that must be considered in fashioning a sustainable future theology of the planet. While not as indebted to the cosmological and evolutionary-based theology of Teilhard de Chardin as others in the "listening" camp such as Albert Fritsch and Thomas Berry, Carmody nonetheless emphasizes with them the need for the human agent to listen to nature as both prelude and practice in fashioning an appropriate response to the environmental crisis. Moreover, his primary motivation, like others in the "listening" purview, is not to respond to the Lynn White Jr. controversy directly, nor simply to fashion a new theological approach in light of ecological destruction. Rather, the focus seems to be on responding to the ecological challenge on a quasi-theological-spiritual level, invoking the world's great religions in an attempt to uncover spiritual resources to help us rekindle or find anew an ability to relate and listen to nonhuman nature.

Albert Fritsch

Jesuit engineer and theologian Albert Fritsch, who, among many other things, provides alternative-energy appliances, such as solar ovens and refrigerators, in his ministry among the poor of Appalachia, blends science and technology, theology, and spirituality in his distinctive work.[20] Like Berry, he is influenced by the work of Teilhard de Chardin, exploring Teilhard's notion of cosmic evolution within a liturgical context (1987), and he also speaks of the earth as teacher and of the importance of listening to nature, understanding one's own bioregion as a source of theological reflection, and critiquing consumerism from an ecological vantage (1992). Listening to nature, he argues, is not an idle pastime but rather an "acquired skill":

> Listening to the earth...takes some effort and quality time, requiring us to turn off appliances, radio, automobile, the created noises which fracture contemplation and silence. Earth sounds are different, for they become part of nature's symphony, relaxing and soothing our frayed nerves. Many with perfect hearing never listen. They may go through

an entire year without being aware of crickets or song-birds. Human-made noises overwhelm them and they become Earth-deaf ones. (1992: 41)

Fritsch's notion of earth-deaf people parallels Thomas Berry's contention that contemporary society has become "autistic" when it comes to the natural world. Unlike Berry, however, Fritsch builds into his analysis a clearly articulated option for the poor, emanating in part from his work in impoverished Appalachia. For him, there is a clear nexus between oppression of the poor and oppression of the earth, for in his ministerial experience, the same coal-mining companies that ravage the land also ravage their miners, through company-store practices, union busting, and insensitivity to black lung disease among their workers.

In interweaving social and ecological justice concerns, Fritsch argues for a linking of an ecological perspective with an enlightened view of human self-interest. Perceiving the human species as placed atop an interlocking ecological pyramid, Fritsch argues that humans enrich themselves when benefiting other members of the earth pyramid (Fritsch 1980; see Bakken, Engel, and Engel 1995: 95–96). Unlike Berry, Fritsch seems to have a more sanguine outlook on the potential of technology to help in the healing of the earth, as well as a more optimistic perspective on the role of humans in helping effect sustainable and appropriate development (Fritsch 1993). For Fritsch, there does not seem to be a forbidding "Technozoic era," in which humans create a vast waste-world based on industrial exploitation, as there is in Berry's writings.

•

This approach, as evinced by Carmody, Fritsch, and, to a varying degree, Berry (as will be discussed later), posits a human role that is responsive and attentive to nature and strives to build upon existing cultural and religious institutions — Christian, interreligious, and secular — in order to respond to the ecological crisis. Its critique of consumer culture and call for a more simplified lifestyle, when combined with its emphasis on listening to nature, nudges it into a spirituality of the earth, one that to different degrees takes into account a concern for the poor as well as the planet and all its creatures. In this sense, it is a holistic, at times mystical approach, but one nourished often by hard-hitting social analysis.[21]

Conclusion

In reviewing these sundry readings and categorizing them loosely into apologetic, constructive, and listening approaches, one is struck by the momentousness and urgency of the task to which our global ecological crisis calls us. The works cited represent just a fraction of the spadework that has been and is being done in the area of theology and ethics to come to grips with our environmental emergency.

All three approaches reveal that the "vocation of the human," as Douglas John Hall has termed it, is a salient question in the emerging ecological literature. In light of the horrifying prospect of environmental degradation we now face at the close of the twentieth century, all three approaches are prompted to pose some basic questions: What is our role as humans? What is the goal of human civilization? What does progress mean? What kind of world do we wish to leave to future generations? What metaphors or motifs from the Judeo-Christian tradition or elsewhere may be beneficial in helping the human community to "befriend" the earth? What *on earth* are we doing?[22]

It seems that a more explicitly political, transformative expression of ecological theology is of paramount importance in attempting to respond to such questions. Just as liberation theology was able to galvanize many Christians to deal with oppressive political and economic conditions in Latin America and elsewhere in the South, ecological theology, if it is to be effective, must strive for similar galvanization around oppressive ecological forces. In light of this concern, the remaining chapters represent an attempt to articulate a framework for a political theology of the environment. The tradition upon which I draw is represented by five important paradigms: the Gaia theory, process theology, the new cosmology, ecofeminism, and liberation theology. Each of these paradigms is assessed in light of the authors' treatment of the role of the human and in light a liberationist approach articulated principally by Latin American liberation theology. These paradigms, examined from this twofold vantage, I argue, represent important steps toward establishing a political theology of the environment, in which concern for marginalized persons and impoverished and exploited nature are blended in life-giving and pragmatic ways.

Chapter 2

The Gaia Hypothesis

The Earth as a Living Organism

---

*Most of us sense that the Earth is more than a sphere of rock
with a thin layer of air, ocean, and life covering the surface.
We feel that we belong here, as if this planet were indeed our
home. Long ago the Greeks, thinking this way, gave to the
Earth the name of Gaia, or, for short, Ge.*

— JAMES LOVELOCK, *The Ages of Gaia*

Gaia: A Framework for Exploring
the Function of the Human

The Gaia hypothesis has become a significant framework for exploring the environmental crisis because it fuses scientific insight and religious imagination in a potentially energizing and transformative way, challenging persons across a broad spectrum of disciplines to deal in an integrative fashion with the ecological crisis. Moreover, just as the Copernican Revolution forced humanity to alter its self-proclaimed centrality within the universe, so may Gaia hold the potential for a similarly foundational cultural transition.

First articulated by British atmospheric chemist James Lovelock, the Gaia hypothesis, succinctly, suggests that Earth is a self-regulating, self-sustaining entity that continually adjusts its environment in order to support life. Though a science-based conception, the Gaia hypothesis has sparked a swirl of religious, New Age, and philosophical reflection since its initial articulation in 1969 and challenges certain long-held assumptions about evolution, the importance of the human in determining environmental change, and the relationship between life and the environment itself

In this chapter, I first outline the scientific statement of Gaia advanced by James Lovelock and his collaborator, microbiologist Lynn Margulis, as well as some of the scientific critiques of Gaia. Second, I explore how Gaia theorists treat the role of the human, a treatment that has distanced them from many environmentalists. Third, I explore practical, philosophical, and theological responses to Gaia. Fourth, I critically evaluate elements that may be helpful in constructing a political theology of the environment.

The Gaia Hypothesis: What Is It?

James Lovelock, believing that university environments hamstring scientific inquiry, has supported himself through independent contracts and his abundant inventions. While serving as a consultant for NASA during the 1960s, Lovelock worked on the Viking Project, which assessed whether life existed or were even possible on Mars. To probe these questions, Lovelock examined what sustained life on Earth and, arguing from his strength as an atmospheric chemist, found his answer in the composition of Earth's atmosphere, with its delicate balance of oxygen, hydrogen, nitrogen, methane, and traces of other elements.[1]

Liberated from "Martian chronicling," Lovelock concentrated on the nature of Earth's atmosphere:

> The result of this more single-minded approach was the development of the hypothesis that the entire range of living matter on Earth, from whales to viruses, from oaks to algae, could be regarded as constituting a single living entity, capable of manipulating the Earth's atmosphere to suit its overall needs and endowed with faculties and powers far beyond those of its constituent parts. (Lovelock 1979: 9)

Unlike Mars, with an atmosphere composed mainly of carbon dioxide, Earth, Lovelock concluded, has a dynamic and self-regulating atmosphere. Just like an oven thermostat that maintains a constant temperature, Earth's atmosphere sustains a stable balance of gases and temperature supportive of life. Because Mars has no suggestion of such a matrix or dynamic atmosphere, it is lifeless, Lovelock concluded.

Needless to say, having spent millions on a Viking probe to Mars to explore the question, NASA was not pleased with Lovelock's findings. Lovelock wryly observes that the first Viking spacecraft landed on Mars in 1975, and neither it nor the subsequent Viking probe presently sitting on Mars ever detected life (Lovelock 1990: 7), thereby lending support to the findings of his less extravagant experiments.[2]

For Lovelock, the Gaia hypothesis proposes that the biosphere has the ability to adjust itself continually in order to keep Earth "healthy," that is, able to sustain life. It achieves this through the manipulation of the physical and chemical environment (Lovelock 1990: 11). Estimating that life first emerged on Earth some 3.5 billion years ago, Lovelock notes that the fossil record indicates that Earth's climate has changed very little during that period. This constancy perdures despite the estimated 25 to 30 percent increase in the sun's intensity during that time. Why? Lovelock pondered other questions: Why isn't the sea saltier, when a saline percentage over 6 percent could be fatal to life? Why has the sea's salinity remained steady at 3.4 percent? Why has the total volume of water on Earth apparently remained constant during the past 3.5 aeons? Why is Earth's atmospheric oxygen level at 21 percent, the upper end of life sustainability? (If it were at 25 percent, for example, the world would be a fireball.) For Lovelock, the answers lie not with happenstance but with a self-regulating Gaia (Lovelock 1979: 9ff.). Gaia is a vital, self-regulating organism whose environment is life itself.[3]

In an effort to eschew a highly sterile scientific name for his proposal (such as the Biocybernetic Universal System Tendency, which he briefly contemplated), Lovelock consulted friend and Bowerchalke neighbor William Golding, the celebrated British novelist, who suggested the term "Gaia," the name given to the earth goddess in ancient Greece (Joseph 1990: 30). The name, redolent with mythic, poetic, and religious resonance, was immediately chosen.

In Lovelock's understanding, the fact that climatic and chemical properties of Earth work together to maintain the optimal conditions for life suggests coordinated activity. "For this to have happened by chance," Lovelock jocularly surmises, "is as unlikely as to survive unscathed a drive blindfolded through rush-hour traffic" (Lovelock 1979: 10). Research into the makeup of the atmosphere convinced Lovelock that it was such a complex, intriguing blending that it could not have emerged by accident, for almost everything about it belied the laws of equilibrium chemistry (Lovelock 1979: 67ff.). Lovelock notes that when oxygen first was produced in the atmosphere, it must have been a devastating pollutant, but it was Gaia that evolved microorganisms that could process oxygen.

Lovelock compares Gaia's atmosphere not to a goddess, however, nor to a living organism, but to an extension of a living organism (i.e., a cat's fur, a bird's plumage, or paper on a wasp's nest), seeing it as "an extension of a living system designed to maintain a chosen environment" (Lovelock 1979: 10).

For Lovelock, life is not surrounded by a passive environment to which it has accustomed itself. Rather, life creates and reshapes its own environment (Margulis and Sagan 1986: 267). Whereas traditional earth scientists maintain that Earth's climatic pattern is more geological than biological and is therefore less robust and more vulnerable to lasting injury, the Gaia hypothesis purports that Earth is like a self-regulating animal and may have organs that are especially important, such as the rain forest and wetlands, which are more vital to the global environment than are other parts of the system (Joseph 1990: 2). In other words, while Gaia may sustain the loss of its "big toe" (i.e., the blue whale), it can ill-afford to lose its "lungs" (i.e., the tropical rain forests).

Lovelock's evocative insight is that Earth's chemically volatile yet dynamically sustained atmosphere suggests a uniquely vital planet, in contradistinction to the nonvital atmospheric stability of Venus and Mars. He terms this phenomenon "the Goldilocks effect" — "not too hot, not too cold, but just right" (Sahtouris 1989b: 60).

Gaia: Historical Antecedents

One could argue that historical antecedents of the Gaia theory reside in the work of G. F. Hegel, Baruch Spinoza, Alfred North Whitehead, and Herbert Spencer, who all spoke of nature in terms of an organism. Moreover, Aldo Leopold, deemed the father of the modern conservation movement, spoke of Earth as an "organism" possessing a certain degree of life. As philosopher Anthony Weston also points out, the Gaia theory has a particular relevance to our time, with its general systems-theory and interplanetary expeditions (Weston 1987: 219). Evolutionary philosopher Elisabet Sahtouris notes that early in this century, the Russian scientist V. I. Vernadsky viewed the biogeochemistry of the planet as a unity, but his work was not known to Lovelock until after the Gaia thesis was proposed (Sahtouris 1989b: 57). Lovelock himself points to the nineteenth-century Scottish scientist James Hutton, the father of geology, as a Gaia forerunner. Hutton spoke of Earth as a "superorganism" and was one of the first scientists to conceive of Earth in a systems context (Joseph 1990: 83).

Lynn Margulis: The Wizard of Ooze

With the help of Lynn Margulis, formerly married to Carl Sagan and a microbiologist at Boston University, Lovelock has refined his thesis and has been able to reinforce his ideas scientifically with reference to Margulis's research on microorganisms.[4] Known amusingly as "The Wizard of Ooze" owing to her investigation of microbes in swamps, mudflats, and marshes around the world, Margulis maintains that symbiosis and cooperation have been as central to biological evolution as has the competitive conflict for survival that marks Darwinian theory (Joseph 1990: 8). Through her work in Laguna Figueroa in Baja California, Margulis has become convinced that microbes work in concert through automatic biological processes to keep their environments livable. She has helped originate the theory of endosymbiosis, which postulates that two or more species can cooperate so closely that eventually they become one species (Joseph 1990: 44).

For Margulis and Dorion Sagan, interrelation, rather than competition, is the leitmotif of nature. Like Lovelock, they see the biosphere as "seamless," a grand, integrated, and living organism. They assert that the first bacteria acquired almost all the necessary knowledge about living in an integrated schema. "Life did not take over the globe by combat," they contend, "but by networking" (Margulis and Sagan 1986: 15). Attempting to show the importance of microorganisms for Gaia, Margulis is quick to demonstrate that life on Earth has existed for 3.5 billion years, and for the first 2 billion, only bacterial microorganisms existed. Mammals, including the human, she goes on to speculate, may exist solely to provide warm homes for such microorganisms (Margulis and Sagan 1986: 15–18) — a humbling thought for those who used to sit near the summit of the Great Chain of Being.

Gaia's Reception within the Scientific Community

For Peter Bunyard and Edward Goldsmith, coeditors of the British journal *The Ecologist: Journal of the Post-industrial Age,* the Gaia hypothesis suggests that the biosphere, together with the atmospheric environment, constitutes a unified natural system. This system is the fruit of organic forces that are highly coordinated by the system itself. Gaia has, in effect, created herself, not in a random manner, but actually in a goal-directed fashion. This is suggested by the fact that the system is highly stable and able to maintain its equilibrium despite internal and external dilemmas. It is actually a "cybernetic" system and thus must be seen as a grand cooperative project. As Bunyard and Goldsmith argue: "If Gaia is a single natural system that has created herself in a coordinated and goal-directed way, then Gaia is clearly the unit of evolution, not the individual living thing as neo-Darwinists insist" (Bunyard and Goldsmith, eds., 1989: 7). In fact, they speculate, Gaia might be evolution itself. Competition becomes not the primary feature but a secondary one, and survival of the fittest becomes not a highly individualistic exercise but a cooperative attempt to weed out certain species for the benefit of the organic commonweal. They insist that now there is more evidence for Gaia as an evolutionary process than there is for neo-Darwinism (Bunyard and Goldsmith 1989: 9).

The Gaia hypothesis, while garnering highly respected proponents such as Lynn Margulis, has also its share of critics in the scientific community. Gaia is particularly distressing for neo-Darwinists, who view evolutionary change as stemming from the natural selection of organisms that, through random mutations at the genetic level, are somehow better adapted to the struggle for life and can bequeath to the future more "successful" progeny (Bunyard and Goldsmith 1989: iii).[5]

Molecular biologist W. Ford Doolittle, accustomed to viewing evolutionary change at micro rather than macro levels, is skeptical about the intimation of foreknowledge and advance strategizing on the part of Gaia to deal with sundry crises, that is, the introduction of oxygen into the atmosphere and the increased intensity of the Sun. Is it really possible for genes within the cells of tiny organisms, he wonders, to moderate such massive phenomena as gas composition and atmospheric temperature? For him, the Gaia theory is "a motherly theory of nature without a mechanism" and is thus insupportable (Doolittle 1981: 60–63; see Margulis and Sagan 1984: 68–69).

Oxford University zoologist Richard Dawkins, also informed by a neo-Darwinist perspective, is among the most vigorous opponents of Gaia. In his refutation of Lovelock's theory, Dawkins claims that Earth as a Gaian system would have had to have been the lone success story out of a long series of planetary failures, contending that it is impossible for a lowly organism or even more so its genes to have any idea of what was required on a planetary scale. Dawkins cannot see how it can be logical that other planets did not share Gaian tendencies (Dawkins 1982: 236; Bunyard and Goldsmith 1989: iii). Elisabet Sahtouris observes that when trained evolutionists such as Dawkins assess the Gaia hypothesis, which "falls outside the major Darwinian paradigm of selfish individualism," they find it difficult to "refrain from regarding Gaia as the latest deification of Earth by nature nuts" (Sahtouris 1989a: 70).[6]

In March 1988, the Gaia hypothesis was subjected to its most sustained scientific scrutiny when the American Geophysical Union, an international association of geologists and geochemists, dedicated the entire week of its biannual Chapman conference to Gaia. Leading scientists from around the globe gathered to debate the premise and details of Lovelock and Margulis's findings. While it is hard to determine whether the majority of scientific skeptics were converted, the Gaia hypothesis has, since the conference, increasingly been called the Gaia theory in scientific circles (Sahtouris 1989b: 55). Lawrence Joseph, the colorful journalistic chronicler of Gaia, observes that since the 1988 conference, about one hundred scientific and technical articles have been written on the Gaia theory. Many of the authors of these articles seem less concerned with the verity of the theory than with how it has led them to novel questions and approaches in their respective specializations, some of which challenge the fundamental orientation of their disciplines (Joseph 1990: 13).

All scientific theories, of course, are as reflective of the culture from which they spring as they are of the empirical methodology on which they claim to rest. Gaia is no less culturally shaped than was Darwin's evolutionary theory, hatched during the inchoate Industrial Revolution, replete with its ethos of liberating marketplace competition and "survival of the fittest" in expanding industrial capitalism. Mary Clark, a biologist at San Diego State University and author of the *Ariadne's Thread,* notes a correspondence between social conditions and scientific reflection in Gaia:

Scientific insight is often molded by social milieu. We in the US see competition and violence in our lives, so we go out and look for it, and find it, in nature. There may also be substantial evidence for symbiosis and cooperation in nature, but it is the habit of science to ignore details incompatible with generally accepted models. The Gaia hypothesis helps us to be critical of the visions we have of the natural world, which are usually based on an individualistic, competitive world view. (Quoted by Joseph 1990: 59–60)

Lovelock himself states that the Gaia hypothesis may be an antidote to the traditional modern view of nature as a primitive force to be simply beaten back, subdued, and mastered (Lovelock 1979: 12). In light of the scientific debate surrounding Gaia, Lovelock responds: "I don't really care whether the Gaia hypothesis is right or wrong, so much as whether it causes one to ask valuable questions.... Science is never right or wrong absolutely. This is a dreadful misconception" (quoted by Joseph 1990: 79).

The Role of the Human in the Gaia Theory

While many environmentalists initially warmed to the Gaia theorists, perceiving them to be natural allies in the eco-struggle, Lovelock and Margulis proved to be reluctant eco-partners. Part of the reason for this distancing lies in the minimal place the human holds in the overall Gaia theory as articulated by Lovelock and Margulis. For the Gaia theory originators, Gaia is a self-regulating system, a "creature," that moves forward into the future regardless of what humans do.

In his first full-blown, popular articulation of his theory, *Gaia: A New Look at Life on Earth,* Lovelock clearly distinguishes himself from mainstream environmentalists. In this imaginatively written work, Lovelock asserts that, contrary to the gloomy forecasts of environmentalists, life on Earth is robust, hardy, and extremely adaptable, as his analysis of Gaia regulation over the aeons intimates. He suggests that large plants and animals are in fact probably less important than are bacteria deep in soils and seabeds. He compares "higher species," for example, trees and mammals, to glitzy salesmen and show models used to display products — helpful but not essential. He goes as far as to say that even nuclear war would probably not affect Gaia drastically (Lovelock 1979: 40–43).

Pollution, for Lovelock, is as natural as sea and sand and is therefore not fulsome but simply organic, an inevitable byproduct of "life at work." The early biosphere, he argues, must have experienced pollution and the depletion of resources, as we do in the modern world. He notes that the first entity to use zinc beneficially probably also produced mercury as a poisonous waste product. Microorganisms were later produced to break down the mercury, representing perhaps life's most ancient toxic waste disposal system (Lovelock 1979: 27–28).

While conceding that the devastation through modern industrial and technological development may prove "destructive and painful" for our own species, Lovelock doubts that it threatens the life of Gaia as a whole. (The ethical questions surrounding the "pain" for the human species are left unexplored.) In fact, he continues, "the very concept of pollution is anthropocentric and it may even be irrelevant in the Gaian context" (Lovelock 1979: 110). Acknowledging his lack of concern for the place of humanity within the Gaian framework, Lovelock admits that his work "is not primarily about people and livestock and pets; it is about the biosphere and the magic of Mother Earth" (Lovelock 1979: 112).

Lovelock, in ascribing a peripheral role for humanity in the Gaian framework, neglects to take into account socioeconomic factors of pollution. For example, in discussing Rachel Carson's galvanizing work *Silent Spring,* which analyzed how DDT and other pesticides were destroying birds and other wildlife, Lovelock asserts that DDT "will probably be more carefully and economically employed in the future" (Lovelock 1979: 115). Lovelock's pollyannish perspective is belied by the increased sale of DDT to the Third World after its use was banned in North America.

Contending that chloroflorocarbons (CFCs) are also "natural," Lovelock initially dismissed the fears of environmentalists that human-made CFCs resulting from aerosol cans, refrigerators, and air conditioners could have any sizable impact on ozone depletion. Methyl chloride, produced by the seas, he countered, breaks down ozone, as do CFCs, showing that too much ozone is as dangerous as too little for Gaia (Lovelock 1979: 80, 105). Gaia, he suggested, has the situation under control. Lovelock, however, in 1988 conceded that he had blundered. He admitted he may have been wrong to oppose those who wanted to legislate a reduction in CFCs, saying he would now support such legislative restrictions in light of the disturbing evidence of ozone depletion.

Revealingly, Lovelock, regarding humans as insignificant within the emergence of Gaia, was reluctant in this instance to advocate any change in ecologically disastrous human behavior. His oversight may be an example of a scientist, captivated by his own theory, giving in to the hubris of his own discipline, which claims to "know" the intricate and still ineffable workings of Earth. As Lawrence Joseph notes:

> When pressed, [*Atmospheric Environment* editor James] Lodge confided that "with Gaia on his mind, Jim [Lovelock] was not about to overestimate the destabilizing influence of any single system, including ozone. The theory was new and exciting, and perhaps Jim was a bit infatuated with the whole idea." Lovelock was so in love with his own theory that he was blind to any facts — even important ones that he had discovered — that contradicted Gaia. (Joseph 1990: 162)

Lovelock's dismissal of the important ozone depletion problem, a condition he brought to light through his own research, is a fascinating and important case study.[7] It highlights how scientists, enthralled by their own theories, can ignore data and minimize mammoth problems that belie their visions. It uncovers the limiting subjectivity of science and its all-too-human dimensions and demonstrates how science is susceptible to social, political, and psychological pressures. Convinced that Gaia was robust and all-controlling, Lovelock had difficulty admitting that the pesky unfeathered bipeds of the human race could significantly injure it.[8]

On the environmental-sensitivity barometer, Lynn Margulis fares little better than Lovelock, partially owing to the minuscule role she also ascribes to the human within Gaia. As suggested earlier, because animals are "Johnny-come-latelies" to Gaia, Margulis intimates that animals, including humans, are merely delivery systems or incubators for the microorganisms that really control Gaia's functioning (Margulis and Sagan 1984: 68). In fact, Margulis and Sagan speculate that the greatest psychological barrier to acceptance of the Gaia hypothesis is that it questions the special role of the human in creation. If microorganisms can plan, what's so special about human intelligence? Margulis suggests: "Not much." She claims that Gaia can still be seen primarily as a microbial production and that humans are relegated to "a tiny and unessential part of the Gaian system. People, like the Brontosaurus and grasslands, are merely one of the many weedy components of an enormous living system dominated by microbes" (Margulis and Sagan 1984: 71).

Not to deny completely a role for the human, Margulis proposes that humanity has the potential to be an anxious "early warning system" for Gaia, detecting how Gaia might be injured by various human activities or other changes. Moreover, we humans might be able to colonize other planets and deflect oncoming asteroids in the future, thereby protecting Gaia.[9] Such a diminutive role, she maintains, should not make us "depressed." Rather, Margulis counters, "we should rejoice in the new truths of our essential belonging, our relative unimportance, and our complete dependence upon a biosphere which has always had a life entirely its own" (Margulis and Sagan 1984: 73). As Lawrence Joseph surmises, "Compared to the three-and-a-half-billion-year momentum of the microorganisms, Margulis cannot help but snicker at the vainglory of our little species" (Joseph 1990: 51).

Gaia Responses: Pragmatic, Philosophical, and Theological

During the 1980s, in addition to sparking debate within the earth sciences, Gaia served as a galvanizing concept for New Age persons, globalists, and religious figures concerned about the environment. Dean James Morton of the Cathedral of Saint John the Divine in New York commissioned a Missa Gaia by the eco-music (or "Earth-jazz") group, the Paul Winter Consort. Gaia Books in London, inspired by Lovelock's vision of Earth as a single, living organism, prepared *Gaia: An Atlas of Planet Management* and *The Gaia Peace Atlas: Survival into the Third Millennium,* with contributions from scientists, church leaders, politicians, population experts, doctors, and environmentalists, all dedicated to preserving the earth from decimation and arguing for the need to reharness human energy from war-making to earth-keeping.[10] Books on Buddhism and Gaia, and myriad reflections on Gaia goddess imagery from an ecofeminist perspective, also emerged.[11] These responses, which can be classified as pragmatic, philosophical, and theological, all discuss the role of the human within the Gaia framework, but to varying degrees of success.

A Pragmatic Response: Kit Pedler

Curiously, one of the most serious and sustained examinations of Gaia's implications comes from the late Kit Pedler, an imaginative, if not eccentric, British medical doctor, research scientist, and science fiction writer. In his *The Quest for Gaia*, Pedler argues that the Gaia theory is a new revolutionary force that has been unleashed on the world. Technologists, he argues, have made the egregious blunder of assuming that nature is passive and neutral, a vast piece of blank paper on which they could draw their dreams. Instead, Pedler contends, the life process that surrounds us is characterized by an intelligence capable of self-rectification and regulation, an insight provided by Lovelock (Pedler 1991: 10).

65

For Pedler, the mind of Gaia is in a continuous state of evolution and revolution, always modifying its own contours to ensure stable conditions for the maintenance of the life process. As he comments, "It is not, 'if you can't beat them join them,' but 'we have to join them in order to survive'" (Pedler 1991: 51). With Lovelock and Margulis, Pedler states flatly that we will never have the power to destroy Gaia and suggests that the thought itself bespeaks of humankind's hubris, proud of its destructive power.

Nonetheless, unlike the Gaia theory originators, Pedler does ascribe a hefty role to the human in living within Gaia. Pedler contends that we must reorient ourselves to live in harmony with Gaia; otherwise we face extinction. For Pedler, we are in Gaia; there is no way to extricate ourselves from it; we are not above or superior to it. He suggests that no sustainable future for humanity can be attained unless human concerns are put second to Gaian concerns.

Pedler notes, for example, that most of the fuel for electricity generation goes into making waste heat, or entropy, rather than into generating electricity. The only sustainable path for humans, he claims, is to establish a way of living that creates no net entropy increase to the earth (1991: 33). To help decrease entropy, Pedler advocates the elimination of meat consumption, processed bread, and canned food and drinks. He also calls for the elimination of freezers. All these proposals are based on his principle of reducing entropy. In fact, because the industrial society itself conflicts with the basic rules of Gaia, it too must be abandoned. (The sociological and economic dimensions of this abandonment are regrettably unexplored.)

Instead of delineating social ramifications of such societal dismantling, Pedler takes the Gaia thesis personally and shows how it can be incorporated into our health, eating, brushing of teeth, dress, hobbies — indeed, almost every aspect of our day-to-day living. In a Gaian society, baths are out, men don't shave, and people avoid antibiotics, wash their clothes with soaps instead of detergents, and wear natural fiber clothes.[12]

Philosophical Responses

There are, at present, few sustained philosophical treatments of the Gaia hypothesis. This is not surprising, given the theory's recent vintage and its scientific focus. Perhaps the philosophic community is waiting for the scientific community's verdict before embarking on an enterprise whose subject matter may prove ephemeral.

William Irwin Thompson

At any rate, William Irwin Thompson, a philosopher and cultural historian, has made Gaia something of a personal vocation in recent years. Formerly professor at MIT as well as York University in Toronto, Thompson is presently director of the Lindisfarne Association, a relatively loose-knit concatenation of intellectuals dedicated to engendering what they term a global culture. Believing that scientific theory is inevitably grounded in a grander philosophical and cultural narrative, Thompson sees in Gaia a scientific story that could assist in stitching together a common planetary culture (Thompson 1991: 168). Claiming that Gaia is a new way of understanding our world, he avers that "ecology will be the political science of the future" (Thompson 1987).

For Thompson, our common understanding of "nature" is a fiction, a cultural construct influenced by Sierra Club calendars and the bucolic landscapes of eighteenth- and nineteenth-century British painters such as Constable and Gainsborough. "Nature is the horizon of culture," Thompson argues, and depending on one's context, one's horizon will vary. Lovelock and Margulis help us to see this, he believes, for in the Gaian framework, the division between animal, vegetable, and mineral is erased. All is "nature," wherever and whenever we look in the Gaian schema. The Gaia theory focuses on Earth processes, which offer insight into how culture operates and how we understand interrelationships among created realities (Thompson 1991: 172–73).

Although briefly involved in New Age currents, Thompson in 1983 began looking for new avenues to a "planetary consciousness" and found in Gaia a promising vehicle. Believing that history is inevitably paradoxical, Thompson claims that humanity can never know fully what it is about, for the reasoning mind gains insight into one reality only by casting shadows upon another. The world is thus "a structure of unconscious relations," and the relations of a global culture can only be the product of a process seemingly motored by avarice and fear. Gaia thus represents a concrete cosmology within which these antinomies of history become comprehensible. As David Cayley points out, "Gaia is the larger systemic mind of which we are the unconscious parts. We cannot be conscious of this greater mind by definition, but we can identify ourselves with it, and it is this identification which animates Bill Thompson" (quoted in Thompson 1991: 180–81).

What is the role of the human in the Gaian framework? For Thompson, it appears to be simply to sit back and reconcile itself to a process in which humans may be nothing more than a transitory phase. Rather than managing the planet, we are merely passengers, much like ants on a log, Thompson muses, drifting downstream, actively trying to steer that over which we have no control (Thompson 1991: 182). In promoting Lovelock and Margulis through his Lindisfarne Association, Thompson, it appears, is also promoting the limited role for the human in the Gaia process. He appears less involved in social action for the future sustainability of the planet than in "planetary consciousness raising" so we might reconcile ourselves to our microscopic function within the all-embracing Gaia.

Anthony Weston: Gaian Ethics

Anthony Weston, a member of the Department of Philosophy at the State University of New York at Stony Brook, has a particular interest in environmental ethics, as well as the ethics of technology and medicine. He has explored what he terms the sundry "forms of Gaian ethics" in an article for *Environmental Ethics* (Weston 1987). While claiming that Lovelock's Gaia hypothesis is very suggestive, Weston points out that what precisely it "suggests" is rather nebulous. He notes that Lovelock and Margulis both emphasize Gaia's powers, rather than human responsibility, and that Lovelock has at times characterized ecologists as "misanthropes" and "Luddites" (220). Weston suggests, however, that there are at least two other ethical approaches one can adopt with regard to Gaia: one is commensurate with contemporary philosophical ethics, and the other is more akin to "deep ecology."

First, Weston postulates, for the sake of argument, that one could regard Gaia not simply as a living entity but as a person, thereby forcing not a recasting of ethical assumptions but merely an expansion of our understanding of person to include other realities. In this manner, we might challenge not the ethical centrality of persons but the presupposition that only humans can be counted as persons (223). While such an approach appeals to a long ethical history of the rights of persons, Weston finds it anthropocentric in light of the current ecological situation and also too facile a maneuver. For Weston, Gaia ultimately is not a person but a novel locus of values (225).

Second, noting the correspondence between deep ecology and the Gaia theory, Weston comments that both view humans merely as one species among many in the vast sweep of Earth's processes, offering what deep ecologist Arne Naess calls a "total field" conception. In this understanding, we humans can only comprehend ourselves as elements of a much fuller and older life process. In this understanding, humans sense the destruction of Earth. We feel in our bowels, as it were, the destruction of the rain forest; hence our visceral connection to Gaia helps us empathize and therefore resist the destruction of the planet. Since we are an inextricable part of Gaia, this argument continues, we feel Gaia's pain.

Weston counters that such an approach presupposes a level of communication and identification among Earth's species that even the Gaia theorists do not detect. For example, in Lovelock's Daisy World experiment, Weston comments, the daisies don't communicate — they merely respond individually to changes in sunlight. While more developed species have greater sensitivities, it is not clear that these are physiological. The Gaia metaphor can be stretched too far to claim an intelligence for Gaia, an intelligence that simply may not exist (228). Weston also argues that such an approach devalues nonanimate matter, such as rocks and hills, and he worries about the environmental costs of such a devaluation. "Persons are not the only things that have value," he notes, "and neither is life itself" (228).

What is an acceptable Gaian ethic? For Weston, the answer lies not in substituting Gaia for one ethical framework but in assimilating Gaia within the already extant variety of environmental values. Gaia doesn't necessarily have only one meaning or one interpretation but could have many varied meanings, and it could help point us toward the interrelationship of various value systems. Weston suggests further that such an integration of Gaia into our ethical understanding should not be rushed (230).

Theological Responses

Douglas Hall: Reintegrating Creation

In Amsterdam during May 1987, James Lovelock and Canadian theologian Douglas Hall, along with a handful of others, discussed the ecological crisis. Invited by the World Council of Churches as a follow-up to the WCC's 1983 Vancouver call to engage the churches in a commitment to "justice, peace, and the integrity of creation," the British scientist and Canadian theologian emerged with a discussion paper entitled "Reintegrating God's Creation." Intriguingly, Hall, in his paper, does not deal with the Gaia hypothesis directly. Rather, he discusses the nature of the term "integrity of creation" and the human role in light of destructive ecological habits. (Hall wondered if the scientific community will give any credence to Lovelock's Gaia hypothesis, which strikes him as somewhat outlandish.)

As a Christian theologian, Hall professes that he cannot support those who advocate a human retreat from intervention in the world, such as some deep ecologists do. Rather, he proposes a contextual and strategic theology, one that walks the narrow path

between what he terms "prometheanism" (a destructive glorifica-
tion of human power) and passivity (Hall 1987: 32). Hall offers
three roles for the Christian: steward (which he further develops
in a book by the same title), priest, and poet.

The steward symbol, based in biblical texts and church tradition, conveys solidarity, accountability, and responsibility —
all providing a caring leadership. The priest symbol is founded
on representation, in which the priest represents God before the
"creature" and represents the "creature" before God. Hall maintains that the priest is called upon to be an empathetic and
compassionate mediator in reintegrating the world broken by
environmental despoliation. The third symbol, the poet, has its
roots in the prophetic tradition of ancient Israel, celebrates the
creaturely joys and visceral pain of being part of the created
world, and speaks not only for itself but also for other creatures
with whom it inhabits the universe (34–36).

For Hall, then, the role of the human is central to an environmental theology. However, Hall does not specifically contex-
tualize this human role in a Gaian framework. Though Hall was
literally in dialogue with Gaia, as it were, during his conversations
with Lovelock, he does not use Gaia as an overarching paradigm. In fact, neither he nor Lovelock ever refers to it in their
working paper.[13]

Thomas Berry: Gaia in a Cosmological Context

For Thomas Berry, a self-proclaimed "geologian," the scientific
wellsprings of the Gaia theory are part of a continuum through
which a new sense of the sacredness of the cosmos is coming from
modern science. With his own work deeply influenced by contemporary physics and astronomy, as evidenced by his collaboration
with mathematician Brian Swimme on *The Universe Story,* Berry
argues that theories of relativity, quantum physics, the uncer-
tainly principle of Heisenberg, the sense of a self-organizing
universe, and the more recent chaos theories have gotten us beyond Cartesian mechanistic thinking and into a more interrelated
understanding of our world. Gaia is part of these developments.

In "The Gaia Theory: Its Religious Implications" (1994), Berry claims that the Gaia hypothesis needs a new cosmology. For Berry, the universe is the primary revelatory event, and hence knowing and relating the story of the universe's unfolding, from the big bang or "primordial flaring forth" some fifteen billion years ago to the present, are of primary religious significance. In Berry's view the human is now in the driver's seat of geological evolution, moving us out of the Cenozoic era into either the "Technozoic" era, in which we continue to plunder the planet, or the "Ecozoic" era, in which we live within the functioning of the planet. The choice is ours.

Thus Berry, unlike Lovelock, ascribes a significant role to the human. Not only are we now the architects of evolutionary history — we are the beings in which the universe becomes self-conscious and through which it is able to reflect upon itself. Such a momentous role for the human in the cosmos has caused some to critique Berry's thought for its potentially dangerous anthropocentrism. In essence, Berry uses the Gaia theory as a springboard for his own musings on the mystical dimensions of the cosmos (see chapter 4, below). More often than not, his religious views are connected more to the views of animistic or shamanistic faiths than to Christian tradition. As several commentators have pointed out, Berry's cosmological vision rarely is distilled into Christian categories, and his universal story lacks a coherent plan of social action, a point made by Jon Sobrino, Paul Knitter, and Gregory Baum.

Conclusion: Gaian Implications for a Christian Political Theology of the Environment

The Gaia theory, as some of the practical, philosophical, and theological commentators suggest, raises a host of questions for those wishing to engage in a political theology of the environment. As intimated above, many of these questions revolve around the role of the human in the Gaian schema. Are we humans mere transient blips, a short-lived, destructive species with little lasting impact on the planet, as Margulis, Lovelock, and

William Irwin Thompson propose? Are we to refrain from eating meat, stop shaving, eliminate baths, and, while we're at it, throw out our industrial society, as it were, with the bathwater, as Kit Pedler proclaims? Should we assimilate Gaia into a preexisting set of environmental values, reconciling ourselves to a pluriform ethical schema, as Anthony Weston proposes? Shall we take the cooperative model advanced by Gaia as a blueprint for an ethic of earth-healing, as advanced by Rosemary Radford Ruether? Are we called to be stewards, priests, and poets in light of the ecological crisis, as suggested by Douglas John Hall? Or are we the self-consciousness of the universe, as postulated by Thomas Berry, whose role for the human is to place Gaia within a cosmological context?[14]

Beyond these questions, however, are the pressing social justice issues and concerns of a political theology of the environment. Is Gaia useful for a Christian social justice perspective on environmental destruction? Does Gaia provide a suitable framework for articulating the role of the human within such a social justice perspective? A social justice perspective views the world as a political economy, that is, as a structure of power relationships in which there are haves and have-nots. Can Gaia be understood as a political economy in addition to an earth economy in which the poor nations, particularly of the South, bear the brunt of ecological destruction?

A social justice perspective posits a preferential option for the poor. Is such an option viable within a Gaian framework? Lastly, a social justice perspective ascribes special responsibilities to persons and governments of Northern nations in effecting a just global community. Can Gaia sharpen our analysis of and insight into North-South differences and help develop a model of action that takes into account these differences?

Gaia *is* helpful for a social justice perspective in several ways. First, as Lovelock himself comments, Gaia helps us look at the world not as a mechanistic Cartesian engine but as an interrelated, vital, and cooperative enterprise in which interdependency rather than competition is the hallmark of life. Second, Gaia is useful for a social justice framework by revealing that the context in which human praxis is waged is one of critical and unavoidable interconnectedness. A key insight of European political theology, Third World liberation theology, and feminist theology is that a transformative theology must be contextual. Gaia forces us to expand our notion of context beyond social, economic, and political dimensions to include a critical planetary dimension.

Gaia also has, however, serious limitations for a social justice perspective. First, in human terms, it is ahistorical. It lacks an analysis of existing power structures as well as historical patterns of inequality in which political praxis occurs. Moreover, it underestimates the destructive potency of the human species. By viewing humans as simply one life-form among many, and a largely inessential one at that, Gaia woefully undervalues the human ability to destroy the life-systems of the planet. Hence Gaia ultimately lacks a framework for critically assessing and challenging exploitative human activity.

In conclusion, it can safely be said that Gaia is indeed an important interlocutor for a political theology of environment, providing a crucial framework of interconnection and cooperation. Its ultimate value lies, perhaps, in the fact that it prompts us to envisage our world in a novel, challenging, and inspirational way, as the burgeoning Gaia literature attests. The question as to whether or not the theory is "true" is, in the end, secondary to whether it helps us link justice and peace *to* the integrity of all creation. Gaia, I believe, can help us forge this still fragile but necessary nexus, as long as we remain aware of both its evocative power and its grave limitations.

Chapter 3

Process Theology

Intersubjectivity with Nature

Process theology, for a variety of reasons, is crucial to explore in attempting to discern the contours of a political theology of the environment.

First, process theology, as evinced particularly by John B. Cobb Jr., has been among the earliest and most sustained Christian paradigms to take our present ecological crisis seriously. It has attempted, building on the works of Alfred North Whitehead and Charles Hartshorne, to remain faithful to the Christian tradition while incorporating into its ambit more recent scientific investigations involving quantum physics and advanced molecular biology. In this sense, it has tried to make Christianity relevant to a modern context in which secularization, broadly understood, has been a hallmark.

Second, process theology has tried to find an appropriate role for the human in light of our present ecological challenge. In its critique of certain strands of the Christian tradition, it has jettisoned the highly individualistic notion of the human agent bequeathed to us by the Enlightenment and classical Protestantism. In its stead, process theology has advanced the notion of the "person-in-community." In so doing, it advocates what it terms an "ecological" rather than "mechanistic" model of nature that sees the human more as a participant with than as master of or "steward" over nature.

Finally, process theology in North America has explicitly attempted to embrace German political theology, feminist theology, and, to a lesser extent, Latin American liberation theology, revealing a self-critical approach and an openness to social and economic analysis while nevertheless offering challenges to these theological movements.

In this section, I shall cursorily discuss the general outlines of process theology and then focus briefly on the work of three of its chief North American proponents who have focused on ecological concerns: John B. Cobb Jr., Jay B. McDaniel, and Catherine Keller. In so doing, I shall attempt to delineate, concisely, salient elements of process theology's understanding of nature, its conception of the role for the human, and its implications for Christianity's reflections on the environment.

What Is Process Theology?

"Process theology" — the term was first used by Bernard Loomer in 1946 — is primarily the theological application of the "process philosophy" of Alfred North Whitehead and Charles Hartshorne. In general, the term "process philosophy" denotes any philosophical stance that revolves around the notion of flux or becoming.[1] For many process theologians, a central tenet is that the "substances" of Aristotle and Saint Thomas are actually "societies," aggregates of actual entities. Whole events come and go; societies to whose existence they temporarily contribute perdure and are thus deemed the "substances" of commonsense experience (Bracken 1987).[2]

Creation is viewed as a continuing process, not as a finished product, and process theologians find this the most compelling way to interpret the order and nature of life (Ford 1974; Bracken 1987). Relatedly, God is seen not as all-powerful but as all-loving. God's potency is suasive, not coercive, leading Cobb and McDaniel, for example, to speak of the divine as a "lure" (Cobb and Griffin 1976; McDaniel 1990b). A chief understanding of God is as one who suffers with humanity, a notion that Cobb views as a point of convergence with political theology (see Cobb 1982b).

David Ray Griffin succinctly pinpoints four aspects of process theology that lend themselves to an ecological orientation.

First, there is no dichotomy between humanity and nature. All nonhuman individuals have intrinsic value, and thus there is an inherent antidote to Christian anthropocentrism. Second, in process theology, not all living beings are of equal intrinsic value. Unlike Albert Schweitzer's "reverence for life" schema or deep ecology, process theology claims that certain life-forms, owing to their "richness of experience," have higher intrinsic value than do others.

Third, because the basic components of life are seen as momentary events rather than enduring substances, relations to others are internal to each individual. One's personal well-being is hence bound up with the well-being of the rest of the world. Thus, we must be concerned not only with an individual's intrinsic value but also with ecological value as well. Finally, the "others" mentioned in such events include God. God permeates all of nature and is present in each individual, from a proton to photoplankton to a blue jay to a human. Each species is thus deserving of respect as a manifestation of the divine (Griffin 1992: 384–85).

John B. Cobb Jr.: The Quest for a Just, Participatory, and Sustainable Society

The creative action of God which concerns us is the creation that takes place now, moment by moment, in our environment and in ourselves. In each moment God confronts the totality of the past with new possibilities. How the world responds, whether in acceptance or rejection of these possibilities, God does not determine. He created by persuasion in and through the free decisions of his creatures. To believe in God is to trust his creative work amongst and within us, to adapt ourselves to it, to attend to it as it operates in all creatures, to sensitize ourselves to it as it works in us, and to respond to its call to new risks.

—JOHN B. COBB JR., *Is It Too Late? A Theology of Ecology*

In 1969, having been prompted to read Paul Ehrlich's *The Population Bomb* by his son Clifford, John B. Cobb Jr. had a self-described *metanoia* experience. While his career until that point was largely concerned with incorporating the process thought of Alfred North Whitehead and Charles Hartshorne into a theological perspective, the serious state of environmental degradation would thenceforth be an important and sustained concern for Cobb. As he recalls: "For the first time, I saw, vividly, the ways in which increases in consumption and population feed on one another and bring insupportable pressures to bear on the earth's resources. The danger to our future and that of our children struck me with almost unbearable force" (1972: 1).[3]

In this section, I will review the fruit of Cobb's theological concern for the environment, paying especial attention to its depiction of the role of the human and his characterization of nature. I shall also pose some critical questions regarding Cobb's provocative insights.[4]

Process Theology and the Ecological Worldview

The overarching thrust of Cobb's theology is to make sense of Christian faith in light of modernity. Indeed, as he himself claims, he experienced a faith-crisis when he first attended the University of Chicago. His somewhat sheltered and pietistic faith was shattered by the insights of modernity. It was only with the embrace of Whitehead's process theology that Cobb was able to reconstruct a theology that engaged modern developments in science and made sense to him in a period of secularization.

For Cobb, all reality is physically interrelated. For him, this insight is one of the great contributions of modern science, especially systems-theory, which assays to demonstrate how all matter is "kindred" in some sense. Cobb delineates the scientific and theological dimensions of this perspective most fully in *The Liberation of Life: From the Cell to the Community* (1981), which he co-wrote with biologist Charles Birch, though these ideas percolate throughout his other writings. Echoing the "philosophy of organism" perspective of Whitehead, Cobb seeks a twofold liberation regarding life: (1) liberation from the "tyrannical" tradition that views organisms as objects rather than as subjects;

78

and (2) liberation of social structures and human behavior from manipulation and domination to "respect for life in its fullness" (Cobb and Birch 1981: 2).

Cobb critically examines what he terms the mechanistic, deterministic, and "vitalistic" models of nature that have been championed by Newtonian and Darwinian science. Moreover, Cobb claims that certain ensuing metaphors, such as "web of life" and "balance of nature," while evocative and important, unfortunately lack the specificity of scientific understanding, rendering them too glib to be of pragmatic usefulness. Cobb posits rather an ecological model that builds on contemporary scientific understandings of the interrelation of all biotic matter. Ecology and evolution are inseparable realities. The ecological model, as articulated by Cobb, studies flora and fauna within their environments, and hence protection of habitat becomes a central, rather than peripheral, scientific concern.

Manifesting the process orientation toward "events" rather than static "substances," Cobb provides a succinct description of this model:

> The ecological model holds that living things behave as they do only in interaction with the other things which constitute their environments. It does not deny, of course, that many features of their behavior are determined by structures of the organism itself or that much has been learned when these structures have been examined by scientists with the mechanistic model in mind. But the ecological model proposes that on closer examination the constituent elements of the structure at each level operate in patterns of interconnectedness which are not mechanical. Each element behaves as it does because of the relations it has to other elements in the whole, and these relations are not well understood in terms of the laws of mechanics. (Cobb and Birch 1981: 83)[5]

For Cobb, behavior within the ecological model of life can most adequately be explained as an "event" rather than as a "substance." Within this framework, subjectivity or experience is ascribed to all such events, and because for Cobb all experience has value, events themselves have intrinsic value. Therefore all things have a modicum of intrinsic value either in themselves or in their constituent parts. For Cobb, such an understanding is irreconcilable with what he views as the predominant anthropocentric ethical heritage, which has relied on mechanistic and positivistic worldviews. Cobb claims that theologians concerned about the environment are hamstrung by a paucity of categories in Western science that seek to build such a model. He asserts that when we see ourselves as outside nature, we are more disposed to destroy nature, thinking cryptically that our destruction of the environment will not ultimately destroy us.

While claiming that the traditions of idealism (Kant), empiricism (Locke), and materialism (Marx) all contributed key elements at critical junctures in the cavalcade of Western thought, Cobb argues that none of them attributed significant reality to "things in themselves." Centering on the human rather than the nonhuman world, each of these intellectual currents never fully grappled with the possibility of nonhuman nature's ethical claims upon us.

The ecological worldview suggests that our first wrong turn occurred when we supposed we could isolate some elements from the whole and could cull the truth from them in abstraction. This required the development of a conceptuality built upon abstraction. While conceding that much can be learned from such an approach, Cobb counters that "only a knowledge that is ecologically related to all knowledge is appropriate to a reality that is ecologically interconnected" (Cobb 1988a: 111).[6]

Cobb notes that though there have been celebrated countervailing voices within Western thought, their reflections on nature have often been muted or ignored. He mentions, for example, how the radical ecological teachings of Saint Francis of Assisi and Albert Schweitzer have largely engendered superciliousness or mild shame among otherwise sympathetic commentators:

Francis of Assisi is greatly admired throughout Christendom, but we smile condescendingly at his behavior toward birds and animals. Schweitzer is widely recognized as one of the great men of the twentieth century, but we are a little embarrassed by just that behavior of his which shows that he took seriously the principle of reverence for all life. We tolerate these strange actions as the pardonable foibles of a saint and genius. (Cobb 1972: 124–25)

In other words, we savor the cream and not the grist of these visionaries when it comes to their ecological insights. Given the dominant anthropocentrism of the tradition, Cobb intimates, such radical environmental teachings, even by acknowledged spiritual giants, are not to be taken seriously.

Curiously, however, while sensitive to Schweitzer's reverence for life, Cobb is also critical of it. He claims that Schweitzer's absolutist approach to life offers no way of discriminating value among various life-forms. As a physician, Schweitzer was involved in the killing of bacteria threatening human life, Cobb notes, yet his own theory, according to Cobb, offers no basis for prioritizing life-forms or justifying killing of those life-forms.

Cobb strives to adopt a more nuanced position. Rather than holding that every life is of "infinite or absolute value," Cobb gainsays "that any finite thing is of any infinite worth" (Cobb 1981: 144). Instead, Cobb uses the notion of "richness of experience" to serve as a measure for prioritization of life, a notion he finds useful in determining the appropriate use of animals and ethical use of abortion.

Humans: Part of the Continuing Evolutionary Process

Within this ecological paradigm, for Cobb, the human is not the zenith of nature but merely a distinctive part of nature, a product of the evolutionary process. While the human has unique powers, it nonetheless is still adapting to and shaping its environment, like all other evolutionary creatures. In this worldview, because richness of experience, rather than substance, is central, the notion of the human as an agent becomes problematic. For Cobb, to conceive of an agent who acts is to regress to the notion of substance. Such an agent would have to exist prior to and independently of the activity and be largely untouched by that activity. For Cobb, nature contains no evidence of such an agent. Rather, "the activity itself constitutes nature" (Cobb 1988a: 109).

Moreover, just as there are no agents of activity distinct from the activity elsewhere in the world, Cobb argues, "so there is no self who is the subject of experience apart from the activity that is the experience in the human being" (Cobb 1988a: 109). Claiming that this ecological understanding is concurrent with that of David Hume and Buddhism, Cobb maintains that there is a flow of experience that simply has that richness and just that degree of identity through time that it factually possesses — nothing more and nothing less.

In stressing the need to see humans as part of nature, Cobb suggests that we are not distinct in our ability to feel and act, since other animals also share in these activities. Though the human is interdependent, it remains independent; interdependent does not mean identical. While the notion of the human as "steward" has merits, Cobb prefers the notion of the human as a participant in a process of healing and growth. Such a metaphor indicates that while the human has responsibilities to fulfill in the healing process, the human is not in control of that process but merely plugs in, as it were, to a larger emerging event (Cobb 1972: 85–91). While Cobb claims alliance with deep ecologists, such as George Sessions and Arnie Naess, who assert that human beings are merely one species among others, he contends that the Judeo-Christian understanding of humanity gives us a different role. Cobb argues that the human person is unique and manifested this uniqueness early on with the use of tools and a hunting and gathering economy. Each human life is not merely a product of its genetic inheritance and environment. It is also a creative response to life, one that incorporates the element of transcending, which, through grace, leads us to do the unexpected and unimagined (Cobb and Birch 1981: 108).

Reflecting the thought of Douglas John Hall, Cobb argues that the biblical injunction of dominion has been misunderstood by interpreters of the Bible. Dominion has been taken to justify destruction of the earth, though the scriptural call has always involved responsibility for creation and accountability. But even if we were to focus solely on dominion, Cobb notes, "this policy would still come about through human decision and would thereby reflect our dominion" (Daly and Cobb: 1989: 387–88).

In demonstrating his distinctiveness from a dominion-based position, Cobb responds to Paul Shepard's *Nature and Madness* (1982), which suggests that humans, rather than embracing the modern self as capable of change and improvement, should be what they were in an earlier time and, like other animals, "be what they are." The idea is that the prophetic-Enlightenment tradition has led to human projects destructive of both humanity and nature and is irredeemable, leading to an ecologically destructive anthropocentrism that cannot be shed. While Cobb concedes Shepard's point that humanity was better off, biblically speaking, before the Fall and before tasting the fruits of good and evil, especially the evils of modern technology and warfare, he assails Shepard for advocating the impossible task of duplicating a past situation, "a life in which the knowledge of good and evil is gone." Such a notion is a fallacy.

Cobb maintains that the only realistic choice in our fallen state is the prophetic biblical tradition, one that is nurtured by self-transcendence and leads, as in the case of Gandhi or Martin Luther King Jr., to a consciousness of systemic evil and an effective critique of sinful structures. Cobb writes:

> There is, then, really no alternative to the prophetic stance in fallen history. The choice is between calling for the return to the Garden and proposing some different end both from where we began and from where we have been since then. Shepard chooses the Garden; we choose a different end. (Daly and Cobb 1989: 390)

For Cobb, while all life has value, not all life is of equal value. The measure for determining a hierarchy of value in process thought thus becomes not an absolute value for all creatures but "the richness of experience of each life form." In this sense, Cobb undermines a universal, absolute value placed on human life. As Cobb explains, the intrinsic value of experience bestows rights. Those who have the ability to experience have the right to savor such richness of experience to the best of their abilities. While they have the right to have their lives respected, and wherever feasible, safeguarded, such rights are not absolute in a strict sense. "The only absolute," Cobb contends, "is respect for life itself" (Cobb and Birch 1981: 205).[7]

For Cobb, Life, with a capital *L,* is the scientifically indicated yet intuitively sensed "ground of being" referred to by Paul Tillich and Karl Rahner. In Cobb's writings, there is a conflation of Life with God. He follows Whitehead's notion of God as Life, for not only is God's immanence the life-yielding precept of the world, but this life-yielding precept is itself alive. God is the ultimate example of the ecological model of life, maintaining, as it does, that living things are constituted in part by their environments (Cobb and Birch 1981: 195–96). In equating Life with God, Cobb proclaims that God has no favorites, or "preferential options":

Life favors all living things, and precisely for that reason does not take sides in our inevitably competitive existence. Life favors both the fox and the hare, supporting the success of both hunter and hunted. Life favors all the runners in the race, and hence has no favorites. (Cobb and Birch 1981: 198)

Though Cobb sees process theology as a form of political theology, as his book *Process Theology as Political Theology* suggests, his notion of Life as God is problematic for such a nexus. Such a God, who has no favorites and takes no sides, is in clear contrast to liberation theology's preferential option for the poor and its insight that in cases of rich versus poor, the biblical God always takes the side of the poor, as should the church.

Homo Economicus

Just as Cobb's ecological model posits the person-in-community with nonhuman nature, his notion of economics puts persons-in-community with other participants in the human economy. Thus Cobb's "Homo economicus" becomes "Homo economicus-in-community."

Cobb proposes this notion of person-in-community to counteract what he sees as the extreme individualism that marks laissez-faire capitalism. Seeking to reorient economics to serve human needs and respond to human dilemmas, Cobb strives for an alternative to socialism and capitalism. With economist Herman Daly, he proposes a "steady-state economy," one oriented not toward growth but rather, in the terminology of the World Council of Churches, toward a "just, participatory, and sustainable" economy, a theme he explores most fully in *For the. Common Good:*

> The individualism of current economic theory is manifest in the purely self-interested behavior it assumes. It has no real place for fairness, malevolence, and benevolence, nor for the preservation of human life or any other moral concern. The world which that economic theory normally pictures is one in which individuals all seek their own good and are indifferent to the success or failure of other individuals engaged in the same activity. There is no way to conceive of a collective good. (Daly and Cobb 1989: 159)

This quest leads Cobb to critique forcefully free-trade agreements that disrupt local sustainable economies so they can allegedly partake in the global marketplace, which is increasingly run largely by transnational corporations. Such models, with the aid of the World Bank and International Monetary Fund, have led to structural-adjustment policies that are not only socially but ecologically destructive. In elaborating his critique, Cobb looks to premodern models, such as feudalism, to see what they may offer, in an attempt to recover premodern ideas without sacrificing the fruits of modernity such as individual rights and freedoms and political equality. Cryptically, he also, in this vein, assails national economic control in favor of decentralization of the economy, advocating giving, in the case of the United States, individual states more power over welfare payments and their own economic planning.[8]

An Unoptimistic Hope

Throughout his writings, Cobb evinces a stubborn, almost mystical hope, one nurtured by his sense of the prophetic biblical tradition and his process-informed Christian faith. Part of this hope also stems from Cobb's notion of the Spirit as always at work in the world in the guise of Life itself — budding, changing, striving for novelty and continuance (Cobb 1972: 142–43). The ability of the human to engage in transcendence, as suggested above, leads to novelty, not predetermination; thus "the chance to love," in the words of poet W. H. Auden, "is always open till we die." The transformative power of grace yields grounds for hope; because of grace, resignation and release are not choices for the Christian. "We know we are not masters of our history," Cobb surmises, "but neither are we mere victims" (Cobb 1992: 11).

Thus, in Cobb's work, we discern an ecological model of nature that emphasizes human interrelation and interdependence with the nonhuman world, a role for the human that attempts to eschew a view that perceives the human as superior to and master over nature, and an attempt to hold up the leavening potency of Christian grace for creating a sustainable future within our economic, academic, and religious establishments. In so doing, Cobb's thought has "sired" a new generation of process ecological theologians, the most prominent of whom we now consider.

Jay B. McDaniel: Animal Rights and a Life-Centered Ethic

An ecologically sensitive Christianity...might be called a "life-centered" version of creation inclusive theology.... I use the term life-centered to name an alternative to that human-centeredness which has characterized so much modern Christian thinking.... To be centered in life is not to worship life at the expense of God, but rather to be interested in the well-being of life along with God. My proposal ...is the very God in whom Christians trust is interested in the well-being of each and every life. A God of this sort is life-centered. We are faithful to this God by being similarly centered.

—JAY McDANIEL, *Good News for Animals?*

Though an intellectual scion of John B. Cobb Jr. and an exponent of process theology, Jay B. McDaniel brings a distinctive vision to a "life-centered" Christianity. McDaniel has an understanding of nature that is filtered through the lens of animals, as it were, and, more precisely, animal rights, rendering him unique among the process theologians concerned professionally about the environment.[9]

In *Of God and Pelicans* (1989), McDaniel vividly describes a formative experience in his relationship with animals. As a ten-year-old hunting with his father, he shot a deer. Seeing it writhe in pain, McDaniel was told by his father that he must shoot the animal again. Unnerved by the animal's suffering, he could not steady his rifle. After relinquishing his gun to his father, who finally shot the deer, Jay asked if animals could "feel," though he now already knew the answer (1989: 111).

McDaniel, in his theology, is concerned about animals' suffering, particularly in the agricultural and cosmetic industries. This is exemplified in the very title of his book *Of God and Pelicans,* which makes reference to the relation between God and the "second chick" hatched in a pelican nest. Normally, McDaniel explains, a female pelican lays two eggs at a time; the first pelican chick is nurtured and fed, while the second is forced out of the nest by the first chick and prevented from returning by its parents. Ninety percent of the time, this "backup chick" dies of abuse or starvation. McDaniel's starting point here again is animal suffering, but one ingrained in an evolutionary process. How can God design such a seemingly cruel pattern? Does God care about the well-being of the second pelican chick? For McDaniel, the answers lie in the process understanding of God, a God who is not all-powerful but all-loving (1989: 22–23).

McDaniel, following Cobb, argues that God's potency is in persuasion, not coercion. He maintains that the natural world holds a certain creativity independent of God's creativity and that through this, evolutionary patterns can emerge that even God cannot prevent, a God who remains empathetic if not somewhat enfeebled in the face of such anguish. This evolutionary perspective depicts God as all-present but not all-controlling. In this process understanding, God is the universal "experiencer," or, one might say, Supreme Empathy. God suffers not only with humans but with nonhumans as well. Thus, while God, McDaniel writes, cannot prevent the suffering of the second chick, whose predicament lies in evolution's creative pattern, God can "redeem" its suffering (1989: 24–25). Comparing God's love to parental affection, McDaniel argues that God wants to redeem parts as well as the whole, the individual pelican chick as well as the whole pelican species. "As the mother of all pelicans," he writes, "she would want to redeem the individual backup chick as well as the entire family of pelicans" (1989: 42). McDaniel explains that this does not imply that God loves all creatures in the same manner or with equal vigor. There might be more to love in a chimpanzee than an amoeba, he claims, owing to the former's superior "richness of experience," a concept Birch and Cobb delineate, as we have seen. Yet he stresses that God loves each creature on its own terms and for its own sake (McDaniel 1994c: 80).[10]

McDaniel goes on to speak of the second chick's "redemption":

Perhaps as contributing to God, then, the pelican chick might find redemption, for as divine harmonizing occurs, the chick's experiences are linked with everything else in the universe in a way that transcends the brokenness of creation as he experienced it. A harmony is achieved in God that is not achieved on Earth. This eschatological harmonization does not involve a forgetfulness of the chick's life on its own terms. Rather, to whatever extent possible, it involves a creative integration of his life on *his* terms with all other lives on *their* terms. It is the realization in divine experience of an eschatological community of love. The chick is redeemed by contributing to, and being remembered in, the everlasting life of God. (1989: 44)

While the attempt to redeem the suffering of individual animals in this fashion is hopeful, it does raise a bevy of questions. Could such an approach be used to justify animal suffering at the hands of humans? Is it a pie-in-the-sky type of message that could be used by agribusiness and the meat industry to justify their commoditization of and cruelty to animals? Just as traditional church teaching in some eras told poor and exploited groups that their reward would be great in heaven, thereby conveniently eschewing involvement in struggles for social justice, might this understanding of redemption have a similar resonance for those working with animals?

Moreover, McDaniel, following Cobb's understanding that the Holy Spirit is reflected in part in the movement of Life, argues that God takes no sides in such evolutionary patterns of suffering. "In the struggle between the two chicks," McDaniel contends, "God is on the side of each" (1989: 39). How does such divine equanimity square with a biblical and liberationist understanding that sees God as taking the side of the poor, oppressed, and downtrodden? How does this aspect of process theology jibe with God's and the church's "preferential option for the poor," which has been highlighted in liberation theology?[11]

More broadly, McDaniel is interested in the role of individual creatures within larger ecosystems, striving, in a sense, not to lose sight of the individual trees amidst the forest. For him, the God of process thought, which, as we have seen in our treatment of John

Cobb, is imaged more as a lure than as a monarch, calls us into a nonviolent, covenant relationship with animals:

> If, as process thinkers suggest, the Lure of God is always to-ward the fullness of life, the peace churches show that, in human life, the "fullness" toward which God calls is itself nonviolent. We are called by the very Heart of the universe to be gentle and caring in relation to one another...as is God....Though our four-legged relatives may not be able to live in full peace with one another or with us, we hu-mans are "made in God's image." As empowered by God's Spirit, we can live in peace with one another and with them. (1994d: 85)

McDaniel claims that he, like all process theologians, grieves over the massive suffering of domesticated animals at the hands of humans, arguing that such affliction is immoral. He hopes that in the future such suffering will end, either owing to moral per-suasion or legal coercion (1988: 93).[12] For McDaniel, this solely instrumental view of animals, also reflected in the cosmetic in-dustry, where beauty products are animal-tested, is not only an ethical problem but a spiritual challenge as well. It arises from the understanding that animals exist simply for our own use, as means to our ends, and that we can therefore treat them any way we find useful. More so than Cobb, McDaniel seeks to respond directly to the *spiritual* issues involved in environmental destruc-tion. He suggests five ways in which an ecological spirituality might more appropriately perceive animals: (1) as having intrinsic value; (2) as kindred creatures loved by God; (3) as "extensions" of God's body; (4) as spiritual guides, and (5) as images of God.

In this context, McDaniel advocates vegetarianism as a Chris-tian act of solidarity with both the earth and the poor. He notes how much of the world's grain supply presently goes to feed livestock rather than hungry children, how the North American meat habit is a driving force in the destruction of rain forests for grazing land, and how 90 percent of the deleterious organic waste-water pollution in the United States is caused by livestock

(1990a: 64–79). He endorses the WCC's threefold lifestyle alteration, which calls Christians to (1) avoid cosmetics and household products that have been cruelly tested on animals; (2) avoid clothing and other fashion items whose production has been historically linked to cruelty to animals; and (3) avoid patronizing forms of entertainment that treat animals as mere means to human ends. As to the last of these: we are called to seek benign forms of entertainment, ones that nurture a sense of the wonder of God's creation and reawaken that duty of conviviality we can discharge by living respectfully in community with all life, the animals included (McDaniel 1990a: 78).

McDaniel, like Cobb, is not opposed to certain animal uses, as in some types of animal research. He does suggest, though, that attempts be made to reduce the number of animals used in such manner, to substitute with alternatives for animals whenever feasible (e.g., with computer models or tissue cultures), and to develop techniques that minimize animal discomfort and pain (1990a).

But what are the criteria for using some animals and not others for such purposes? For McDaniel, the determining factor is the level of sentience or what Birch and Cobb call the "richness of experience." McDaniel writes:

> To be sentient is to be able consciously or unconsciously to take into account, and thus enjoy, environmental influence. All living beings, including cancer cells, do this to one degree or another; hence all living beings have intrinsic value. But some, the more complexly organized, enjoy amid their sentience greater harmony or intensity — greater "richness of experience" to use Birch and Cobb's phrase — than others. By virtue of this richness, they have greater intrinsic value. If a life must be taken, and if instrumental considerations are equalized, it is best to take the life of the being with the lesser capacity for sentience, and hence the lesser degree of intrinsic value. Thus, in choosing between a cancer cell in a woman and the woman herself, the cancer cell can be sacrificed. (1988: 95)

This explication, however, raises a host of questions. Who ultimately determines a being's richness of experience? Might such a criterion conveniently be used by powerful elites to justify exploitation of impoverished persons, for example, or the mentally handicapped, or prisoners, or anyone else deemed to have less richness of experience? Does this not speak of a type of conception of hierarchy that has been deleterious in the human treatment of the nonhuman world, a conception that the process thinkers have rightly critiqued? The sentience yardstick for determining a value of a being's life remains problematic.

McDaniel, building on a phrase of Cobb's, argues that in pursuing an ecological theology, he is pursuing "a way that excludes no ways." While this does not suggest that every idea is acceptable, it does entail a radical openness to novel thought in keeping with a process perspective. Hence, McDaniel embraces Buddhism and feminism in his quest for an ecological theology, and, though critical at times of some precepts, he nonetheless incorporates some of these traditions' insights into his theological construct.[13]

The Role of the Human

As suggested, McDaniel, like Cobb, sees the human as part of nature, not as somehow transcending it (1989: 25). Moreover, McDaniel does not underestimate the great power of the human to alter, for good or ill, the natural landscape. McDaniel shows a great sensitivity to the social and economic forces that oppress both nature and poor persons, and his "way that excludes no ways" demonstrates a critical engagement with liberation and political theology (though to a lesser extent than does John Cobb). Thus, whether criticizing the meat and poultry industry, assailing the dumping of toxic waste (1990: 84), deploring the horrific petrochemical pollution in Cubatão, Brazil, or criticizing the machismo that leads to the killing of animals and other humans to prove "manhood" (1989: 111ff.), McDaniel is ever-mindful of the social, economic, and cultural structures that lead to a denigration of the nonhuman world.

For him, the role of the human, in light of its vast power, is one of responsibility, both to future and to nonhuman generations (1990a: 85). He builds upon Douglas John Hall's notion of "dominion-as-stewardship" and is at once wary of his own terminology. As he explains:

Of course, even if we assume that dominion means stewardship, the very idea of stewardship can be problematic. The idea easily lends itself to attitudes of separation from the rest of creation. If dominion-as-stewardship is to be affirmed, emphasis must be placed on the fact that stewards themselves are creatures among creatures, human nodes in the broader web of life. (1989: 74)

Even the *imago Dei,* for McDaniel, refers to a distinctive capability of the human to care for creation with a "stewardly compassion" that mirrors God's.

But what about dominion? Should this notion be retained? McDaniel replies affirmatively, for it denotes an irrefutable fact: humans do today have a certain reign over the earth. He argues that this concrete dominion is expressed through urbanization, resource exploitation, agriculture, and other features of modern industrialization. Moreover, our dominion, according to McDaniel, is "irreversible":

By United Nations estimates, the human population will be around 6.3 billion by A.D. 2000 and 11 billion by the end of the next century. It would be impossible for 6.3 billion people to live on the planet without exercising inordinate rule over other creatures and their habitats, if only to meet basic needs for food or shelter. To meet these needs, much manipulation will be required, for good or ill. (1994c: 74)

What we need is the notion of "right dominion," McDaniel argues, which builds upon a notion of dominion-as-stewardship that denotes "kindly use in a spirit of respect." Such a notion encourages us to increase the quality, not the quantity, of human life, with diminished abuse of domesticated animals and decreased impact on habitats and wildlife. "It invites us to develop societies," McDaniel writes, "that are ecologically sustainable even as they are socially just" (1994c: 75).

The Notion of Shalom

As intimated, McDaniel, much more so than Cobb, as we have seen, and Keller, as we shall see, is interested in fostering an ecological *spirituality.*[14] A central motif of such a spirituality is the notion of "shalom," often translated from the Hebrew as "peace," though it suggests not only the absence of violence but the fullness of life.[15] "Shalom is harmony eternally observed and internally felt" (McDaniel 1990a: 18).

Eschewing "unrealistic romanticism," however, McDaniel is very quick to point out that, given predator-prey relations, such a peaceful harmony is an impossible ideal in our present plane of existence. He wryly observes:

> There may be a kind of external harmony in the overall ecological system in which the wolf eats the rabbit, but it is doubtful that the rabbit feels this harmony...while she is being eaten. As long as one rabbit experiences disharmony, the fullness of shalom has not been realized. (McDaniel 1990: 18)[16]

At best, then, we can hope for approximations of shalom, a culture in which we would use technology responsibly and strive for a minimization of human destruction of the natural world and greater "ecstasy and trust, wholeness and solidarity" (McDaniel 1990a: 18–19).

As a Christian, McDaniel believes that the fullness of shalom is realized in Jesus Christ, whose life, death, and resurrection are "witnesses" to this vision and indicators of the "mystery" of the incarnated Word. For McDaniel, as a process theologian, this "Word" suggests the lure of the divine. In Jesus, he contends, we perceive the "lure" enfleshed. In his humanity, Jesus at times embraced God to the extent that his hopes and God's hope became enmeshed. In a statement that illustrates his process orientation, McDaniel notes, "He [Jesus] became transparent to God's Lure in such a way that God's lure became his Lure" (1990a: 160).

McDaniel's ecological spirituality, as has been suggested, has several chief elements:

1. a hope not for a utopia but [for] a more sustainable and equitable world;

2. an emphasis on the interconnectedness of all things, the intrinsic value of all life, and the compassion of God for all life-forms;

3. openness to other religions;

4. a faith which sees God immanent in each living being as a "lure toward wholeness," shaped by a Buddhist understanding, and thus claiming that neither God nor the world is changeless;

5. a panentheistic manner of envisioning divine mystery, which suggests that such mystery is the mind or heart of the universe, and the universe is the "body of God";

6. a refusal to "absolutize" itself, and thus a willingness to always be open to growth, to a process of becoming.[17]

For McDaniel, in the womb of process thought lies the creative synthesis that will nurture an authentic ecological spirituality:

> For process thinkers, the life well-lived is one that is open to the divine heart. Openness of this sort is faith, and it is an art rather than a science. It involves a trust in a Presence who cannot be manipulated through conscious control and whose depths cannot be fully exhausted by conceptual formulas or religious doctrines. The fruits of openness include value-pluralistic thinking, care for others, a hunger for justice, the enjoyment of relational power, and union of thought and feeling, a discovery of oneself as creatively integrative, an

appreciation of nature as organic and evolutionary, and a reverence for life. (McDaniel 1989: 144)

In McDaniel, then, we see threads of John Cobb's insight spun in new patterns, especially around the notion of sensitivity to animals, and stitched together in an overarching concern for an ecological spirituality, one that is intended to lead to a greater sensitivity to the earth, its systems, and its creatures.

Catherine Keller

Like McDaniel, Catherine Keller is a former pupil of John B. Cobb Jr. Yet, whereas a sensitivity to animals is the galvanizing concern for McDaniel, Keller is animated by a feminist perspective in her ecological theology, a theology that remains under the umbrella of process thought.

In her major work, *From a Broken Web: Separation, Sexism, and Self* (1986), Keller thanks her "teacher John Cobb" not only for sharing his process vision but also for "unflinchingly encouraging my feminist preoccupations" (1986: xi). An associate professor of theology at Drew University, she dates these preoccupations to her student days at Claremont, when Thiasos, a group devoted to the study of women in religion, invited Mary Daly to speak. The momentum of Daly's thought, Keller notes, "as well as the organizing and aftermath of the total event, rerouted my thinking and writing" (1986: xi).

The Role of the Human: Toward a Selfhood of Creative Integration

For Keller, the predominant cultural ethos of the Western world maintains that an individual attains authentic identity only if clearly separated from others and from the rest of the enveloping world. Constructing boundaries, rather than bridges, becomes the chief enterprise of true selfhood and is waged under the notions of "independence" and "autonomy." The quest for separation becomes the only legitimate enterprise in establishing a mature, viable, and independent self. Alluding to Alan Watts, Keller contends:

> One of the prime hallucinations of Western culture — and I would add the paradigm of dominance — is the belief that you are a skin-encapsulated ego. And just as the skin defends you from the dangers of the physical world, the ego defends you from the dangers of the psychic world. This leads to what I have termed the separative self. . . . For our culture it is separation which prepares the way for selfhood. (Keller 1995a: 274)

This manner of conceiving the self, in patriarchal Christianity as well as Western thought, as atomistic and autonomous, she argues, has been deleterious for both men and women.

For men, such a notion of autonomy has inhibited intimacy and the ability to express feelings of dependence upon others. Building on Nancy Chodorow's *The Reproduction of Mothering: Psychoanalysis and the Sociology of Gender* (1978) and Carol Gilligan's *In a Different Voice: Psychological Theory and Women's Development* (1982), Keller postulates that the atomized self in patriarchal culture may have its provenance in the culturally engendered separation of young boys from their mothers. The notion of the self as an isolated ego may itself be a projection of male experience of the atomized self:[18]

> Separation and sexism have functioned together as the most fundamental self-shaping assumptions of our culture. That any subject, human or nonhuman, is what it is only in clear division from everything else; and that men, by nature and by right, exercise the primary prerogatives of civilization: these two presuppositions collaborate like two eyes to sustain a single worldview. (1986: 2)

The adverse effects of this worldview for women are dually manifested. First, it has prompted men's perception of women as

"other," an otherness that has led not to a celebration of boun-
tiful differences but to objectification and the idea of an inferior
"other" that could be controlled. Second, women, who perforce
must adhere to this predominant atomized notion of the self as
the only ontological "game in town," as it were, can either become patriarchal like their male counterparts or, as happens more
frequently, see their role as distinct and complementary to men,
leading to obsequiousness and destructive self-sacrifice.

What is the alternative? For Keller, influenced by process
thought as well as George Herbert Mead's notion of intersubjectivity, a more accurate and less deleterious understanding is
that of the "permeable self."[19] Such a self recognizes the porous-
ness of its boundaries and maintains a "sense of moment to
moment presence" to its experience. All that occurs in one's experience is part of the individual. In this conception, Keller states,
one does not simply dissolve into that experience; rather one
recognizes that one *is* that experience. Although a fundamental
dimension of one's being consists of a constant flow of environmental influences, past experiences, and bodily influences, that
which constitutes the self as a self is the "creative spontaneity"
that sifts and plays with these influences, integrating them in
novel ways (Keller 1995a: 275).

The self is therefore free; it makes choices in the way it integrates experiences and influences; it is creative and relational.
"The self," Keller argues, is thus a verb, not a noun, forever in a
swirling process of becoming.

Nature in Eschatological Perspective

In keeping with her critique of the notion of the atomized self,
a notion nurtured in a modern climate that tended, particularly
beginning with Descartes, to perceive nature as a machine, Keller
shares the process interpretation of nature as evolutionary and
ecological, interrelated rather than mechanistic. For Keller, we, as
"connective selves," are inseparable from all other beings in the
universe at a metaphysical level. To perceive this all-encompassing
relationality, she argues, requires an expansion of our metaphys-

ical vision, one that includes "feeling" in its gaze. Building on Whitehead, she contends that fluidity and interpermeability, historically associated with the feminine, are really the hallmarks of all beings. "Every entity in the universe can be described as a process of interconnection with every other being" (1986: 5, 155–215).

The question that emerges here, however, is whether or not a realization of the interconnection of all life will necessarily lead to a greater respect for all life. A pregnant mother, for example, recognizes her interconnection with her fetus, yet some pregnant mothers choose to smoke and drink alcohol. Doesn't this challenge the somewhat assumed and sanguine connection Keller draws between realization of the connectedness of all beings and realization of a more just and less destructive culture? What is the possible underside of this interrelated self?[20]

Though other process theologians discuss interrelation, as we saw especially in Cobb, Keller adds a distinctive twist. For her, this interrelationship has become eschatological. She claims that we are now experiencing "the greening of eschatology," wherein apocalypse is today spoken of in "natural" terms. Apocalyptic fears ensuing from global warming, the melting of the polar ice caps, potential widespread flooding, increased droughts and mercurial weather patterns now haunt even suburban North Americans. What is unusual, Keller notes, is that talk about the weather has lost its innocence and rendered apocalyptic rhetoric a commonplace:

> You exchange pleasantries with a stranger and find a casual allusion to the weather — for instance when it is unreasonably warm, or cold, or when the weather weirdly bounces — rudely insinuating the end of the world. The foreboding feeling of irretrievable and unforeseeable damage reverberates in the brief silences, as we nod and shake our heads, break eye contact, change the topic. (Keller 1995b: 30–31)

Alluding to Bill McKibben's *The End of Nature* (1989), Keller contends that during the close of the twentieth century, nature can only be understood as a product of human agency, whose destructiveness is not a judgment upon us but rather that for which we will be judged. Actuarial science will henceforth have to seriously reconsider what is an "act of God" and what is an act of the human. The notion of a natural disaster, Keller argues, may soon sound like nostalgia for a lost cosmos (1995b: 34).

Christian faith becomes trivial unless we look at green apocalyptic reality, she argues. Christians have to revisit their notion of a new earth transformed by God in light of its transformation by humans — only then can they discern if the notion has led to a diminishment in the interest in nature.[21] Like Jay McDaniel, Keller speaks of biblical "shalom," which is expressed, she argues, in intensely natural and historical terms:

Hope in the Hebrew Scriptures is not for life without death but for a long, full life, lived under the shade of one's own vine and in the fullness of a community healed of the alienation of nature and culture (the lion and the lamb cohabiting, the little child leading . . .). In a way not unlike that of Native Americans today, the prophetic vision harkened back to a tribal sense of "the land," imagined as new Israel, new heaven and earth, new Jerusalem. (1995b: 44)

While ascribing a minimal apocalyptic dimension to Jesus' teaching, which was cast in messianic language by Saint Paul, Keller claims that only in the Book of Revelation does one encounter an elaborated New Testament apocalyptic narrative, a narrative that is seemingly dominated by fear more than love and that constitutes "the ultimate case of bad weather" (1995b: 44). Yet the mythic structure and nonlinear presentation of the Book of Revelation, she claims, leave it wide open to embrace by both reactionary and liberationist camps.

Ultimately, for Keller, eschatology, as a doctrine, cannot be understood separately from the doctrine of creation, just as the doctrine of creation cannot be comprehended apart from its eschatological framework, that is, the "new creation." We are all called to work with the Spirit of creation to bring about this new creation. In a statement combining both her understanding of nature and her "marching orders" for the human vis-à-vis nature, Keller writes:

> We cannot create or recreate this life. Our responsibility for the new creation is not to terraform planets and otherwise play God. It is to participate in our finite, interconnected creatureliness with metanoic consciousness — that is, facing up to the " 'man'-made" apocalypse.... As earth-bound Christians, we may indeed embrace a utopian realism, bound to the rhythms of earth and its indelible history, but nonetheless still "bound for the promised land" — a promising place and time which is the possible healing of this one. (1995b: 47)

Keller thus has a somewhat humble notion of the human role within an integral relationship with nature. Nature does not exist independently of the human, and the "greening of the apocalypse" does not gainsay a new utopianism, one that accepts our responsibility for what we have done to the planet yet builds a new program of relationships based on the "promised land" of fertile and nonoppressive human relations with nonhuman nature and between men and women.

•

Keller, then, while working within the process ambit, brings feminist analysis to bear on a notion of selfhood. By moving away from a separative self to a more integral notion of selfhood, the dual oppressions of women and nature, she implies, can be diminished or avoided. With our destruction of climate patterns built up over 4.5 billion years of earth history, our interrelationship with nature, which is an ontological reality, has reached eschatological proportions in the fading of the twentieth century.

Her project, though, does raise some questions. First, how appropriately or successfully can Whitehead's thought, written within a patriarchal worldview, be transplanted into a feminist

101

cultural critique? Can one ever truly extirpate an idea from its so-cial and cultural context? Second, what might be the underside of Keller's notion of self, the person in process, the creative, syn-thesizing self that is offered? Is the possible underside of this self, which could perhaps be even darker than the autonomous self, being overlooked in the quest for "something new to emerge"?

Contributions and Questions of Process Ecological Theology

As among the first and most prolific contemporary Christian theological voices addressing the environmental issue, John B. Cobb Jr., Jay B. McDaniel, and Catherine Keller have served as lighthouses for many who have not known how to navigate the waters of ecological theology. They have rendered, and continue to provide, a trenchant and "leavening" service to the cause of a religiously informed environmental ethic, particularly through their construction of a "relational self."

While process theology has been critiqued on a general level by a host of scholars (Pixley 1974; Hill 1976; Clarke 1979; Whitney 1980; Burrell 1982; Smith 1987), I am also concerned here with contributions and questions arising specifically from the environmental implications of process theology.

Contributions

An Expanded Context

What does process ecological theology offer a political the-ology of the environment? Process theology holds out to a social justice perspective an expanded theological context. Po-litical and liberation theologies have convincingly asserted the importance of context in discerning a proper theological response to human marginality owing to economic and political structures. Process theology indicates that the *environment* and the human-nonhuman interrelationship must be seen as a primary context in discussing the construction of liberation from marginalizing structures. The notion of an integration of the human and nonhuman worlds is an important ingredient that has not been historically accented by liberation and political theology. Why is this notion critical? Principally because it allows us to respond to and analyze marginality as a fundamental oppression of the earth's life-systems — an oppression that not only marginalizes humans in relation to social and economic power but also marginalizes specific human populations in relation to the environment, the context of all life.

A Recasting of "Marginalization"

As the point above implies, process ecological thought asserts that one's personal well-being is bound up with the well-being of the rest of the world, for interrelationship is the leitmotif of the process understanding of life. This attributes an intrinsic value to all nonhuman individuals and manifests that humans and their nonhuman worlds are invariably intertwined. In delineating this interrelationship, process theology provides a new model for the notion of "marginalization." Traditionally, a social justice perspective has examined human marginalization within economic and political systems. World-systems-theorists such as Immanuel Wallerstein, André Gunder Frank, and Eric Wolf, building upon Marxist insights, have shown that economic development is inextricable from economic underdevelopment, that wealth and poverty in a world capitalist system are two sides of the same coin, as it were. The process perspective, in showing that the environment is our primary context, constructively challenges a social justice perspective to acknowledge that a struggle for liberation must include in its analysis not just political and economic structures of marginalization but also structures that marginalize nonhuman realities — land, species of flora and fauna, air, water, and so on — as well as the special marginalization of those in closest proximity to those nonhuman elements, such as preliterate societies and First Nations. Social analysis, process thought suggests, must be stretched to include access to clean water, clean air, untainted food and soil, and a healthy environment in which to raise children. These issues of environmental marginalization are continuous with issues of political and economic marginalization.

This environmental understanding of marginalization has specific implications for the way in which marginalization is viewed: poverty becomes not just a Third World or inner-city phenomenon but adopts a planetary dimension. Consequently, we are all ultimately diminished as Earth becomes "oppressed," as it were. There is no more "my backyard" in this ecological scenario. There is, in a sense, a new "commons," which leads to a different sense of interconnection between the haves and the have-nots, one that includes socioeconomic *and* environmental concerns.

An Alternative to the Stewardship Model

While process ecological theology builds upon the notion of dominion-as-stewardship, as noted by McDaniel, it also goes beyond it. "Stewardship" implies a certain managerial control that humans can exercise over nature. While cognizant of the human power to affect nature profoundly, process ecological theology, with its notion of interrelationship and its insight that our lives and those of other beings are deeply bound up with one another, connotes a deeper intersubjectivity of all life than does the "stewardship" model. There are life-forces that exceed the control not only of human hands but of divine fingers as well, as we have seen especially in McDaniel's and Cobb's treatment of evolution. We thus become not stewards but intersubjective participants in a larger process of life.

Questions

Despite the aforementioned contributions, process thinkers do not uniformly seem to recognize that the environmental context, although fundamental, is not an abstract relationship but rather a relationship systematically organized through differences of race, class, gender, ethnicity, and so on. The environment is not an ahistorical context; it does not exist as an abstract ontological ground-of-being but as a concrete reality configured within specific human histories corresponding to racial, class, gender, and ethnic divisions. Consequently, interrelationship and marginality are always manifest in social, economic, and political terms. Process theologians, of course, do not reject this connection, yet they do not appear to incorporate it systematically into their process paradigm. It seems more an extrinsic concern rather than an inherent element of process thought.[22] A social justice perspective, however, does more than acknowledge the connection between human poverty and environmental devastation; it argues that political and economic marginalization and environmental degradation are a single, systemic, and historically constructed phenomenon. It does this primarily through the notion of a preferential option for the poor.

Whither a Preferential Option?

Equating the Holy Spirit with the force of life in the evolutionary process poses a particular concern to a social justice approach. A social justice vantage speaks of a preferential option for the poor. How does such a biblical and traditional approach jibe with the notion that the God of life, in process thought, does not take sides but loves predator and prey equally? Where is the notion of sin in process thinking? And the notion of justice?

While process ecological theology notes the integration of the human with the natural world, as well as the human's ability to destroy the planet, there seems to be a significant aspect of the human missing. The human animal is distinctive in that its survival is based on moral systems, not simply ecological ones. These systems consequently involve a sense of sin. We do not act simply out of instinct, nor do we simply react to our context. We have a unique agency. While this is partially addressed in Keller's notion of the integrative self that creatively sifts exterior influences before fashioning behavior, the idea that our agency is always articulated within a moral system seems to be unaccented in process ecological theology. A preferential option for the poor establishes a moral framework for understanding "interrelationship" and gives the human agent a distinct moral agency (and responsibility) within a world plagued by both environmental and social injustice.

Richness of Experience: A Continuing Hierarchy?

Moreover, the preferential option for the poor counters the political ambiguity in process theology's positioning of the human in the hierarchy implied by richness of experience. The notion of "richness of experience," as outlined by Cobb and McDaniel, positions the human within a hierarchy in which humans again are the zenith, judging who or what has inferior sentience or richness of sensation. What is problematic here, from a social justice perspective, is that such criteria could be used by virtually any social group to justify virtually any social situation. While the "richness of being" construct is intended to counter "speciesism" (which claims that one species is inherently superior to another), it in itself does not address questions of human relational injustice (i.e., hierarchies of wealth and poverty). It cannot, for example, critique from its own logic the claim of Lawrence Summers, who as chief economist for the World Bank noted in 1989 that the logic of dumping toxic waste in Third World countries was "impeccable" and that the nations of Africa were vastly "underpolluted" (quoted in the *Montreal Gazette,* March 28, 1982).

While a preferential option for the poor is also a "relational" precept, it is one intended to highlight the structural inequalities inherent in existing political-economic-environmental arrangements and to call for their transformation. While "richness of being" denotes a natural, ontological order of being, a "preferential option" points to an unjust human order, embedded in "sin," with the human agent responsible for and at the center of social transformation.

Conclusion

Process ecological theology, as noted, emphasizes the human interrelationship with all reality. Nature is no longer perceived as separated from the human but is seen as so interrelated with the human that we must reconsider our economic systems (Cobb), our treatment of animals (McDaniel), and even our notion of eschatology (Keller) in light of that relation. Yet this overarching insight, while critical to a liberative environmental consciousness, remains chiefly descriptive rather than cogent. Interrelationship does not inherently lead to solidarity. In contrast, the preferential option for the poor problematizes human agency in terms of structural inequality, the notion of sinfulness, and the need for social and spiritual liberation. Unlike the neutrality of the process God of life, the God of the social justice perspective takes sides.

What happens when process ecological thought is joined with a social justice perspective? At least three things.

First, the human-environmental interrelationship becomes a profoundly moral one, in which moral issues come to the fore. Cobb's notion of person-in-community, McDaniel's sensitivity to animals, and Keller's green eschatology, while all implying a special human responsibility, are given a particular focus in a social justice perspective, one that looks at these realities "from the bottom up," as it were, from the underside of human and nonhuman exploitation.

Second, this human-environmental interrelationship is seen as continuous with political-economic patterns of marginalization. The disjunction between the wealthy and poor is seen in the expanded context of what parts of the natural environment are reserved for the wealthy and what elements are reserved for the poor. Just as economic wealth is disproportionately allotted, increasingly natural wealth — clean water, breathable air, fertile soil — is also being divided along the fault lines of economic disparity. One sees that many of the same forces oppressing poor persons are also oppressing the earth, leading to the possibility of a dual solidarity with oppressed persons and oppressed elements of the natural world. Social justice and environmental justice thus become inextricably linked.

Third, the notion of shalom, articulated so eloquently by process ecological theology, is given a more directed focus. The biblical notion of shalom is undercut somewhat by process theologians' claim that God is not in control of evolutionary development. Along with this questioning of the creative dimension of evolution, the suggestion exists that such a notion of shalom can never be achieved. And if by some chance shalom were to come, it would probably come not from God, who is all-loving but not all-powerful, but from the inherent creativity of the evolutionary process. In a social justice perspective, however, this achievement of shalom becomes more compelling. In demonstrating solidarity for poor persons and attempting to achieve justice and social, economic, and political emancipation for all persons, such a perspective offers pragmatic ways to help approximate this biblical notion of peace. Joined with process ecological theology, the justice and peace concerns are united with "the integrity of creation," and "shalom" becomes not an impossible utopian vision but a clarion call to action, demanded not by a neutral God of life but by a biblical God who requires justice.

Chapter 4

The New Cosmology

The Universe as Context

═══════════════════════════════════

The story of the universe has been told in many ways by the peoples of Earth, from earliest periods of Paleolithic development and the Neolithic village communities to the classical civilizations. . . . In all these various circumstances the story of the universe has given meaning to life and existence itself. . . . In the modern period, we are without a comprehensive story of the universe. . . . With all our learning and with all our scientific insight, we have not yet attained such a meaningful approach to the universe, and thus we have at the present time a distorted mode of human presence on the Earth. We are somehow failing in the fundamental role that we should be fulfilling — the role of enabling the Earth and the entire universe to reflect on and to celebrate themselves, and the deep mysteries they bear within them.

— THOMAS BERRY AND BRIAN SWIMME,
The Universe Story

The so-called new cosmology is a prominent development in Christian approaches to the environment and, for myriad reasons, is increasingly significant to explore for a Christian political theology of the environment.

First, the new cosmology, as articulated primarily by cultural historian Thomas Berry and mathematical cosmologist Brian Swimme, suggests a distinctive context for doing theology — the universe itself — claiming that it is only when we embrace this cosmological perspective that we will fashion structures, stories, and religious ideas that help us eschew destructive ecological patterns.

Second, the new cosmology is an element of a larger theological approach that attempts to address what is seen as an imbalance engendered by the Christian emphasis on human salvation to the diminishment of creation itself. Such an approach, inclusive of what is called "creation spirituality," articulated by Matthew Fox and others, argues that a reaccenting of creation in theological discourse may help Christians respond more judiciously to life's ecosystems. Its critique of corporate and religious establishments, as well as consumerism, originates not in social analysis but rather in a highly distinctive creation-based framework.[1]

Third, the new cosmological approach, like process theology, attempts to make the Christian voice responsive to twentieth-century scientific discoveries, particularly those relating to the universe, through the disciplines of physics, astronomy, biology, and mathematics.

Finally, in keeping with its universal focus, the new cosmology builds, in a not uncritical fashion, upon the work of Teilhard de Chardin and posits a special role for the human as the self-consciousness of the universe, with special powers to alter the course of geological evolution. This perspective is significant, for it has been embraced by many Roman Catholic sisters and other Christian groups, including liberation theologians, as we shall see, dedicated to a growing and influential "eco-ministry" within the church.

The New Cosmology: What Is It?

We need to know the story, the universe story, in all its resonance, in all its meanings. The universe story is the divine story, the human story, the story of the trees, the story of the rivers, of the stars, the planets, everything. It is as simple as a kindergarten tale, yet as complex as all cosmology and all knowledge and all history.

—THOMAS BERRY, *Befriending the Earth*

110

Sometimes referred to as "the new story" or "the universe story," the new cosmology is a scientifically informed mythic narrative of the origin and integration of the universe, stars, solar systems, the earth, humans, and life itself. It is an attempt to portray "the big picture" of creation, amalgamating recent scientific data and mythical and religious sensibilities, all with an eye toward discerning the proper place of the human within the cosmos. For the new cosmologists there is no more grand or important story to relate.

New cosmology asserts that popular and religious understandings of the universe have not kept pace with twentieth-century scientific discoveries. The universe as cosmos (a given, fully formed, static entity) has been replaced in scientific understanding by the notion of cosmogenesis (the universe as an emerging, dynamic, and integral phenomenon containing a distinctive narrative). New cosmology attempts to help people, including scientists and theologians, relate this emergence to religious and ecological consciousness.[2] The ambitious agenda of the new cosmologists is to relate the "great adventure" of the universal story, from the "primordial flaring forth" or "big bang" some 15 million years ago, through the development of galaxies and supernovas 10 to 14 billion years ago, the emergence of the solar system, the development of Aries (the first prokaryotic cell on Earth), right through the unfolding of the human species and the rise of contemporary civilizations (Berry and Swimme 1992).

According to Thomas Berry, the principal theological proponent of new cosmology, tremendous social and historical shifts have always compelled the human community to generate new social visions or stories. He claims that Saint Augustine provided a grand narrative in *The City of God*. Augustine's work, written partially in response to the burning of Rome in A.D. 410, helped inspire and create the spiritual energy for the medieval world, with its triumphs and tragedies.

Similarly, Francis Bacon (1561–1626), the great propagandist of the Scientific Revolution, introduced another historical vision. Reflecting on the rationalization of society, Bacon envisioned a better order in earthly affairs through scientific control and manipulation of the processes of nature. His ideas not only helped fuel the Industrial Revolution but became, Berry claims, its cosmological framework.

As a cultural historian, Berry reflects on a "new story" and its implications for all human institutions. This new story, according to Berry, is crucial because it helps generate the requisite "physic" energy to lift us from the environmental crisis. The modern story, with its belief in progress through technological advancement and mastery over nature, has lost its appeal, he claims. It can no longer galvanize our civilization, for its underside — nuclear war, genocide, ecological destruction, social and economic disparity — has become too manifest to ignore.

The notion of "story," then, is central to new cosmological thinking. New cosmologists argue that people in the Western world feel alienated from their major political, economic, and religious institutions and have to feel "bonded" again. For new cosmologists such as Berry, that bonding rests ultimately in the unity, the interconnectedness, of the universe, something Christians, Jews, Muslims, atheists, Hindus, and indigenous peoples all have in common.[3]

The universe yarn is portrayed by new cosmologists as one of drama, suspense, tragedy, and celebration millions of years before we humans ever stood erect to gaze at a star-strewn sky. The language, at times technical and scientific, can also be lyrical, almost mystical. As Thomas Berry and Brian Swimme write in *The Universe Story:*

> We live in a world of green maple leaves, of cirrus clouds brushed in dry strokes on a darkening blue sky, a world where sea gulls shriek over the entrails thrown from the fisherman's home-bound trawler rocking and yawning in their great ocean drifts, the half-moon lifting above the horizon. (Berry and Swimme: 1992: 21)

In this universe story, all matter, all reality, is not only interconnected but "bonded," suggesting an affective dimension to interrelationships within the cosmos. Moreover, all matter is

112

marked by "differentiation," whereby uniqueness, not duplication, is the norm, and by "interiority," in which every particle or creature expresses the profound mystery of existence (Berry 1995b: 42–43). While the universe is a self-energizing and celebratory event, it is not without its shadow side. Resistance, energy, and dreams, in this cosmology, are the provenance of violence in the universe, from the shattering blast of a supernova to the lethal burst from a gangland machine gun. The violence of the universe, Thomas Berry and Brian Swimme argue, is somehow bound up with its creative energy. In the universal narrative, they write, "we witness a burst of glory, an amplification of the universe's beauty, and a dangerous and joyful release of power." (The ethical implications of such a statement are not directly explored — a critical point developed further in the conclusion of this chapter.)

Thomas Berry: "Geologian"

The traditional religions in themselves and out of their existing resources cannot deal with the problems that we have to deal with, but we cannot deal with these problems without the traditions. They cannot do it within their own resources as they exist at the present time, but it cannot be done without them. Something new has been added, a new experience, a new context, and we must now function out of this new context.... There is, in a sense, a new revelatory experience of the divine through our present understanding of the time-developmental universe.

— THOMAS BERRY, *Befriending the Earth*

A Roman Catholic priest, cultural historian, and scholar of Asian religions, Thomas Berry brings a rich and eclectic background to the study of the earth and the development of the new cosmology. Born in 1914 in Greensboro, North Carolina (one of thirteen children), Berry took his first vows with the monastic Passionist order in 1935.[4] Until his ordination in 1942, Berry read deeply in the area of the church fathers, Christian theology, and Western cultural history, as well as classical Greek, Latin, and translated Indian and Chinese writings. From 1943 to 1947, Berry, as a graduate student at Catholic University of America, worked with anthropologist John Cooper, whose fieldwork involved Algonquin-speaking Native Americans, as well as Frederick Engle-Janosi, who exposed Berry to the work of Giambattista Vico, hailed by some as the first modern philosopher of history.[5] Berry's dissertation on Vico helped provide a context for Berry's framing of history within grand cultural epochs, which has continued in his environmental writings. After a teaching stint in China truncated by the Cultural Revolution and three years in postwar Germany as a NATO chaplain working with orphaned children, Berry visited England, where he had an opportunity to meet Christopher Dawson, whose *Religion and the Rise of Western Civilization* left a profound impression on Berry's analysis of the cultural role of religion. From 1966 until 1979, Berry coordinated the History of Religions Program at Fordham University, which offered the only doctoral program in world religions at any Catholic University in the United States. From 1970 until 1995, he directed the Riverdale Center for Religious Research, which he founded in order to examine the human role not only within the dynamics of the earth's life-systems but within the unfolding universe as well.

The Influence of Teilhard de Chardin

One of the most important influences upon Berry's thought is Jesuit paleontologist and theologian Pierre Teilhard de Chardin (1881–1955), whom Berry considers one of the greatest theologians since Saint Paul. Why is Teilhard so significant? For Berry, there are three main reasons. First, Teilhard depicted the universe as having a "psycho-spiritual" dimension as well as a "physical-material" dimension, an insight that Berry builds upon in asserting that the universe is a "communion of subjects, not a collection of objects" (Berry 1995b: 39). Second, Teilhard integrated human history within the history of the universe itself, confirming the insights of physicists such as Freeman Dyson of Princeton University. Berry argues, as does Teilhard, that the emergence of the human species was not simply a random occurrence but an event that in some way was rooted in the very origins of the universe itself. Third, Berry credits Teilhard with advocating a move away from heavily emphasized concern over the redemptive process to a greater emphasis on the creation process in the Christian tradition, a move that Berry embraced as president of the American Teilhard Association (Berry 1982, 1991).

Yet, for Berry, Teilhard's theology was not without its own limitations. Entranced by the idea of progress and devoted to technological advancement, Teilhard was unable to discern humanity's destruction of the natural world and suggested that should there ever be an environmental problem in the future, science would discover other forms of life (Berry 1982; 1991: 24–26).[6] So enthralled with the advancements of human society, Teilhard, according to Berry, was unable to discern that in the "glory of the human" lies the decimation of the natural world (Berry 1982).

The Earth as Subject

For Berry, modern society has become entranced by the technological dream, which promises a "wonderworld" but delivers a "wasteworld," replete with acid rain, fouled waters, toxic solids, polluted air, and extinct species — in short, a closing down of the life-systems of the planet. In its stead, Berry wishes to highlight "the dream of the earth." Building on the Gaia thesis of James Lovelock, Berry perceives the earth as a subject, not an object, as an integrated, living organism, which has now yielded power over its destiny to the human.[7] As a human community, Berry contends, we must grow out of our adolescent phase, in which we plundered the earth and the aboriginal peoples closest to Gaia, and adopt a more mature and respectful approach to the earth, listening to the earth's dream and living our lives in accordance with its dictates. We must cease trying to control the earth in mechanistic fashion and listen to its message. Sadly, we have become "autistic," he claims, when it comes to listening to the earth and to nature (Berry 1992). Manifesting a mystical sensibility, Berry writes:

> In a kind of mental fixation we have become autistic in relation to the natural world. We have closed it out as an acceptable world. We impose our mechanistic systems on our surroundings until we have attained an abiding beatitude beyond all contact with the natural life communities to which we belong and without which we cannot survive.... We need to hear the voices of the natural world, the voices of the mountains and rivers, the voices of the ocean and the sky and the wind. (Berry 1992: iv)

Ironically, one of the greatest agents of the earth's degradation, modern science, is also the source of the new vision of functional cosmology that Berry seeks to develop. By revealing the genetic interconnection of all life, charting the sustained development of the cosmos, and, recently, speaking of the mystery, rather than the predictability, of creation, modern science, for Berry, has opened a window onto the story of the universe that is pivotal if we are going to view ourselves as part of the "cosmogenesis."

The Human as the Self-Consciousness of the Universe

For Berry, the universe is a celebratory event in process, and it is in the human person that the universe becomes self-conscious. Consequently, Berry advocates the restructuring of all education and professions to become earth-oriented. Economists, under his curriculum, would look at the "gross earth product" rather that the gross national product; colleges would teach the story of the universe's unfolding rather than just the saga of Western civilization; lawyers would develop legislation for a "biocracy" rather than a democracy; and so forth. While Berry warns against over-romanticizing primitivism, he maintains that North American Indians, with their interior sources of renewal and wisdom of the earth, "are our hope for the future." "The fate of the continent," he writes, "the fate of the Indian, and our own fate are finally identical" (1988: 193). The indigenous perspective is a great countervailing voice to the four great patriarchal systems which Berry accuses of contributing mightily to the destruction of the planet: the classical empires, the church establishment, the nation-state, and the modern corporation (1988: 146ff).[8]

Though a cleric, Berry is noticeably "un-Christocentric" in his writing. As mentioned, Berry claims that the Western religious traditions have focused too heavily on redemption to the detriment of creation. Consequently, he advocates that the universe, not the Bible, be seen as the "primary revelatory event." He seems sympathetic to Lynn White's excoriation of the Christian tradition and notes that, though other non-Christian civilizations destroyed their natural surroundings, none of these had a "millennial entrancement" combined with such sophisticated technological skills as has Christian culture. He thus concludes that it is no accident that the most destructive forces for the earth were engendered in a Christianized West.

For Berry, humans have now entered an "ecological age," whose conditions demand that (1) human technologies function in an integral manner with earth technologies; (2) we face up to the tremendous order of magnitude of the changes needed in our way of thinking and acting (no mere fine-tuning here); (3) sustainable progress be progress for the entire earth community; (4) technologies take care of their waste products; (5) a functional cosmology be developed; (6) the violence of nature, as well as its beneficence, be accounted for; and (7) the new technologies be bioregional rather than global or national (1988: 65ff.).

As Berry contends, "All human professions, institutions, and activities must be integral with the earth as the primary self-nourishing, self-governing and self-fulfilling community. To integrate our human activities with this context is our way to the future" (Berry 1988: 88).

The Context for Humanity: The Revelatory Universe

I consider that our new understanding of the universe is a new revelatory experience. It is not revelation in the sense

117

that the Bible is revelation, but it is nevertheless revelatory.
It is the way in which the divine is presently revealing itself
to us. . . . The universe itself is the primary sacred community.
It is the primary religious reality.
　　　　　　　—THOMAS BERRY, *Befriending the Earth*

Many theologians posit a starting point at which the human community experiences the divine. For Friedrich Schleiermacher (1768–1834), the influential German theologian whose insights led to a variety of modern interpretations of theology, this starting point was a general feeling of absolute "dependence" on God. For Karl Rahner (1904–84), one of the premier Catholic theologians of this century, it was the self-communication of God through grace. For Berry, it is the sense of awe and mystery in the universe.

According to Berry, the universe, the solar system, and the planet Earth "in themselves and in their evolutionary emergence constitute for the human community the primary revelation of that ultimate mystery whence all things emerge into being" (Berry 1987: 107). As Brian Swimme, Berry's principal scientific collaborator, notes:

> For Thomas Berry the universe is primary. He enters with no distracting agendas drawn from conciliar documents (e.g., statements of popes or bishops). He does not attempt to see the universe as a gloss on the Bible. From his point of view, to attempt to cram this stupendous universe into categories of thought fit for scriptural studies or systematic theology is to lose the very magnificence that stuns us in the first place. Our encounter with the universe must be primary, for the universe is primary. In his view, the stars, the mountain ranges, and the clusters of galaxies demand and are worthy of our deepest regard. Our attention must be turned to the vast drama and majesty of the universe if we are to discover our role at the species level. (Swimme 1987: 85)

Shifting from the Cenozoic Age to the "Ecozoic" Age

What is happening in our times is not just another historical transition or simply another cultural change. The devastation of the planet that we are bringing about is negating some hundreds of millions, even billions, of years of past development on the earth. This is a most momentous period of change, a change unparalleled in the four and a half billion years of earth history.
> —THOMAS BERRY, *Befriending the Earth*

For Berry, the main task of the human agent in this new ecological age is to adopt mutually enhancing human-earth relationships. Berry refers to this as making the shift to an "Ecozoic period," a term he uses to signal the end of the Cenozoic period or the era of geological history from 65 million years ago to the present that saw the development of grasses, flowers, birds, and mammals. Berry calls the latter the "lyric" period of geological history. The other option is to shift to a Technozoic era, which Berry contends will only result in the death of human life.

Berry's new cosmology points to the six conditions of an Ecozoic age, all of which involve a fundamental repositioning and reconceptualization of the human agent in relationship to nature.

1. The universe must be viewed as a community of subjects, not objects. Christianity, in particular, must expand its notion of community to include the elements or subjects of nature. We don't think of community, Berry claims, as a rapport with the trees, the wind, or the water because we don't see our communities as part of the universal community.

2. The earth must be acknowledged as a single reality; it can not be saved in fragments, for it is an integrated unity.

3. We must recognize that the earth is a one-time endowment. We don't get a second chance. If we kill the earth, it's all over. Neither God nor humans can reconstitute extinguished species.

4. Humans must see themselves as derivative and the earth as primary. All professions consequently must be realigned to reflect the primacy of the earth.

119

5. Human responsibility for the earth must be grounded in a religious sensibility that professes a reverence for all life, from bluebirds, butterflies, and insects to the trees, or as Albert Schweitzer says, to even a worm on a rain-drenched road.

6. The Ecozoic era demands a new ethical principle that recognizes the absolute evils of biocide, the killing of the life-systems (such as tropical rain forests), and geocide (the killing of the planet) (Berry 1991).

Brian Swimme: From Mathematics to Mystery

When we reflect on the creativity and forgiveness, the wisdom, insight, and perdurance required of humans in our moment of crisis, we understand the need for the tremendous power of the universe for our work, our survival, and our celebration of life.... We must become these cosmic dynamics and primordial powers in new human form.
— BRIAN SWIMME, *The Universe Is a Green Dragon*

The other principal progenitor of the new cosmology, Brian Swimme, earned his doctorate from the University of Oregon in mathematical cosmology — the study of the laws that drive the evolution of the universe in space and time. A professor of cosmology at the California Institute of Integral Studies, he directs the Center for the Story of the Universe and is a long-standing collaborator with Thomas Berry.

Unlike Berry, however, Swimme focuses more on the scientific and empirical data surrounding the unfolding of the universe. Moreover, Swimme uses the new cosmology to critique consumerism in a direct way, tracing many social and cultural ills to a lack of a new cosmological perspective. Whereas Berry attempts to lead religious traditions into a scientifically informed cosmological perspective, Swimme endeavors to lead modern scientists into a mythically and religiously imbued cosmological framework.

For Swimme, the universe is not a calculable puzzle but a wondrous mystery, unraveling the presence of God in each moment of its emergence. In his writings and videos, Swimme portrays the development of the universe as a spellbinding drama, full of suspense, valor, tragedy, and celebration that took place aeons before humans ever stood erect to behold the evening sky.

Raised in the Roman Catholic tradition, Swimme explains that the connection between the physical and the spiritual was an inherent one for him:

> Because I went to a Catholic University [as an undergraduate], Santa Clara University in California, the idea of a science and religion synthesis — I studied Teilhard de Chardin — was natural. When in graduate school suddenly these questions dropped out, that was most surprising to me. It was so unusual that we'd just be focused on the mathematics and not be asking some of the deeper philosophical questions. (Personal interview, May 18, 1994)

Yet, for Swimme, the divine is the origin of the universe, not only the birth of the universe, and is present in every instant. One of the most important discoveries of the entire twentieth century, for Swimme, is the nature of space:

> Space isn't an empty thing, but is actually the source of everything. . . . From the point of view of physics, we call this a quantum vacuum, but in my own interpretation and that of others, I identify the quantum vacuum with the super-essential darkness of God, . . . the ground of all being. They are different words for the same reality. So the divine in a certain sense is the origin of the universe instant by instant. (Personal interview, May 18, 1994)

For Swimme, the divine is what both sustains and transforms the universe, the energy that supports as well as shapes all emerging reality. In his later writing, Swimme refers to this as the "all-nourishing abyss" (Swimme 1996).[9] The two wellsprings of Swimme's work are a sense of awe that the universe inspires

121

and the sense of destruction he feels when looking at humanity's treatment of the earth.

One recurring critique of Swimme's schema has to do with the great emphasis it places upon the human. Given that the human-centeredness or anthropocentrism of Western culture has greatly contributed to ecological destruction, one wonders whether Swimme's assertion that the human is the "self-consciousness" of the universe might be problematic from an ecological perspective. Moreover, one wonders about the implications of Berry and Swimme's contention that humans are now in the driver's seat of geological evolution, whereby they can augur in a Technozoic or Ecozoic era.

Swimme reflectively responds to such concerns:

> That's one of those really important questions that requires a lot of care. In my mind, I tend to think of these as two poles, both of which have to be avoided. One is kind of the *status quo* idea that it's all here for us [humans], our playground....We need to be talked out of that, I would say. On the other hand, I also think that to say that the human is just one species among others — I regard that as an overcompensation. If we were to accept that view,...the rest of the earth community would suffer immensely, because the rest of the species are not capable of cleaning up the toxins we spew out. Its such an interesting challenge. We have to somehow be responsible concerning this power, while at the same time [maintaining] this profound humility in regard to our particular status. (Personal interview, May 18, 1994)

Following the Cosmos in a Consumer Society

In a trenchant critique, Swimme argues that consumerism has become the world's most pervasive faith: in a sense it's the official cosmology ingrained in children worldwide as they watch television advertisements. In the United States, he claims, before the average child enters the first grade, she will have watched over thirty thousand television commercials — a remarkable in-doctrination. Calling advertisers the planet's "most sophisticated religious preachers," Swimme speaks of the need to reacquaint the world's youth with the story of the universe, rather than the story of consumer capitalism (Swimme 1996: 10–19).

For Swimme, consumerism rests on the assumption that the cosmos consists of dead objects rather than animated sub-jects — a view, he claims, that leads to loneliness, alienation, and depression:

> Consumerism is a prison whose walls and bars are the items advertised everywhere. We dedicate ourselves to getting the objects so that we can be encased by them. For most hu-mans, even in the best consumer circumstances, such a way of life proves unsatisfying to the core. It is simply not human finally to live a life sealed off from all conscious contact with those powers at work throughout the Earth and universe and within every one of our cells. So intolerable is this sense of being out of it, of being left out, of being without any cen-tral meaning for the world, we will resort to any route to ease the pain. (Swimme 1996: 34–35)

How do we escape from this alienated landscape? For Swimme, consumerism offers one alternative: drugs. The alternative that he proposes is the new cosmology, which opens both children and adults into a universe consisting not of dead objects but, as Berry also contends, of vital subjects. In this worldview, alienation is an impossibility, for we are intimately connected with all reality, sharing the common origin of the "big bang."

The Role of the Human

Swimme maintains that the human is "the most intricate and most profound and most dangerous being in creation." As such, the human "can no longer be neglected," he argues, in attempts to understand the cosmos itself (Swimme and Fox 1992: 24). For Swimme, the violence of the universe, such as the explosive energy of the big bang, is somehow mysteriously reflected in human violence — and in both, violence often is the flip-side of creativity. The explosive birth of stars leads to beautiful planets, and human wars often galvanize incredible technological advancement.

For Swimme, as for Berry, the human — powerful, creative, violent, yet open to mystery — is the point at which the universe becomes conscious of itself. Unlike Berry, however, Swimme uses a scientific illustration to exemplify this role. Adopting a dramatic sensibility in telling the universe narrative, Swimme tells the story of Albert Einstein pouring over his mathematical equations in his Berlin apartment on November 22, 1914, a moment when the world, Swimme claims, was changed forever. That evening, Einstein created his general theory of relativity. But, according to Swimme, that is only part of the story. What really happened that evening was the Newtonian world was destroyed and the Einsteinian world was created. Einstein at that moment discovered the expansion of the universe, a revelation that he himself was frightened by, to the extent that he modified his equations to come up with a different calculation. Years later, while gazing through Hubbell's telescope and seeing the expansion of the universe for himself, Einstein called this tampering with his equations the greatest blunder of his career.

For Swimme, however, that night was not simply a milestone in science but an instance in which Albert Einstein was a piece of the Milky Way galaxy reflecting on itself. In keeping with the new cosmological understanding of the role of the human, Einstein had become the locus in which the universe became aware of itself: he had become part of the self-consciousness of the universe (Swimme 1996).

The human role, then, for Swimme, becomes one of realizing that we are at once the center of the universe, the consciousness of the universe, and endowed with a responsibility for learning and perpetuating the principles of the universe as we discern them. This assertion raises a bevy of questions, as we shall see.

The New Cosmology:
Contributions and Critical Concerns

Contributions

One of the principal achievements of the new cosmology is to articulate the ecological crisis in a distinctly evocative manner. While many Christian theologians, as we have seen, are deeply concerned about ecological destruction, few write with the spiritual or mystical resonance of Berry and Swimme. While process, ecofeminist, and liberation theologians stimulate environmental activism through their critical social analysis, the new cosmologists galvanize ecological activism based on a sense of awe, mystery, and myth. While trenchant social critique is an important dimension of social transformation, the new cosmology utilizes myth, symbol, and mystery to mobilize social environmental action. In this way, new cosmologists are tapping into the symbolic and spiritual resources of society in a distinctive and effective way.

Relatedly, new cosmologists provide a traditional but recently deemphasized context for theology, that is, cosmology. While political and liberation theologians have developed a context for doing theology out of political and economic oppression, new cosmologists broaden our notion of context to include the emerging universe. This suggests, however, more than simply adding the universe to our list of theological contexts (i.e., "add cosmology and stir"). Rather it describes a whole new ontology, a new mode of being that profoundly alters our self-understanding. In the new cosmological scenario, the notion of interconnection or solidarity is potentially expanded. Humans stand in a type of connectedness not only with marginalized persons or endangered species but with all existence, owing to our common origin in the "primordial flaring forth" some 15 to 20 billion years ago.

Finally, unlike traditions that draw distinctions between orthodoxy (right thinking) and orthopraxis (right conduct), new cosmologists collapse these categories. There can be no correct action without correct thinking, new cosmologists maintain, thereby potentially eschewing a dualism between thought and ac-

125

tion in the human. Just as in certain Native American traditions there is no dichotomy between religion and politics or religion and social life, so with the new cosmologists there is no split, in a sense, between understanding and acting. For new cosmologists there can be no liberation, no redemption, no salvation that will emerge out of diseased or pathological thinking. (As Brian Swimme notes, "Diseased landscapes are the products of diseased mindscapes.") Any solution proposed to economic disparity, pollution, drug abuse, or sexism will be destined to fail if it comes out of a contemporary, dysfunctional, and obsolescent modern worldview. The suggestion here is that a worldview that distinguishes between thought and action is fundamentally flawed.

Critical Concerns

The new cosmology presents the universe as "a text without a context," the only self-referential entity that exists. This statement raises a host of questions. Can there actually be such a thing? Does any text exist without a context? Certainly in light of postmodern critiques, building on Wittgenstein's notion of language as representational, this assertion seems questionable. The assertion becomes even more suspect in light of the new cosmology's emphasis on narrative, "the new story," as a paradigm not only for ecological sustainability but for a new way of relating to existence. Jürgen Moltmann once noted that those who read the Bible on an empty stomach read it differently than those who read it after eating a full meal. Thomas Berry suggests that we should put the Bible on the shelf for twenty years and listen to nature (and, by extension, the universe). Yet do those who gaze upon the universe with empty stomachs read the "universe story" differently than those who gaze upon creation with full stomachs? As human beings we are culturally, politically, and economically embedded, a reality to which the new cosmologists pay little sustained attention in their analysis. Given the socially structured nature of humanity, is it ever possible, therefore, to view the universe a-contextually, outside of a political, economic, social, or moral framework, as the new cosmology suggests?

Moreover, does such a claim obscure the political, economic, and social inequalities that frame the way human beings perceive and experience reality? While Thomas Berry, for example, has been critiqued for not having a concrete plan of social action (Baum 1987; McFague 1992), might he also be critiqued for portraying a universe that is indifferent to such inequalities and, hence, to human suffering? Unlike the God of liberation theology, for example, who suffers with the poor and downtrodden, and whose own experience of suffering is the gateway of solidarity with contemporary victims of injustice, the universe of the new cosmology as a self-referential entity seems to preclude any notion of solidarity or intimacy with human suffering. This is a universe that does not necessarily "bend toward justice." Rather, one could interpret this universe to be like "Old Man River" in *Showboat* — it just "keeps on rolling" through the "pain and sorrow" of slave society and "don't say nothing."[10]

Part of the problem with the self-referential identification of the universe is that it is constructed using scientific discourse in a less-than-critical fashion. Both Berry and Swimme base their claims about the universe story on contemporary science, thereby adding an aura of stentorian authority to their assertions. In addition, there does not appear to be a critique of science as a representational enterprise or social analysis of science as a politically, economically, and culturally contoured system of thought — an insight developed principally in feminist and postmodern thought (see Keller 1990; Hardy 1981; Schiebinger 1993). These theorists have rightly pointed out that science itself is not a text without a context — that is, it is not the value-neutral, objective, self-referential purveyor of "truth" that it has claimed to be in modernity. Berry and Swimme, without reference to these critiques, seem to suggest that science itself is a-contextual (that it is not embedded in social, political, and economic realities) and that with the aid of contemporary science they can convey a universe story that transcends all contexts and contains a universal resonance. In this respect, it seems, they have, through a "language without a context," created a "universe without a context."

As suggested, one of the potential hazards of a "text without a context" is that the entire issue of its contextualization is obscured. Berry and Swimme, for example, make three successive assertions: (1) that the universe is self-referential; (2) that the universe story is a definitive story and is accessible to all people; and (3) that the adoption of the universe story will lead to an ecologically sustainable future, the "Ecozoic era" as defined by Berry. There does not seem to be anything inherent in these assertions, however, preventing a CEO of a transnational corporation from savoring the stars at his or her beach house on the weekend while employing children in a Third World sweatshop. More importantly, however, there doesn't seem to be anything inherent in the new story to prevent that same CEO from adopting the new cosmology to promote his own capitalistic projects and products. ("Everything in the universe is connected," for example, is a cosmological shibboleth that could be utilized extensively by telephone companies and computer software firms.) Because it is removed from a specific context (i.e., a program of social action), the new story can be slotted potentially into virtually any context, whether it be that of radical environmentalists, white liberal Christians, or neoconservative capitalists. By not providing a concrete program of the story within a larger justice framework, the new cosmologists have perhaps left their story vulnerable to a panoply of appropriations.

This new narrative, moreover, while remaining open to a variety of appropriations, also seems to weave together conflicting strands. On the one hand, as a narrative imbued with a sense of mystery, awe, and sacredness, it is polyvalent. It attempts to speak to the religious, spiritual, and psychic sensibilities of the human to foster and develop an appreciation of an emergent universe and an understanding of the human role within it. Berry sees this as a story that transcends cultural differences because it taps into the sense of awe and reverence all human cultures have for the cosmos. On the other hand, it is unclear on whose terms this sense of awe and wonder is expressed. Do Berry and Swimme intend that this scientifically informed universe story be appropriated by various cultures around the world and transformed in light of their local contexts? Their discourse intimates that the new cosmology is not simply one story among others but "the" universe story. In this sense, their paradigm is not so much an invitation as it is a manifesto, a normative way of perceiving the universe and our role within it.[11]

This manifesto-like aspect of the new story raises a further query: Is there an element here of a monolithic cosmology? In their attempt to replace the old monolithic story of modernity, with its baleful ecological consequences, are Berry and Swimme attempting to construct a new hegemonic discourse? Interestingly, Berry and Swimme, both Catholics, are constructing a cosmology that is consistent with the way in which hegemonic discourses are constructed in the Roman Catholic intellectual tradition. Just as religious ideas for change are centralized, codified, and promulgated, often in the form of an encyclical or conciliar document, in Roman Catholicism, the new story, it seems, is also codified and disseminated as a definitive teaching. In this sense, is the new story being proposed simply as a new myth that speaks to our spiritual sensibilities or as a "new catechism" that determines normative vantage points for perceiving both the universe and the role of the human within it?

In addition, there is a suggestion in the new cosmology that the purveyor of this new catechism is not simply a person or group of persons but the universe itself. Berry, arguing that every era needs a story, reflects on how the great storytellers of the past — Augustine, Aquinas, Dante, Bacon — gave imaginative focus to their respective eras. Claiming that we are now "in between stories," Berry, it seems, is proposing not himself but rather the universe itself as the next great storyteller. There is the suggestion that nature and the universe itself are the story-weavers of the next age of human and geological history; the universe is communicating a story, and our role is to listen to it and understand our place in the narrative.

Such a proposal suggests not only an anthromorphization of the universe, a very slippery prospect to be sure, but a transcendent story beyond human critique, a story to end all stories. Unlike the narratives of Dante, Aquinas, or Newton, the universe story, as articulated by the new cosmology, is timeless and above critique. It is the story of the unfolding of life itself. While Augustine, according to Berry, provided the imaginative world that helped give birth to the Middle Ages and was subsequently replaced by another cosmological raconteur, the universe story, it seems, which Berry hopes will catapult us into the Ecozoic era, will, in the new cosmological schema, never be eclipsed. There is the implication that the variety of criticism to which the great storytellers of the past have been subjected are somehow irrelevant to the universe story, a text without a context, the story of life itself.

Moreover, the new cosmology claims a special role for the human that is problematic from both an ecological and a social justice perspective. For Berry and Swimme, the human is the being in whom the universe reflects upon and celebrates itself. As Berry writes, "It is not that we think on the universe: the universe, rather, thinks *itself* in us and through us" (Berry 1991: 21). Furthermore, the human is in the driver's seat of geological evolution, directing the course of earth history out of the Cenozoic period, the last 65 million years of Earth history, and toward either the Technozoic or the Ecozoic era. Is such a prominent human role as the self-consciousness of the universe and now architect of geological evolution deleteriously anthropocentric? Does it belie many ecological theologians' call for a more humble self-understanding in light of human devastation of the life-systems of the planet? In the modern era, thinking we knew what was best for the planet, we have forced thousands of species into extinction and perhaps irrevocably altered ecosystems we thought we could "manage." If we were to embrace the human role articulated by the new cosmology, what is to stop us from further destroying the planet or other parts of the universe? Might seeing ourselves as the self-consciousness of the universe steer us more toward hubris rather than humility? Isn't it possible that allotting such a magnificent role to the human might add to the human tendency to see itself superior to other species and do more to develop and promote human projects to the detriment of the nonhuman world?

Finally, there is a suggestion in the new cosmology that one's morality changes as one alters one's worldview — in essence, that the crisis we now face socially or environmentally is at root a crisis of perception.

While cosmological shifts are important for social change, it is crucial to recall that cosmological shifts always take place in a political, economic, and cultural context. While the new cosmology hints at this through its incisive critiques of the global corporation and consumerism, it does not dwell on ecological destruction as taking place within a context of winners and losers, those who are benefiting from the earth's destruction and those who are being destroyed by it. What does not seem to be underscored in the new cosmology is that environmental change takes place within a context of oppression, and environmental activism is a political act as well as a cosmological act. The role of the human in this regard is not merely as a conveyor of or listener to the universe story but as a political being: making choices about power, control, domination, and liberation. Unlike the new cosmology, a social justice perspective suggests that we not simply listen to the universe and assist in its unfolding but rather help the universe unfold and bend toward justice. In this sense, the human becomes not the consciousness but the conscience of the universe.

Chapter 5

Ecofeminism

From Patriarchy to Mutuality

Racism, sexism, class exploitation, and ecological destruction are four interlocking pillars upon which the structure of patriarchy rests.
— SHEILA COLLINS, *A Different Heaven and Earth*

Ecofeminism, for several reasons, is a pivotal development for those fashioning a political theology of the environment.

First, ecofeminist theology, as espoused particularly by Rosemary Radford Ruether, has been at the vanguard of a religiously oriented social ecology, which attempts to delineate the connections among social, cultural, religious, economic, political, and ecological exploitation. Consequently, ecofeminism is built upon social analysis that scrutinizes interlocking dualisms perceived to be oppressive of both women and nature.

Second, ecofeminist theology has endeavored to locate a liberative role for the human amid such intersecting circles of exploitation. Through a critique of patriarchal dimensions of classical philosophy and the Judeo-Christian heritage, as well as Enlightenment traditions of the autonomous and objective self and the perception of nature as mechanistic and nonsacred, ecofeminists seek a transformed notion of the human that erases hierarchical, patriarchal dualisms undergirding patterns of dominance. For the theological ecofeminist, the encounter with the divine should lead to a human role marked neither by dominance nor by exploitation, but by mutuality.[1]

Third, as a theology of emancipation, ecofeminism adopts a self-critical and transformative stance. Its objective is not merely to understand ecologically and culturally pernicious structures but to transform them with sustained critique and sustainable alternatives.

What Is Ecofeminism?

While there are myriad approaches within ecofeminism, a common insight is that in Eurocentric societies there is a forceful nexus between the manner in which women and that in which nature are viewed, specifically, with trepidation, resentment, and denigration (Spretnak 1993: 261). Ecofeminists find within a Western patriarchal framework an unmistakable "logic of domination" that extends to the nonhuman world.

Ethicist Karen Warren asserts that just as patriarchal culture fosters racism and sexism, it also engenders "naturism":

Ecofeminists insist that the sort of logic of domination used to justify the domination of humans by gender, racial, ethnic, or class status is also used to justify the domination of nature. Because eliminating a logic of domination is part of a feminist critique — whether a critique of patriarchy, white supremacist culture, or imperialism — ecofeminists insist that naturism is properly viewed as an integral part of any feminist solidarity movement to end sexist oppression and the logic of domination which conceptually grounds it. (Warren 1990: 132)

Interlocking Dualisms

In order to comprehend this logic of domination, ecofeminists study the interrelated dualisms of Western culture: male/female, mind/body, human/nonhuman, culture/nature, white/nonwhite, heaven/earth, independence/interdependence, and so on (Daly 1990; Adams 1995). Such dualisms, it is argued, reduce diversity into an either-or scenario.

133

Not only does this rigid separation undercut a mutuality that may exist between the two categories, but it also renders the second part of each dichotomy both inferior to and in the service of the first, ecofeminists argue. Hence, women serve men; nature serves culture; animals serve humans; nonwhites serve whites; and so forth (Adams 1995: 2).

Ecofeminism has traced the dualisms that mark European patriarchal culture to (1) classical philosophy and the Judeo-Christian heritage (Rosemary Radford Ruether and E. Dodson Gray); (2) modern European mechanistic thought and Enlightenment focus on autonomy and objectivity (Carolyn Merchant and Vandana Shiva); and (3) the evisceration of Earth's sacredness in light of a transcendent "Sky God" (Charlene Spretnak, Starhawk, Sallie McFague) (Adams 1995: 2).

Historically, ecofeminists claim, women and the physical world have experienced similar exploitation under a structure of male supremacy. The interconnection of woman and nature has been reinforced by the personification of nature as female, as seen in the terms "Mother Nature" and "Mother Earth" and the tradition (now jettisoned) of giving hurricanes female names. While some of these identifications have nurturing intimations, other terms reveal an exploitative side to such identification, such as "virgin land" or "virgin stands of timber" — places yet to be cultivated by males. Moreover, the term "raping the land" derives from the violent sexual assault of women (McCoy 1984: 132).

Regarding religions, ecofeminists observe that the prevailing patriarchy of Western civilization is grounded in a spirituality that attempts to transcend nature and the body — particularly the female body. Such a patriarchal spirituality connects body, women, and nature and then preaches transcendence of the body and nature, thus sanctifying oppression (Adams 1995; Spretnak 1993: 261). Consequently, ecofeminists attempt to foster ideas and practices that perceive both nature and the body as sacred and spiritually revelatory.[2]

Rosemary Radford Ruether tersely defines the theological aspects of ecofeminism:

The *theology* of ecofeminism brings feminist theology into dialogue with a culturally based critique of the ecological crisis. Patriarchal ideology perceives the earth or nature as a female or as a feminine reality. As such, nature is considered to be inferior to men. As a material being having no spirit, no life in and of itself, nature is only a tool to be exploited by men. The cultural roots of the ecological crisis can be found in this common perception of both women and nature as realities without spirit and tools to be exploited by dominant males. (Ruether 1994: 199)

A New Wave of Analysis

Ecofeminist analysis objects to separating culture into separate spheres — for example, politics from spirituality, human from nonhuman nature — seeing such divides as patriarchal dualisms. And yet it critiques any syncretisms that eschew political analysis. As Carol Adams writes:

We are deeply engaged with political and economic struggles, as well as with the challenge to articulate ecofeminist theory. This is why ecofeminism has been called the third wave of feminism. Ecofeminism may have grown out of earlier feminist theory, but it revises this theory by its position that an environmental perspective is necessary for feminism. In demonstrating how a patriarchal culture "naturalizes" the domination of nature, of women, and of different races, this third wave of feminism can play a significant part in linking feminism with other social movements. (Adams 1995: 3)

In response to claims that ecofeminism is widely diffuse, Adams claims that ecofeminist analysis is not characterized by unity of thought, but by solidarity. Moreover, this solidarity is joined by interrelationship, transformation, and embodiment — the common threads of ecofeminist spirituality (Adams 1995: 4–8).

In the following sections, we will review the work of three prominent ecofeminists — Rosemary Radford Ruether, Sallie Mc-

Fague, and Vandana Shiva — noting both points of conflict and convergence in their approaches to ecofeminism, their understanding of nature, and the role of the human.

Rosemary Radford Ruether:
Appealing to the Prophetic Tradition

Women must see that there can be no liberation for them and no solution to the ecological crisis within a society whose fundamental model of relationships continues to be one of domination. They must unite the demands of the women's movement with those of the ecological movement to envision a radical reshaping of the basic socioeconomic relations and the underlying values of this society.

— ROSEMARY RADFORD RUETHER,
New Woman/New Earth

Rosemary Radford Ruether[3] was among the first to show the connection between female and natural oppression (Adams 1995: 2; Bouma-Prediger 1995).[4] Ever since the publication of Ruether's *New Woman/New Earth* (1975), analysis of the twin oppression of nature and women has been a centerpiece of ecofeminist writings. As Ruether comments:

Since women in Western culture have been traditionally identified with nature, and nature, in turn, has been seen as an object of domination by man (males), it would seem almost a truism that the mentality that regarded the natural environment as an object of domination drew upon imagery and attitudes based on male domination of women. (Ruether 1975: 186)[5]

Culture Critique

Ruether's power as a theologian lies largely in her ability to cut wide swaths through cultural patterns of oppression and structure them in a consistent narrative. Because of her training in the

136

social and intellectual history of Christianity, her work reveals a historical methodology. This methodology has been used over the years to probe a variety of social issues: racism, religious prejudice, anti-Semitism, sexism, class conflict, colonialism, militarism, and ecological despoliation. In delineating the myriad ideological patterns in the Christian legacy that have condoned violence and subjugation, Ruether concludes that they all stem from a single root. In each of these ideologies, the prevailing social hierarchy and power relationships are affirmed and sanctified by the claim that they emerge from the order of creation and are ordained by divine will (Ruether 1989a: 2).

For Ruether, such a schema is most vividly manifest in sexism. The superiority of men over women is perceived as a reflection of the superiority of God, cast as male, over creation and the church, envisioned as female. This pattern of domination dovetails with a spirit-matter dichotomy. Men are seen as having superior rationality and thus are more suited to places of power. Women, allegedly bereft of these qualities, must by nature take a back seat to male authority (Ruether 1989a: 2–3).

For Ruether, the basic dualisms — alienation of the mind from the body, separation of the subjective self from the objective world, the inferiority of nature to spirit — all have their provenance in the apocalyptic-Platonic roots of classical Christianity (Ruether 1975). Moreover, racism, classism, and human suppression of nonhuman nature are also modeled after this mind-over-body duality. In relationship to the oppression of nature, Ruether brings her theological insights to bear on the implications of sexism for the environment:

The *theology* of ecofeminism brings feminist theology into dialogue with a culturally based critique of the ecological crisis. Patriarchal ideology perceives the earth or nature as a female or as a feminine reality. As such, nature is considered to be inferior to men. As a material being having no spirit, no life in and of itself, nature is only a tool to be exploited by men. The cultural roots of the ecological crisis can be found in this common perception of both women and nature as realities without spirit and tools to be exploited by dominant males. (Ruether 1994b: 199)

Redemptive Lineaments of Our Cultural Heritage

Despite her thoroughgoing critique of the Platonic and Judeo-Christian patriarchal heritage, Ruether does uncover within the classical patriarchal legacy elements of liberation, in which injustice is assailed, and love and solidarity among persons and with the earth are proclaimed. (Such "treasures" are perhaps what keeps Ruether working within the Judeo-Christian religion, rather than outside of it, where other onetime Christian feminists have chosen to toil.)

For Ruether, the Psalms and the prophetic, covenantal tradition of the Hebrew Scriptures and the New Testament hold particular power for an ecofeminist perspective, as does the Judeo-Christian sacramental tradition (Ruether 1989b; 1992: 205–53). The prophetic tradition, according to Ruether, engenders a move in the social location of religion. Rather than speaking for the privileged and powerful, the prophetic tradition speaks on behalf of the poor and marginalized within society. The prophets decry the injustices of the ruling political, economic, and social powers, calling them to account for their subversion of the biblical call for justice and compassion. God punishes in order to foster repentance, and through repentance the society will be restored to the authentic divine wish for humans to live justly with one another and harmoniously with nonhuman nature (Ruether 1989b: 3).

The Hebrew prophetic tradition, Ruether argues, is concerned primarily with the crushing of the poor by the rich and is against the imperial regimes of the Near East that subjugated the tribes of Israel. The agricultural heritage of the Hebrew people, moreover, yields an implicit ecological theology. Human injustice and sin breach the covenant with Yahweh, resulting in divine wrath and natural destruction. However, the covenantal promise intimates the recrudescence of peace and fertility when justice and righteousness in the society are restored.

According to Ruether, the New Testament expands this critical vision to a catholic redemptive community unfettered by an ethnic identification of those who achieve "God's smile" of election. She finds particular promise in the Pauline understanding of a dissolution of difference in the umbrella of Christ, where subordinate relations between Jew and Greek, male and female, slave and master are transformed (Ruether 1989b: 3).[6]

Role of Nature

Given her accent on ecojustice, it is not surprising that Ruether perceives nature as largely shaped by the human, rather than as largely distinct from unfeathered bipeds. For her, nonhuman nature is not an objective reality to which we can simply "return." Rather, it is a product of both evolutionary and human emergence. Nowhere on Earth is there such a thing as "pristine nature," untouched by human hands. Everywhere, the smudge of human pollution is manifest, even if only in trace air, soil, and air contaminants. In this sense, Ruether sees nature as "fallen," owing not to any intrinsic evil but to misguided human advancement.[7] Thus, renewing our relationship with nature is a process of re-creating something novel, not returning to a previous unvitiated state (Ruether 1989c: 149). Here, the project takes on the dimension of a new vision:

> Nature will never be the same as it would have been without human intervention. Although we need to remake the earth in a way that converts our minds to nature's logic of ecological harmony, this will necessarily be a new synthesis, a new creation in which human nature and nonhuman nature become friends in the creating of a livable and sustainable cosmos. (Ruether 1989c: 149–50)[8]

A Gaian Guide

Ruether also engages contemporary scientific theory in her ecofeminist writings, most notably, the Gaia theory. In *Gaia and*

God (1992), she provides a helpful and terse overview of the Gaia hypothesis, a scientific theory — first espoused by British atmospheric scientist James Lovelock — that, as sketched earlier, claims that Earth is a self-regulating, living organism. Speaking of the religious reverberations of Gaia, a term that also denotes the ancient Greek goddess of the earth, Ruether notes that it has become an instrument of ecofeminists who see in an earth goddess a way of avoiding a pernicious male deity. She sagely cautions against, however, such an interchangeable approach to God:

> The term Gaia has caught on among those seeking a new ecological spirituality as a religious vision. Gaia is seen as a personified being, an immanent divinity. Some see the Jewish and Christian male monotheistic God as a hostile concept that rationalizes alienation from and neglect of the earth. Gaia should replace God as our focus of worship. I agree with much of this critique, yet I believe that merely replacing a male transcendent deity with an immanent female one is an insufficient answer to the "god-problem." (1992: 4)

Ruether assumes that Earth forms a living system, thereby accepting a key premise of the Gaia theory, and stresses that we humans are an "inextricable part" of that system. She opposes a Western concept of nature as both nonhuman and nondivine and claims that our ethical standards should reflect Gaia's interdependency. Lynn Margulis and James Lovelock, she notes, have given us a new vision of Earth through Gaia, in which cooperation is as important as competition. "Human ethics should be a more refined and conscious version of the natural interdependency, mandating humans to imagine and feel the suffering of others, and to find ways in which interrelation becomes cooperative and mutually life-enhancing for both sides" (1992: 57). For Ruether, both the Gaia theory of Lovelock and microbiologist Lynn Margulis and the new cosmology of cultural historian Thomas Berry and mathematician Brian Swimme counter the Cartesian mechanistic view of nature and help dissolve traditional dualisms that have had such a deleterious legacy for both women and nature.

140

Ruether, it seems, embraces much of the emerging scientific stories such as Gaia and the universe story, unpacking, however, more of their ethical than their theological implications. In outlining the human agenda in light of such scientific insights, Ruether rehearses the ideas that others in the ecological movement have also advanced: bioregionalism, reduced population, organic farming, an end to militarism and destructive technologies, global economic justice, communities of solidarity and alternative lifestyles, and an ability to listen to nature (a chief feature of Thomas Berry's thought) (1992: 265–72). Somewhat surprisingly, however, the theological questions posed by Gaia are not directly addressed.

In Ruether's earlier writings, the role of the human within this matrix is one of a "gardener" who works with the forces of nature to fructify rather than exploit. This seems slightly superseded, however, as she ponders the human role in the context of Gaia, where we are to learn to cooperate among ourselves in keeping with the workings of the living organism, Gaia.

A New Humanity

Reflecting the thought of Latin American liberation theologians, Ruether proposes that the role of the human, ultimately, is to create a "new humanity" within a "new society," one in which cooperation, rather than domination, is the core principle and sex-stereotyping and culturally nurtured oppression would be curtailed.

Ruether elucidates this "new society":

The center of such a new society would have to be not just the appropriate new social form, but a new social vision, a new soul that would inspire the whole. Society would have to be transfigured by the glimpse of a new type of social personality, a "new humanity" appropriate to a "new earth." (1975a: 210)

Such a society, she muses, no longer directed toward destroying the earth, might have greater time for contemplation, leading not to a quarantined understanding of the self but to one that saw the self in affirmation of others and in solidarity with others, the earth, "and the thou with whom I am in a state of reciprocal interdependence" (1975a: 211).

Third World Colloquy

Since the early 1990s, Ruether has fostered a dialogue between First World ecofeminists and Third World women who draw links between oppression of land and of women.[9] In so doing, Ruether issues a challenge to privileged white North American ecofeminists to move beyond psycho-spiritual understandings of nature, with their "exultant experiences of the rising moon and seasonal wonders," to embrace the realities of the plurality of the world's women, who are poor and exploited in a fearsome manner. Such psycho-spiritual reconnection with nature can become a "recreational self-indulgence," she argues, if the connection with overconsumption and waste is not emphasized. Such self-indulgence will occur, she warns,

> if the healing of our bodies and our imaginations as Euro-Americans is not connected concretely with the following realities:... the top 20 percent of the world's human population enjoys 82 percent of the wealth while the other 80 percent scrapes along with 18 percent; and the poorest 20 percent of the world's people, over a *billion* people — disproportionately women and children — starve and die from early poisoned waters, soil, and air. (Ruether, ed., 1996: 5)

Here, Ruether manifests once again her liberationist provenance as a theologian. Solidarity and a preferential inclination toward the poor, in this case, poor women and children, remain for her the starting points of any viable and transformative theological stance.

Sallie McFague: The Quest for Embodiment Transforming Divine and Human Models

Most Westerners, quite unselfconsciously, believe in the sa-
credness of every individual human being (while scarcely
protesting the extinction of all the members of other species);
believe males to be "naturally" superior to females; find
human fulfillment (however one defines it) more important
than the well-being of the planet; and picture God as a
distant, almighty superperson.... Christianity is surely not
alone responsible for this worldview, but to the extent that
it has contributed to and supported it, the deconstruction of
some of its major metaphors and the construction of others
is in order.

— SALLIE MCFAGUE, "A Square in the Quilt"

Like Rosemary Radford Ruether, Sallie McFague believes that the role of the theologian is not merely description, formulation, or analysis but advocacy and transformation. For her, the theological enterprise must be characterized not by "soloists" striving to pen the monumental, all-encompassing systematic theology but rather by "advocates" of a sustainable future, working collegially and respecting differences among their counterparts (1995: 86–87). Her particular contribution to the ecofeminist perspective, or, as she claims, her "piece of the quilt," is to invite Christian theology to consider new models and metaphors for God.[10]

In *Models of God: Theology for an Ecological, Nuclear Age* (1987), McFague, who has a background in literature, launches an evocative critique of the monarchical model of God that has for so long dominated Christian art, prayer, and worship. Building upon feminist analysis, McFague argues that the monarchical model is deeply anthropocentric, marked by dualistic hierarchies. While the image of God as king may not directly be responsible for hierarchical dualism, it has reinforced, she claims, such splits as "male/female, spirit/nature, human/nonhuman, Christian/non-Christian, rich/poor, white/colored, and so forth" (1990: 210).

Moreover, in the monarchical model, she continues, God is re-moved from the world, distant from "his subjects," and engaged only with the human rather than the nonhuman world. In addi-tion, he is far above his subjects, for royalty is "untouchable." Whatever one does for the world is insignificant in this image, "for its ruler does not inhabit it as his primary residence, and his subjects are well advised not to become enamored of it either" (1995: 91). Finally, in this model, God rules through either con-trol or kindness, eviscerating human responsibility for the earth. The sense is that the heavenly God and Father will look after his offspring — God, not humanity, will serve as caretaker of the earth (1987; 1990: 211; 1995: 91). Ultimately, the preservation of the earth within the kingly model is God's problem, not ours. (Significantly, McFague does not allude to the ancient Christian councils, which depict God not as monarch but as Triune, "over and above" as Father and "in and through" as Spirit. God's im-manence is paid scant attention by McFague, and the notion of God's "indwelling" is virtually ignored.)

Searching for Ecological Models of God

God as Mother, Lover, Friend

In place of the monarch, McFague initially proposes the models of God as Mother, lover, and friend (1987).[11] Such models, which have biblical lineage, can help Christianity, McFague believes, es-chew some of the patriarchal dualisms and domineering aspects of the monarchical model and open up new ways to be in sol-idarity not only with other persons but with nonhuman nature as well.[12]

Describing her theology as "heuristic," McFague claims that theology's traditional quest for truth has often led it to suppress all imaginative metaphors. Because no language about God is suf-ficient, she asserts, novel metaphors are not per se less sufficient than previous ones. In this sense, all share a similar status, and no putative authority can declare that some images refer directly to God while others do not, because, ultimately, none do. Thus, the criteria for choosing some images over others transcends "authority," however defined (1990: 207).

The Universe or World as God's Body

McFague also elucidates the metaphor of the world as God's body (1993), building upon an image proposed by process philosopher Charles Hartshorne (see Hartshorne 1941). McFague believes that only an embodied metaphor of God can escape the dualistic, patriarchal images of the divine that have helped nurture both the oppression of women and the destruction of nature. For her, such an organic model is the cornerstone of a theology of nature that must (1) reflect contemporary scientific understandings of the universe, or what McFague calls "the common creation story"; (2) perceive humans as deeply interrelated with all other forms of life; (3) focus more on creation than redemption; and (4) stress the nexus between ecological issues and justice and peace issues, furthering the connection of "justice, peace, and the integrity of creation" proposed by the World Council of Churches (1990: 207; 1993).

The springboard for all of this, for McFague, is the "common creation story" being told by what she calls "postmodern" science. Seeking a "loose fit" between science and theology, McFague claims that the common creation story is the one creation narrative that all humans, nonhumans, indeed, "everything that is," has in common. It is connected with the big bang theory of the universe's beginnings some 15 to 20 billion years ago. Because the story is "common" (i.e., incorporates all that is), it is different from sundry religious cosmologies; however, while being inclusive, it also maintains radical diversity and individuality (1993: 220).

In keeping with this story, McFague suggests that God is the embodied spirit of the cosmos. This embodiment is a model that entails both personal and organic images and, she argues, is commensurate with interpretation by both the Christian faith and contemporary science, which speaks of a common origin and kinship of all that exists. This model, for McFague, emphasizes our bodiliness and raises the notion of responsibility toward all bodies that are interrelated and mutually dependent (1993: 131–50).

Although other Christian ecological thinkers, such as Thomas Berry (discussed above), also appeal to the common creation story emerging in science, McFague is distinctive in her attempt to embrace a social justice perspective in its adoption. Although not engaged in the type of social and cultural analysis that is the hallmark of Ruether's work, McFague reveals a deep sensitivity to liberation theology and the plight of marginalized and impoverished persons, especially women.

She notes that ecological deterioration hits those who are least responsible for it: the inhabitants of the "under-consuming" nations of the Third World. As she illustratively writes:

To put the matter in a nutshell, a Third-World woman of color (as well as her First-World sister in the ghettoes of major cities) is the most impacted person on the planet. Her greatest ecological sin is probably ravaging denuded forests to gather firewood to cook her family's dinner. The most responsible person is a First-World, usually white, usually male, entrepreneur involved in a high-energy, high-profit business. His (her) greatest ecological discomfort is probably having to suffer through a record-breaking hot weekend when the air conditioner broke down and no repair person would come to fix it until Monday. As more of the earth becomes desert, water scarcer, air more polluted, food less plentiful, the lines between the "haves" and the "have nots" will become even more sharply drawn. Justice for the oppressed will recede from view when resources become scarce. If the human population doubles in forty or fifty years, as appears likely, and the pressure on the planet for the basics of existence intensifies, those with power will do what is necessary to insure their own piece of the disappearing pie. (1993: 4)[13]

Poor People and an Impoverished Planet

In an evocative discussion, McFague implies that nature is the "new poor" and attempts to develop a Christology from her personal/organic model that embraces this new poor. Nature is oppressed as are humans, though here McFague is speaking not simply of women but of all who are oppressed in a patriarchal, consumer-driven culture.

As she explains:

> Nature as the new poor does not mean that we should senti-mentalize nature or slip into such absurdities as speaking of "oppressed" mosquitoes or rocks. Rather, nature as the new poor means that we have made nature poor. It is a comment not about the workings of natural selection but of human sin. (1993: 166)

In keeping with her focus on human sinfulness and responsibility regarding environmental destruction, McFague says the emergence of impoverished nature is a "cold, hard" reality of human transgression. We have, she asserts, ruptured the integrity of creation through overpopulation and consumption, through our instrumentalist approach to nature and to certain disenfranchised peoples, and by our unwillingness to respect the intrinsic and divine value of every aspect of creation. Seeing a nexus between the oppression of poor people and the subjugation of nature, McFague writes:

> This perspective claims that in the twentieth century on our planet, human beings have caused nature to be the new poor in the same way that a small elite of the human population has created and continues to create the old poor — through a gross imbalance of the have and have-nots. Those "other" people (the old poor) and nature (the new poor) are, in both cases, there "for our use." (1993: 166)[14]

147

Role of the Human

What is the role of the human within this organic model of God? For one thing, McFague avers, ecology must become a primary vocation rather than a hobby or avocation. An ecological perspective, one that includes a notion of solidarity with both poor persons and destitute nature, must not be ancillary to the theological enterprise, but central.

Moreover, humans must see themselves not as lords and masters over creation but as products of creation, as derived from nature. In addition, humans have to learn to see themselves not as the "goal of creation" but rather as citizens of the earth (a concept borrowed from Aldo Leopold) and "caretakers of the planet." (This in some way reflects Rosemary Radford Ruether's understanding of humans as gardeners.) McFague maintains that, as caretakers, we must see our interrelationship with all matter; we must serve as guardians given our special destructive patterns; and we must acknowledge our responsibility to fulfill the divine plan for life to continue:

> We have become, like it or not, the guardians and caretakers of our tiny planet. In a universe characterized by complex individuality beyond our comprehension, our peculiar form of individuality and interdependence has developed into a special role for us. We are the responsible ones, responsible for all the rest upon which we are so profoundly dependent. (1993: 109)

> We must learn to live within the rules of our *oikos,* our household, from which the word ecology derives, and act in partnership with God to see that life flourishes. (1990: 216–17)[15]

While compelling, this depiction of the human as caretaker reflects the notion of stewardship held up by many theologians as the proper role of the human in light of the environmental crisis. While such a stance is welcome and represents a quantum leap from the modern understanding of humanity as plunderer of nature, one wonders whether it still maintains too much of a managerial flavor to be perduringly helpful. The radical interrelationship that McFague points to in the new common creation story suggests something far more intimate, something far more mutually constitutive in terms of the human relationship to nature. While the Gaia theorists unfortunately belittle the role of the human in effecting changes in nature (as seen in a previous chapter), they do indicate a crucial point — that we may not be more than "middle" or "upper-middle" management when it comes to running the planet.

As a Christian, McFague sees a compatibility between Jesus' role and our role in light of the environmental crisis. Through Jesus' life and passion, we see a twin response to the solidarity to which we are called — liberation and suffering. We are called to help liberate exploited persons and nature from human greed and sinfulness, while at the same time being asked to suffer for our solidarity, a reality that, as McFague points out, belies any naive or sentimental understandings about communing with nature or quick results in achieving sustainability:

> Given human sin, the possibility for solidarity with the vulnerable to triumph or even make a significant difference is highly questionable, as anyone knows who has worked on any justice or ecological issue. Add to human sin the vagaries of natural evil, and one must accept the inevitability of intense and massive suffering. (1993: 178)

As the heinous assassination of Chico Mendes — a Brazilian rubber-tapper union leader struggling to preserve jobs and the rain forest — indicates, such solidarity with the "new poor" may well be met with the same type of violence that solidarity with the human indigent has elicited in the past. If it is true that the same forces who oppress poor persons also oppress nature, then the list of martyrs in Latin America and elsewhere in the Third World may well soon swell with the names of those who express solidarity both with the poor and with the earth.

149

Vandana Shiva: From "Monoculture" to Diversity

*Patriarchal Development and the Dual Assault
on Women and Nature in the Third World*

*We perceive development as a patriarchal project because it
has emerged from centers of Western capitalist patriarchy,
and it reproduces these patriarchal structures within the
family, in community and throughout the fabric of Third
World societies. Patriarchal prejudice colors the structures of
knowledge as well as the structures of production and work
that shape and are in turn shaped by "development" activity.
Women's knowledge and work as integrally linked to nature
are marginalized or displaced, and in their place are introduced patterns of thought and patterns of work that devalue
the worth of women's knowledge and women's activities.
This fragments both nature and society.*

— VANDANA SHIVA, "Let Us Survive"

Though a physicist rather than a theologian, Vandana Shiva
is one of the foremost ecofeminist writers of the South, and her
work has great import for ecofeminist theology. Her insights concerning the twin oppression of nature and women within the
process of "development" have resonance throughout so-called
underdeveloped nations and, increasingly, throughout the North
as well.[16]

Like Ruether and McFague, Shiva assails patriarchy as a prime
adversary in the ecofeminist struggle. Yet, unlike her First World
counterparts, she perceives patriarchy as having two distinct and
parlous prongs: Western development schemes, which spawn a
new colonialism, and modern science, which is destructive both
of nature and of women's sustainable approaches to the earth.
From Shiva's vantage, "capitalist patriarchy has substituted the
sacredness of life with the sacredness of science and development"
(1996: 73).

This overarching patriarchy, in Shiva's view, forms a "monoculture," which destroys localized knowledge systems, such as
that of women farmers and indigenous cultures, as well as diver-

150

sified economies. In so doing, it replaces such knowledge systems with a top-down, First World, modern growth approach to economic and cultural development. This approach is epitomized for Shiva in World Bank policies, such as Structural Adjustment Programs (SAPs), which, in return for loans, compel Third World nations to open themselves to foreign investment; remove price subsidies of basic food stuffs such as milk, bread, and flour; convert agriculture from diversified, domestically consumed products to cash-export products; and generally remove local governments from decision-making processes in their own economies.[17] (In the words of U.S. consumer advocate Ralph Nader, such programs, linked to "free-trade" arrangements, make the world "safe *from* democracy.")

The "myth" of such a monoculture, Shiva argues, is that it is more productive than a diversified culture, whereas in actuality, it merely "controls more" (1993: 7). It has more to do with power than with production. In a striking parallel, Shiva notes that just as there was a disappearance of dissidents in the 1970s in Argentina under a brutal dictatorship, so now there is a disappearance of local knowledge systems throughout the Third World under the tyranny of the market economy, which brooks no dissent (1993: 1–45).

Western Development: Depleting People and Nature

Grounded in numerous case studies of development projects in India and Sri Lanka, Shiva's penetrating analysis, reflecting while transcending the work of social theorists André Gunder Frank, Immanuel Wallerstein, Fernando H. Cardoso, and Enzo Faletto, argues that development is actually a form of neocolonialism. Rather than improving living conditions of those in the developing world, it has actually increased their poverty. Moreover, it hits women particularly hard, for their work, along with nature's productive capabilities, is both devalued and rendered "invisible." Subsistence economies, those working sustainably with the land and maintained by women, become ciphers in the developmentalist schema:

151

The displacement of women from productive activity by the expansion of development was rooted largely in the manner in which development projects appropriated or destroyed the natural resource base for the production of sustenance and survival. It destroyed women's productivity both by removing land, water and forests from their management and control, as well as through the ecological destruction of soil, water and vegetation systems so that nature's productivity and renewability were impaired. While gender subordination and patriarchy are the oldest of oppressions, they have taken on new and more violent forms through the project of development. (1996: 66)

Shiva perceives development as patriarchal because it rises from the centers of Western capitalist patriarchy and replicates patriarchal patterns within the families and communities of Third World societies. Women's knowledge and labor, she contends, are connected to nature, and as they are replaced by patriarchal, top-down modes of thought and work, both women and nature are fragmented (1988: 1–13; 1996: 65–67).

Today, she asserts, women and the natural environment of the Third World are both striving for emancipation from "development" just as, in years past, they vied for liberation from colonialism (1989: 80–85). In essence, they are struggling to extricate themselves from what Shiva terms "maldevelopment," a form of development bereft of ecological principles, of an ethos of conservation, and of respect for women's skills and knowledge. In their stead, large scale development projects, such as hydro-electric dams, are projected, which are geared more to help local elites than the majority of a nation's population, who are often displaced by such modern development projects.[18]

Reflecting much of the critique of development lodged by Gustavo Gutiérrez and other liberation theologians during the late 1960s and early 1970s, Shiva takes the critique one step further, showing how development destroys nature as well as peoples and cultures. Concerning the developmentalist agenda, she writes:

The assumptions are evident: nature is unproductive; organic agriculture based on nature's cycles of renewability spells poverty; women and tribal and peasant societies embedded in nature are similarly unproductive, not because it has been demonstrated that in cooperation they produce *less* goods and services for needs, but because it is assumed that "production" takes place only when mediated by technologies for commodity production, even when such technologies destroy life. (1989: 82)

Hence, in this view, a clean, flowing river is not productive until it is severed by dams; women using the river to supply water to their families and communities are not involved in productive labor (male engineers, however, involved in water management and large scale hydroelectric projects are doing productive work); forests are not productive until they are "developed" into a single crop plantation for export to help finance the foreign debt (1989: 82).

Like economist Herman Daly and process theologian John B. Cobb Jr., Shiva is critical of economic measurements based on gross national product (GNP) or gross domestic product (GDP) standards. Such scales have no cost-accounting for the destruction of nature, failing to take into consideration the "gross *natural* product." Shiva trenchantly observes that indigenous peoples, indeed any peoples who do not participate wholeheartedly in the market economy, are immediately perceived as poor by those adopting a First World, developmentalist perspective. If they eat grains they have grown themselves, live in homes they have built, and wear locally designed and handmade garments from indigenous fiber, they are seen as impoverished. Subsistence and sustainability are perceived as misery (1991a: 346).

Critique of Modern Science

Just as a modern cash economy approach conflates indigenous economies with misery, so does modern science, according to Shiva, relegate indigenous knowledge and proximity to the land as primitive and inferior. Modern science, she observes, had its birth with Sir Francis Bacon (1561–1626) and helped advance male, middle-class entrepreneurs primarily. It was rooted in a quest for dominance and control over nature, and it disdained both women's skills and natural systems. In this sense, she argues, the modern scientific method has never been value-neutral but rather has always been male-oriented; the ideologies of modern science and gender were mutually reinforcing (1996: 67–70).[19]

For Shiva, modern science has achieved an almost unquestioned epistemological orthodoxy. Given its privileged position, and promoted by powerful First World nations, modern science attempts to supply technological nostrums for social and political problems that it cannot resolve, while simultaneously eschewing responsibility for the problems it itself creates (Shiva 1993). As Shiva observes, though modern Western knowledge has a particular relationship to power, it has projected itself as somehow transcending culture and politics and existing in the ethereal realm of "pure truth":

Its [modern Western science's] relationship with the project of economic development has been invisible; and therefore it has become a more effective legitimizer for the homogenization of the world and the erosion of its ecological and cultural richness. The tyranny and hierarchy privileges that are part of the development drive are also part of the globalizing knowledge in which the development paradigm is rooted and from which it derives its rationalization and legitimization. The power by which the dominant knowledge system has subjugated all others makes it exclusive and undemocratic. (1993: 60)

The Virulence of the Green Revolution

Modern science reached much of the Third World in a direct way with the Green Revolution of the 1960s and 1970s. Envisioned as a technological and political agenda for peace and a way to eliminate hunger, the Green Revolution, Shiva argues, left much of the Third World more destitute and dependent — and ecologically ravaged — than before. She examines Punjab, the breadbasket of India, as a case study of such devastation. The promises of a quick technological corrective and of unprecedented output eclipsed, she argues, a serious quest for an alternative agricultural strategy. For her, such an alternative approach would be based on an acknowledgment of the environmental wisdom of peasant economies. Moreover, it would be rooted in a democratic, sustainable agriculture congruent with the village-oriented, autochthonous economic traditions of Mohandas Gandhi, an advocate of cottage-based industries. Shiva records the diminishment of genetic diversity and soil arability as a result of the chemical-intensive approach to agriculture in Punjab and suggests that the Green Revolution also helped foster the severe social and political strife experienced by the region in the 1980s (Shiva: 1991b).

The Green Revolution eliminates diversity — it becomes a monoculture that squelches or critiques as "primitive" alternative, sustainable, local approaches to agriculture (Shiva 1993: 1–45). A leitmotif of Shiva's diatribe against modern science, as it is enfleshed in the Green Revolution, is the supplanting of social, economic, and ecological diversity for social, economic, and ecological monocultures — the latter of which are vigorously promoted by First World nations, international lending agencies such as the IMF and World Bank, as well as global corporations.

A Baleful Biotechnology

Another perturbing outgrowth of modern science for Shiva is the new biotechnologies, which "tamper with the very fabric of life." While noting that biotechnology has existed in some form for centuries, Shiva explains that these new biotechnologies pose novel social, ecological, and economic threats.

Genetic engineering, for example, allows the transference of genes from one organism to another. Shiva argues that this innovation has the capacity to turn genes into a worldwide resource that can be utilized to mold new life-forms. While noting the positive benefits such biotechnologies have already shown in agriculture, forestry, chemicals, drugs, and foods, Shiva is deeply aware of the potential dangers of these breakthroughs.

First, though developed by small firms and universities, these new technologies are almost entirely controlled by transnational corporations, whose concern for profits sometimes outstrips caution in the use of these new "resources."

Second, citing a statement by scientists working on recombinant DNA molecules, Shiva avers that these new life-forms often pose serious and unpredictable biohazards, such as the possibility of artificial DNA molecules being introduced to *E. coli* bacteria, which could then exchange information with other types of bacteria, leading to their wide dissemination among human, bacterial, plant, or animal populations with unpredictable results (Shiva 1993: 96–131).

Moreover, Shiva punctures the myth that these new biotechnologies are ecologically benign and will lead to "chemically free agriculture." Building on the work of J. R. Kloppenburg and others (see Kloppenburg 1988), Shiva notes that a number of principal agrochemical companies are bioengineering plants that are resistant to their herbicides, in hopes that they will be able to continue to sell their pesticides, while also peddling the seeds that can withstand them. For them, it's a win/win situation. For the Third World farmer, however, the situation is different: "For the Third World farmer his strategy for employing more toxic chemicals on pesticide and herbicide resistant varieties is suicidal, in a lethal sense. Thousands of people die annually as a result of pesticide poisoning" (1993: 112). Shiva advocates a Third World ban on the influx of herbicide and pesticide-resistant crops owing to their health and ecological effects, as well as their economic and social impact, which includes labor disruption and the upsurge of capital-intensive farming (Shiva 1993: 110–13):

> Like Green Revolution technologies, biotechnology in agriculture can become an instrument for dispossessing the farmer of seed as a means of production. The relocation of seed production from the farm to the corporate labo-

ratory relocates power and value between the North and South; and between corporations and farmers. It is estimated that the elimination of home grown seed would dramatically increase the farmers' dependence on biotech industries by about $6000 million US annually. (Shiva 1993: 145)

Women and Ecological Movements

For Shiva, perceiving the connection between women and nature is not novel; what is new is realizing that women and nature are joined in a creative and life-sustaining way, as Third World women demonstrate. In contradistinction to many First World feminists, including Ruether and McFague to a certain extent, Shiva argues that Third World women are not primarily victims but leaders of a new social paradigm in relating to nature. Thus, Shiva labels her work a "post-victimology" enterprise. From her viewpoint, women's movements and ecological movements are the same — both are countervailing trends in light of patriarchal maldevelopment. Women involved in ecological movements seek to liberate themselves from oppression and nature from exploitation (1996: 70–71).[20] (Unfortunately, Shiva does not probe the involvement of women in the destruction and maintenance of patriarchy, nor does she discuss the role of women in the decimation of nature.)

Two of the women's movements Shiva points to are the Chipko and Appiko movements, indigenous, women-based initiatives to save forests and farmlands through "tree-hugging," timber-blockades, demonstrations, and other nonviolent measures. These protests have met with much success in India, and Shiva has served with them as participant and reflector. According to Shiva, these movements have gradually evolved from being based in conflicts over resources to clashes over modern scientific and instrumental approaches to nature — approaches that do not see the intrinsic value of the forest, its innate importance for rural agriculture, and the value and dignity of the women and their experience in working with the land (1993: 20ff.).[21] (Shiva's role in this transformation would be interesting to trace.) These movements are recovering what Shiva calls "the feminine principle," which preserves and protects *prakriti* — the source of all life (1989).

For Shiva, these women's movements are engaged in preserving biodiversity, both ecologically and culturally. Over two-thirds of the world's natural biodiversity resides in the Third World. Many peasants and tribal peoples depend on that biodiversity for their survival. Moreover, their lifestyles represent a cultural biodiversity that will be lost along with the flora and fauna if the "monoculture" of modern global capitalism is allowed to move unimpeded through these societies. Hence the preservation of biodiversity in both the natural and human worlds becomes of paramount importance for Shiva (1993: 133ff.).

The Role of the Human

Shiva takes her cue for the human role from these women's ecological movements. We too must adopt an attitude toward life that is holistic, noncentralized, participatory rather than dictatorial, and supportive of ecological and cultural diversity. The sustenance of life that these women's movements represent must become the anthem of our culture and an organizing precept of society. Such an attitude will provide an antidote to a patriarchal culture of violence against women and against nature. These women, who are "reclaiming life, its sanctity," in search of liberation, are, for Shiva, lighthouses for society in general. They are struggling to recover a "feminine principle" that will help transform the patriarchal support of "maldevelopment."

What would such a transformation entail? First, growth and productivity would be recast according to the production, rather than the elimination, of life. Second, biodiversity rather than homogeneity, in culture, ecology, and economic models, would become respected and would become a logic of production. This would help ensure pluralism and decentralization. Such an approach would strongly assail the World Trade Organization (WTO) and its precursor, the Global Agreement on Tariffs and Trade (GATT), the World Bank, and the U.S. Trade Act, all of which have acted to legalize the patenting of life-forms, to place a market value on human genetic material, to promote large-scale and ecologically harmful megaprojects, and to represent a "monoculture" financed by First World concerns and enforced by First World capital. As a counter to these forces, Shiva's approach constitutes a shift from what she labels "bio-imperialism to bio-democracy" (1993: 88–93). In short, the human is called to a new quarry — not a human-earth interaction based on domination, instrumentality, and homogeneity but rather one based on ecology, equity, and diversity.

Contributions and Questions of Ecofeminism

As the above analysis reveals, ecofeminism provides a rich and diverse approach to environmental concerns. As noted at the outset of this chapter, it advocates not a value-neutral approach to environmental and social concerns but an engaged one. In so doing, it turns to the social and natural sciences for an understanding of the interwoven aspects of patriarchy in Western and Third World societies.

Contributions

A Radical Social Ecology

Unlike other approaches to environmental concerns such as deep ecology or the Gaia theory, ecofeminism embraces political economy as well as cultural, religious, and ecological insights. It argues compellingly that only an integration of such categories can lead to a transformed and sustainable future human-earth relationship. Moreover, because these variables are integrated, ecofeminists are involved in a critique not only of social structures but also of cultural and religious metaphors, images, and social identities. Thus in addition to social analysis, Ruether's critique of ideology proffers the image of "gardener," McFague the metaphor of the "world as God's body," and Shiva the notion of *prakriti* — the source of all life. In this sense ecofeminists helpfully avoid the materialist/idealist split that has derailed much philo-sophical and sociological discourse. Consequently, their appeals for change include not only a restructuring of the World Bank, the International Monetary Fund, and domestic environmental policy but also new models of the divine and of human interaction with nature. This points to not only a transformation in our physical and material relationship with nature — that is, how we use and conserve energy, how we treat natural resources, how we pro-duce food, and so on — but also a change in our religious and philosophical consciousness regarding nature.

The broader implications of this integrated agenda are that the rich vein of feminist analysis can no longer be done in isolation from the natural world. Ecofeminists cogently demon-strate that any feminist analysis that does not take into account ecological destruction is both limited and potentially damaging for any socially just and environmentally enhanced future. In short, they show that to be a feminist one has to also be an environmentalist.

The Notion of the Human as Relational

Ecofeminism also offers an important alternative to the atom-istic, highly individualistic, and separate self bequeathed to us by modernity. For the ecofeminist, the self is primarily relational: it emerges not as an independent, cloistered self-reliant reality but as an "embedded" reality. This self is not independent of or lord over the natural world but utterly dependent on it and yet capable of defining its own relationship with it. Thus the eco-feminists hold out the notion of mutuality with nature without sacrificing the idea of human responsibility toward nature. Un-like the relationality of deep ecology and the Gaia theory, which makes the human largely irrelevant and subservient to nature, the ecofeminist notion of relationality develops a distinctive role for the human, one that recognizes the human power to alter and destroy nature. It therefore demands a sense of responsibility, accountability, and self-criticism.

160

Questions

Is Ecofeminism Gynocentric?

As all ecofeminists agree, patriarchy assigns an essentialism to women as related to nature and therefore inferior to men. Just as nature is to be dominated and controlled by men, so are women. Yet does ecofeminism ascribe to women an essentialism in relation to nature that gives them a superiority? The feminine principle of Shiva as a universal principle to be followed suggests this, as does McFague's maternal God. Do ecofeminists take a hard look at how women's cultures engender and perpetuate patriarchy and how women become agents of ecological destruction? How are women's relationships to nature oppressive and destructive of the earth? How can ideologies of the feminine contribute to a destruction of nature? More importantly, how are women's forms of power rooted in the domination of nature? For example, to what extent is women's control of the household — which in Western culture includes the extensive use of toxic cleaning fluids, pesticides, and herbicides — destructive of nature? To what extent has women's consumerism — a partial product of their entry into the workforce and having greater control over the disposal of their income — been harmful of nature? Such questions suggest that ecofeminism would be strengthened if it eschewed essentialist readings of "women" and continued to focus on the complex and myriad relationship of women with the natural world, as indeed Ruether has begun to do.[22] While certainly not opting for the "biology is destiny" argument, I wonder if solidary feminists have adequately dealt with the realities of biology. Certainly, biology is not destiny, but it is reality and has some independence from culturally conditioned patterns.

Does Ecofeminism Romanticize Nature?

In their search for alternative material and philosophical understandings of the human-earth relationship, ecofeminists, as we have seen, have turned to scientific theories of the natural world. In exploring the Gaia theory, for example, with its emphasis on cooperation rather than competition, Ruether holds up the idea of mutuality as a social goal with a deep connection to natural processes. Shiva proffers the "feminine principle" at work in nature as a paradigm for human interaction with the nonhuman world, and McFague anthropomorphizes nature as the "new poor" in her attempt to incorporate a liberationist theological category. Moreover, both McFague and Ruether view nature as victim; it is "fallen," owing not to any inherent quality of nature but to the rapacious plunder of humanity. Clearly, as the ecofeminists point out, the life-systems of the planet are seriously jeopardized owing to human activity. Yet nature itself is not without its own elements of destruction, loss, and in some cases devastation. Do ecofeminists romanticize the mutuality and harmony of nature while not seriously engaging its violent aspect? While this area is touched on in McFague's work, to a certain extent, the question remains: How do we as humans reconcile this notion of nature's violence with this concept of nature's mutuality?

These questions about the role of violence in nature also raise some substantial queries concerning the incorporation of scientific findings in ecofeminist thought. Much of our understanding of the "violence" of nature has been provided by modern scientific observation. From the "big bang" of 15 to 20 billion years ago, an explosion whose effects we still feel, to the mass slaughter of newly hatched sea tortoises by sea birds as they make their inaugural race to the ocean, nature's violence is systemic and beyond easy ethical categorizations. (Jay McDaniel, as elucidated above, poignantly raises this in his description of the second pelican chick who is forced out of the nest by its parents to face starvation or consumption as part of an evolutionary pattern.) These observations about the violence of nature indicate that nature is not a neat and tidy affair. While Darwin's interpretation of such activity as "survival of the fittest" contributes to a paradigm of domination, as these authors show, there is nonetheless the residual truth of predator-prey relations that perhaps belies a romanticized understanding of what ecofeminists identify as mutuality and cooperation in nature, which is to be emulated by humans. I think it is helpful to distinguish between thinkers who moved from a socialist feminism into ecology, like Ruether, and those who were primarily concerned with the liberation of women and then moved to the environmental aspect. As is evident, McFague is not engaged in a systematic critique of free-trade capitalism as is Ruether or Shiva.

In fact, it is surprising how little some of these authors, for example, McFague, treat the ponderous impact of industrial capitalism on the environment. Ruether is more sensitive to this point, and Shiva is the only one who addresses it from an agricultural base, showing the sustainability of women's peasant agriculture and the ecological horrors of a free-trade, growth-maximizing, world-capitalist monoculture. This raises the larger question of how seriously these authors take the influence of economic structures on the shaping of human consciousness, which a liberationist perspective takes very seriously.

The Limits of Dualistic Discourse

It appears that the ecofeminist critics are not advocating some sort of monism: they recognize the difference between the two poles in the various dualisms noted above but affirm their interaction and interdependence. The question then arises: Does this exclude altogether a "higher" and "lower" between each pair of poles? Since ecofeminists want "humans" to act responsibly in regard to "nature," they seem to credit humans with the higher faculty of critical intelligence. At the same time, there is no higher and lower when it comes to men and women. In other words, each of these dualisms has its own character: they are not all alike. It is therefore not helpful to stress only the similarity among the lower poles of these dualisms, by saying for instance that as women are oppressed, so is nature. One must also point to the difference. For humans inevitably consume nature when they eat and drink, while using and "consuming" women is *always* a crime. In other words, while the antidualism discourse has a useful rhetorical function, it also has its limitations. This nuance is seen, for example, in Ruether's notion of the human as gardener, suggesting a managerial "dualism," if you will, between humans and nonhuman nature (Gregory Baum, personal correspondence).

Conclusion

Despite these queries and concerns, ecofeminism remains a vital and engaging theological approach to a political theology of the environment. It embodies a transformative, political dimension informed by liberationist precepts. The equating of the oppression of the poor with the plunder of the earth reflects the preferential option of the poor that is a defining feature of liberation theology. Moreover, ecofeminism uses the category of solidarity with women in the Third World, as support for the Chipko and Appiko movements shown by Shiva and others illustrates. Here is a concrete commitment to groups struggling to preserve their way of life and their lands. Also, like liberation thought, ecofeminism mines the rich prophetic tradition of the Judeo-Christian heritage (Ruether) and remains self-critical in its approach, using a trial-and-error method and calling for collegiality rather than chauvinism in the theological enterprise. Finally, ecofeminists, like many liberation theologians, see theology as a "second act," the "first act" being solidarity with groups struggling for dignity, freedom from sexism and economic oppression, as well as ecological sustainability.

Of the ecofeminists examined, Vandana Shiva is probably the most sobering and challenging for First World readers. Her critique, coming from the perspective of Third World women and their rejection of a globalizing corporate "monoculture" enforcing a "free-market economy," is a gauntlet cast down for those in the industrialized world. This perspective from the Third World is broadened by liberation theologians, whose perspective on the environment from the underside we next consider.

Chapter 6

Liberation Theology

The Greening of Solidarity

Liberation theology and ecological discourse have something in common: they stem from two wounds that are bleeding. The first, the wound of poverty and wretchedness, tears the social fabric of millions and millions of poor people the world over. The second, systematic aggression against the earth, destroys the equilibrium of the planet, threatened ... by a type of development undertaken by contemporary societies, now spread throughout the world. ... It is time to try and bring the two disciplines together.

— LEONARDO BOFF,
"Liberation Theology and Ecology"

Like ecofeminism, liberation theology has in recent years embraced environmental concerns, starting from a social rather than explicitly ecological perspective.

For a variety of reasons, this melding of liberation and ecological concerns is perhaps one of the most important emergences in the environmental movement, for it unites economic, cultural, historical, political, and religious concerns with environmental discourse in powerful and potentially transformative ways.

Liberation theology, with its clearly defined praxis, preferential option for the poor, and distinctive methodological emphasis on solidarity, offers a concrete and inclusive theological anthropology in its environmental applications. Thus, its novel call for solidarity with the nonhuman world is enriched by a long and in many cases bloody history of Christian solidarity with — and activism on behalf of — poor and victimized persons, particularly in nations of the South.[1]

Moreover, liberation theology emerges from a critique of economic developmentalism based on an understanding of world economic systems (Immanuel Wallerstein) and dependency theories, which argue that the world develops economic cores and peripheries, with the latter locked in oppressive subservience to the former (André Gunder Frank). Thus, when liberation theologians, along with other environmentally concerned Christians, critique "modernity," they do so not in broadcast fashion but rather in a manner rooted in a specific and in many ways compelling history of social-scientific analysis.[2]

In this chapter, after delineating briefly some salient dimensions of liberation theology and its environmental aspects, I will look briefly at the work of two Brazilian theologians who have recently embraced ecological concerns in their liberationist perspective, Leonardo Boff and Ivone Gebara, focusing primarily on their understanding of the human in light of social and ecological concerns.

What Is Liberation Theology?

The term "liberation theology," first used in 1968 by Peruvian theologian Gustavo Gutiérrez, was later developed in a systematic way in his 1971 *Teología de la liberacíon,* translated into thirteen languages and remaining the classic articulation of this theological movement. Though originating in Latin America, liberation theology has found fertile soil throughout Southern nations, as well as in oppressed communities in the North; hence, it is perhaps more accurately described as liberation "theologies."[3]

This theological movement, it can be argued, is one of the most significant religious developments in the latter half of the twentieth century, helping to spur numerous justice and peace statements and projects, church political activism, and North-South solidarity initiatives.

Liberation theology, simply put, attempts to read Scripture "through the prisms of the poor," examining ecclesial and secular history from the underside, that is, from the perspective of the indigent, exploited, and historically marginalized. As Leonardo Boff has commented, traditionally "history has been written by a white hand," by the victors rather than the vanquished, but liberation theologians, through adoption of a preferential option for the poor and a commitment to aiding struggling and oppressed peoples in their quest for human dignity, attempt to show the historical agency of those on the losing side of history, especially the poor and exploited.[4]

Liberation, though a polyvalent symbol, has, according to Gustavo Gutiérrez, three distinct meanings.[5] First, it denotes liberation from all social, economic, political, and cultural oppression. Second, it entails historical liberation, in the sense of poor persons taking control of their own destinies and recognizing "the power of the poor in history," in other words, their own historical potential for individual and societal transformation. Third, it suggests spiritual liberation, an understanding of spiritual emancipation that leads to community with one another as well as community between humans and Jesus Christ (Gutiérrez 1988).

Poverty and Pollution: A Growing Nexus

The connection between destitute persons and diminished ecosystems is increasingly being made in Southern nations. As Eduardo Gudynas, coordinator of environment and development in the Franciscan Ecological Center (CIPFE) in Montevideo, Uruguay, points out, 44 percent of Latin America, 181 million people, lives in poverty, half of those in extreme poverty. But what concretely does this mean? It means that the majority of these people are either unemployed or underemployed; over half have substandard or inadequate housing; and the infant mortality rates of their children is among the highest in the world. Contributing to this misery is contaminated water, fouled air, particularly for urban dwellers, and, in agricultural regions, where 61 percent of Latin America's poor live, loss of land, soil erosion, pesticide and agro-chemical contamination, and severe deforestation (Gudynas 1995: 106–107). Clearly, such devastation is often wrought not by Latin American campesinos but by global corporations. As Ingemar Hedström notes, from 1960 to 1980, beef production in Central America increased 160 percent owing to McDonald's and other fast-food restaurants' search for inexpensive meat production. This expansion resulted in an approximate 50 percent depletion of the four hundred thousand square kilometers of Central America's rain forests, leading to what Hedström terms the "hamburgerization" of Central America (Hedström 1990: 119–20).

These parallel developments, increasing poverty with commensurate environmental devastation, have led many in Latin America, including liberation theologians such as Leonardo Boff, to embrace a "social ecology," which sees poverty as a salient environmental dilemma and poses strategies that seek to diminish both economic and ecological destitution.[6] Such an approach is visible in the over five hundred Latin American environmental, nongovernmental organizations that have sprung up mainly since the early 1980s. These groups, located mostly in urban areas and overall taking a more pragmatic and less radical approach than some of their Northern counterparts, were encouraged by the UN-sponsored 1987 "Bruntland Report," which gave prominence to the notion of "sustainable development," a type of development defined as "meeting the needs of the present without compromising the ability of future generations to meet their own needs."[7]

Leonardo Boff: From Modernity to Ecology

From being the Satan of the Earth, we have to educate ourselves to be its guardian angel, capable of saving the earth, our cosmic homeland and earthly mother.
   —Leonardo Boff, *Liberation Theology and Ecology*

Leonardo Boff, a prolific and celebrated Brazilian liberation theologian whose critiques of ecclesiastical structures led to Vatican silencing and his decision to leave the priesthood,[8] is arguably the most prominent liberation theologian to integrate ecological discourse systematically into his theology. For example, his *Ecology and Liberation: A New Paradigm* (1995) is among the first sustained treatments of ecological concerns by a liberation theologian, and his commitment to an ecological focus is manifest also in numerous articles on the subject as well as his role as an editorial adviser to the Ecology and Justice Series of Orbis Books.[9]

Boff frames his overall response to ecological concerns within the context of what he deems a crisis of the modern world. Such a world is built upon an exploitative and aggressive capitalism that, under current global systems such as structural adjustment policies of the World Bank and the International Monetary Fund, appears content to leave two-thirds of the world's population in abject poverty and the world's ecosystems despoiled.[10] Utilizing the liberationist critique of developmentalism, which advances development of parts of the globe at the expense of underdevelopment elsewhere, Boff brings the rich social analysis that informs liberation theology to ecological discourse:

> Two great problems will occupy human minds and hearts from now on: What is the fate and future of planet Earth if we prolong the logic of plunder to which our development and consumer model has accustomed us? What can the poor two-thirds of humankind hope for from the world? (1995a: 75)

Boff notes that these two questions bespeak twin risks: first, that those persons associated with "the culture of the satisfied" — that is, those elites benefiting from this unbalanced economic system — will further immerse themselves in their "consumer egoism" and "cynically ignore" the destitution of the impoverished majority of the human family; and, second, that the poor, unwilling to accept their "death sentence," will embark upon a desperate quest for survival, which could usher in unprecedented violence and ecological destruction. For Boff, humanity must choose collectively to move from an ethos of exclusive profit to a logic of the common good for not only humans but all beings on the planet (1995a: 76).

Reflecting on the so-called triumph of capitalism with the collapse of the Soviet Union, Boff acknowledges that this historical emergence raises ponderous queries for those seeking societal transformation based on a socialist model. Boff claims unabashedly that global capitalism is creating a new economic imperialism: "We are witnessing a new empire of the type of rationalism, of development and the meaning of existence conceived in the belly of the merchant classes at the beginning of the modern era, and now disseminated throughout the world" (1995a: 101). For Boff, the same "logic of domination" that decimated and enslaved the indigenous populations of Latin America in the sixteenth century is now being waged by multinational corporations from Japan, Germany, Italy, and the United States, in conjunction with Latin American governments. Along with an oppressive foreign debt, he continues, this situation has led to an unparalleled state of human suffering in Latin America, where, in Brazil alone, one thousand children die of hunger daily. "We have never seen death on such a scale as today," Boff writes, "caused by unemployment, low wages, disease, and violence. Dozens of still surviving indigenous peoples are rapidly disappearing. In this way, we shall lose forever forms of humanity of which we have great need" (1995a: 102).[11]

Boff is certainly not a "Luddite" — he acknowledges the many fruits of modernity both in its liberal-representative-democratic as well as in its socialist constructions of society. He claims, however, that these opposing offspring of modernity must now be reconciled. Thus, Boff proposes an "alternative and integral modernity" that will blend the sweeping legacy of science and technology (the harvest of bourgeois modernity) with social democracy for the good of all persons (the insight of "proletarian" modernity) in an enriched understanding of a common future (1995a: 102–4).

Revealingly, though Boff acknowledges modernity's failings, while championing some of its key enhancements, he does not reflect seriously on socialism's neglect of the environment nor its view of the environment as mere commodity, a vantage it has traditionally shared with capitalism.[12]

Boff, in reflecting on poverty, ecology, and "misery," notes that his proposal of an "alternative and integral modernity" is part of a larger project to fashion a new paradigm that bypasses the mistakes of the old, that integrates all humans, not just the fortunate, in a benevolent manner, and that establishes more benign relationships with the environment (1994: 236–38). Hence, there is a need for a social ecology that outlines a social justice framework while acknowledging our part in a larger, holistic ecological dynamic (1994: 239).

The Role of Humanity

For Boff, a person who embodied this new paradigm is Brazilian rubber-tapper union leader Chico Mendes. Mendes, according to Boff, embodied a development model that united social and economic issues. He knew well that the people living in the rain forest — rubber-tappers, indigenous peoples, and so on — needed the forest to survive, and he thus promoted ways of utilizing the products of the forest without destroying its ecosystem, by rubber-tapping, nut harvesting, and so on. All of these practices could be done without destroying the integrity of the rain forest. Moreover, Mendes identified two types of interrelated violence — ecological violence against the environment and social violence against rubber-tappers and indigenous peoples. Both moved to a similar logic — the logic of acquisition through the control of nature and people. What is an alternative model of development? For Mendes, it was one that respects and nurtures the knowledge of nature, trees, soil, and lifestyles (the accumulated wisdom of rubber-tappers and indigenous peoples) while at the same time incorporating novel technologies providing social equilibrium (Boff 1994: 242).

Tragically, Chico Mendes was murdered, apparently by rapacious cattle ranchers, who bloodily illustrate the twin types of violence outlined by Mendes in their quest to have cheap cattle-grazing lands. They are willing to destroy both peoples and forest in their quest for "domination" and "accumulation."

Aspects of Boff's theological anthropology show the influence of process theology and new cosmology. He notes, along with John B. Cobb Jr. and other process theologians, as we have seen, that humans are part of the environment, not above it, entailing a certain moral responsibility and a social-environmental ethic that avoids "naturalism," which claims that nature has unchanging laws to which humanity must be subservient, and "anthropocentrism," which sees humans as lords over nature. Both positions belie the interdependence of humans and nature (Boff 1994: 243).

While humans are a foundational part of the environment, Boff argues, they are distinctly moral subjects and thus have an ethical responsibility toward nature, a responsibility we have largely forsaken. This new ethic demands what Boff calls "ecological justice":

> Ecological justice acknowledges that human beings have a duty of justice towards the earth. The earth has dignity and otherness; it has *rights*. Having existed for millions of years before human beings appeared, the earth has the right to continue to exist in well-being and equilibrium. Ecological justice proposes a new attitude towards the earth, an attitude of benevolence and mutual belonging, while at the same time seeking to repair the injustices committed by the technical scientific project. (Boff 1994: 244)

While Boff echoes the thought of many environmental ethicists in suggesting the earth has "rights," it is not clear in his writings how the earth has rights in the same way humans do. As he observes, humans have a distinctive moral dimension that demands ethics and responsibility. What is the connection between responsibility and rights? If nonhuman nature also has rights, must it also have responsibilities? Can nonhuman nature be judged and held accountable in the same manner as humans? Is rights-language really appropriate in describing the attributes of nonhuman nature? These queries regarding terminology seem unexplored in Boff's works.[13]

Incorporating the New Cosmology

In dialogue with the work of Thomas Berry and new cosmologists, Boff argues that liberation theology should adopt "the new cosmology of ecological discourse, the vision that sees the earth as a living superorganism linked to the entire universe." He continues:

> It should understand the human mission, exercised by men and women, as an expression of earth itself and a manifestation of loving care that exists in the universe; it should understand that human beings — the noosphere — represent the most advanced stage of the cosmic evolutionary process on its conscious level. They are co-pilots with the guiding principles of the universe that have controlled the entire process since the moment of the "big bang" some fifteen thousand million years ago. Human beings were created for the universe and not vice versa, in order to bring about a higher and more complex stage of universal evolution. (1995b: 75)

Boff goes on to say that having adopted this basic view, the starting point must be an option for the poor, which includes the most threatened beings in creation. Moreover, this option asks new questions. The fundamental question is no longer "What future is there for Christianity or Western civilization?" but rather "What future is there for planet Earth and for humankind as its expression?" (1995b: 75).

While Boff creatively adds a liberationist position onto the new cosmological vision, his embrace of the theological anthropology of that cosmology raises questions previously posed about this perspective. If we are "co-pilots with the guiding principles of the universe," why have we as a species taken such a wrong turn? Why have we been so destructive of planetary and human ecosystems? (In other words, what "flight-school" did we attend?) Moreover, if we are in the cockpit of universal evolution and represent "the most advanced stage of the cosmic evolutionary process," an optimistic viewpoint reflective of Teilhard de Chardin's work (evoked by use of the term "noosphere"), who is to say that our destructive patterns are not part of some larger evolutionary plan? Is not the appeal to the "guiding principles of the universe" reflective of the "naturalism" that Boff seeks to avoid? Could not such a view lead to complacency rather than commitment, an acceptance of our elevated status in the universe as somehow cosmically ordained rather than something shaped by our limited understanding and in constant need of critique and revision, as summoned by the Judeo-Christian tradition? As Boff notes: "As sons and daughters of God, and not as despots, we prolong the creative activity of God, cultivating nature, improving it, and multiplying it (as in the case of genetic engineering) responsibly. In this way not only God is creator, but so also, by divine plan, are we" (1995a: 87).

In claiming that we are "co-pilots," "co-creators," as well as the "Satan" or potential "angels" of the earth, is Boff perhaps ascribing a superior status to the human that may border on the anthropocentrism he seeks to avoid? Are such metaphors truly appropriate? Do they adequately reflect the human interdependence with nonhuman nature also touched upon by Boff? Again, if there is a whiff of divine sanction for our "co-creator" status with God as we engage in such ethically slippery activities as genetic engineering and human cloning, might this further fuel the hubris that has led to our smugness and arrogance in our dealings with nonhuman nature?

Ivone Gebara:
Toward a "Holistic" Liberation Theology

We are tired of sterile religious-scientific discourse, of its powers grounded in an All-Powerful, One and Trinitarian God, distant and apart from ourselves. We are tired, to use

the words of Arnaldo Jabor, of seeing the world "divided between those who bewail hell and those who live in it." This refers to the hell of our society, which kills Indians, children, and entire peoples.... The important thing is to renew our lives daily, with tenderness, responsibility, keenness, and great passion, to experience daily our struggle to defend the extraordinary life that is within us, in the unity [and] multiplicity of all things.
      —IVONE GEBARA, "The Trinity and Human Experience"

Brazilian theologian Ivone Gebara, who works among indigent communities in northern Brazil, while writing from an eco-feminist perspective, has, like Leonardo Boff, attempted to expand liberation theology to include the insights of process theology and new cosmology. Moreover, she has related the precepts from ecological discourse to traditional theological categories, such as the Trinity, in provocative and creative ways (Gebara 1996). Though a thorough treatment of her richly textured work is beyond our present scope, a brief consideration of her theological anthropology as it pertains to ecological discourse may help illustrate the complexity of melding liberation theology's colloquy with other paradigms of Christian ecological literature.

In keeping with liberation theology's adoption of a self-critical stance and its "hermeneutics of suspicion," Gebara, in light of her concern for both the dignity of women and the integrity of creation, is critical of liberation theology. While acknowledging that liberation theology has posed the critical question of how one speaks of God in the midst of hunger, misery, injustice, exploitation, and destruction of peoples and has yielded a more collective understanding of sinfulness while stressing the God of life and of justice and a preferential love of the poor, Gebara claims that it has not challenged the patriarchal anthropology and cosmology upon which Christianity rests (Gebara 1995: 209).

Citing the influences upon her work of Pierre Teilhard de Chardin, Fritjof Capra, Brian Swimme, and Thomas Berry, Gebara claims there is a growing suspicion of liberation theology's adoption of the shibboleth that "redemption comes through suffering." As Boff notes, the promise of a new society based on love and justice has not been fulfilled, and attempts to institute it have been thwarted by larger military and economic forces. Gebara claims that many in Latin America are now tired of the unrelenting suffering, the struggles that do not lead to victory, the continuing death and despair. Acknowledging that social and political analysis is important, she also claims that liberation theology must do more. It needs to turn to the air, water, Earth itself, and sense that our environment is part of us. Like Boff, Gebara calls for a "holistic" paradigm, though her vision is based more firmly on ecofeminist principles. As she writes:

> For me, "holistic ecofeminism" has a double purpose. First is the fundamental concern for the oppressed — the voiceless of history — who when they are born are *de facto* excluded from the chance to live a full life because of their economic situation. It is the poor who are the greatest consumers of patriarchal religion because of the consolation it provides! They are caught in a vicious cycle here, but for me it is absolutely key to avoid distancing myself from these voiceless ones. Second is the commitment to put an end to patriarchy in all its forms. (1995: 210)

For Gebara, the Christian task is to resuscitate the human within, not above, the cosmos. In contradistinction to the understanding that the human is lord and master over creation, we are beginning to fashion a notion that we have a particular connection to the waters, air, and land. We see this because we are beginning to suffer because our water is polluted, our food is tainted, and we get sick from the fish from our rivers and lakes. We, like the planet, are ill, highlighting our tremendous interconnection with a vitiated environment. "And so," she writes, "we are beginning to discover our interconnectedness. We humans are not Lords of creation. Instead, we are the Earth's thought, the Earth's reflection of itself" (Gebara 1995: 211).[14]

As noted, this understanding of the human as the thought or self-consciousness of the planet has roots in the thought of

Pierre Teilhard de Chardin and Thomas Berry. The fact that both Gebara and Boff utilize the thought of these men is a tribute to its compelling nature for those who are interested in a liberation perspective. Yet the difficulties of this perspective do not appear to be examined in liberation literature. Does such a perspective bespeak a certain hubris? How can we know that we are indeed the self-consciousness of the universe? Does that point to rather than away from an anthropocentrism that could be ecologically harmful? Does it denote a kind of optimistic evolutionary perspective that sees a progression of consciousness and suggests an "end of history" culminating in the ability of the human to be self-reflective not only upon itself but on all of creation?

An example of how this cosmological perspective is translated into theological categories is provided by Gebara's work on the Trinity (Gebara 1996). She sees the Trinity as a human construct to express the human experience of connectedness to the cosmos, to the earth, to one another, and to God. The Trinity is simply a Christian way of articulating the dynamic process of diversification, multiplicity, and communion that is found in the universal dynamic of life itself. Gebara notes that evil is also present in the relationship, not as something desired by God, the origin of life, but rather as a manifestation of the human "will to Power," as Reinhold Niebuhr described it, the need to control the life-force, to seize it as power with which to hold tight to some of its gifts and keep these gifts from others. Through this process, distortion of this life-process spills over into violence, poverty, and ecological plunder (Gebara 1995).

Thus, the liberative struggle is an attempt to transcend these mangled relations and develop a relationship of mutuality with all creation, as evinced in our understanding of the Trinity. We are called to a redemptive *metanoia,* where our insight of mutuality is translated into just and loving interpersonal, societal, and human-nonhuman relationships.

Liberation Theology and Ecological Discourse: Contributions and Questions

Contributions

As the work of both Boff and Gebara reveals, liberation theology, owing to historical, cultural, and ecological developments, is in process of incorporating environmental discourse as part of a larger construction of a new paradigm. The ability to be self-critical and hopeful in the midst of such massive suffering and ecological destruction is a reflection of the tremendous grace and faith of these remarkable theologians and the communities of which they are a part.

One of the greatest contributions of liberation theories to ecological literature is a grounding for ecological discourse in a specific praxis of solidarity with the poor and marginalized. Building on a rich scriptural and ecclesial legacy, liberation theology, when it approaches ecological issues, does so annealed by the fierce resistance those adopting a liberationist perspective have met both inside and outside of the church, from ecclesiastical investigations and censure to death-squad massacres. Liberationist thought is lubricated, as it were, by the sweat, blood, and tears of celebrated and nameless martyrs who have now, like Chico Mendes, begun to encircle the natural environment in their web of solidarity.

In addition, a liberation perspective brings a disciplined and engaging body of social analysis to the critique of modernity espoused by other Christian ecological paradigms. While acknowledging the critique of the modern individualistic self that sees itself superior to nature, liberation theologians bring a sophisticated social, political, and economic critique of modernity, one written from the perspective of the victims of this initiative. Hence, when they add ecological issues to their discourse, they offer a cogent connection between, on the one hand, the exploitation of First Peoples and the impoverished majority of Latin Americans and, on the other hand, the destruction of the land, air, soil, and beauty of Latin America.

Moreover, they show vibrantly that only an understanding of the human that takes into account the social, cultural, economic, and ecological aspects of human agency will be able to help us climb out of the social and environmental chasms we have created. Liberation ecologists are dealing forthrightly with both the power of the human to destroy life-dynamics and our interconnection with all that is.

Finally, they are attempting to apply their renewed and expanded paradigm to traditional Christian categories, such as the Trinity (Gebara) and grace (Boff). As has been argued by even secular environmentalists (Oelschlaeger 1994), the environmental movement needs the churches in order to effect the deep transformation that is necessary for sustainability, and it is only when these larger paradigmatic issues are contoured to traditional theological categories that these new visions of being human will enter into the lifeblood and practice of faith communities.

Questions

As suggested earlier, there seems to be a somewhat uncritical embrace of certain aspects of the new cosmology and process theology, as well as environmental-rights language, in liberation theology. While such a utilization of these models shows an admirable ability to be self-critical and open to other Christian expressions, liberation theologians, its seems, with their social analysis and commitments, have a distinctive critical perspective to bring to the important contributions of process and new cosmological paradigms.

Moreover, one wonders if liberation theology, in regrouping after the collapse of the Soviet Empire and after the formulation of a renewed utopian vision of society, has reflected upon the deleterious understanding of nature embodied in traditional socialism, as well as upon the kind of hubris that has traditionally accompanied utopian visions. Perhaps this is why there is little critical reflection on the optimistic evolutionary perspective of Teilhard de Chardin. Is there something deeply and incorrigibly harmful and anthropocentric in utopian schemes, as some postmodern theorists tend to suggest? While I believe the answer is ultimately negative, the liberation theologians grappling with ecological discourse may not have treated this question with the deliberation it deserves.

Liberation theology, grounded in social-scientific analysis and commitment to a faith-inspired societal transformation, has clearly demonstrated that the creation of a new social reality begins with a specific context. As a contextual, political theology, liberation theology, in its recent incorporation of ecological discourse, signals an important move from the notion of "justice" as a simply interhuman construct to "sustainability," not only an interhuman but a human-environmental precept. Moreover, unlike Gaian, process, and new cosmological models, liberation theology situates this understanding of sustainability within a very specific and previously articulated perspective, namely, a preferential option for the poor and a solidarity with those striving for human and ecological integrity. Liberation theologians such as Boff and Gebara demonstrate that poverty is a deeply ecological threat, and hence any paradigms, strategies, or proposed solutions to the environmental crisis, if they neglect to address systemic poverty, are ultimately bound for failure and are unfaithful to the Christian gospel.

Additional Contributions of Liberation Theology to Ecological Discourse

As we have seen, emerging out of the poverty, oppression, and injustice of Latin America, liberation theology sought to read the Bible through "the prisms of the poor." In response to the "developmentalist" economic and cultural policies of the 1950s and 1960s, which only led to a wider gap between rich and poor, Gustavo Gutiérrez offered the term "liberation" to reflect more accurately the biblical, cultural, and political aspirations of Latin American Christians. As a contextual term, therefore, "liberation" is very hard to transfer to a different context, such as a North American attempt to fashion a political theology of the environment. Yet several of liberation theology's methodological and intellectual insights into uniting faith and urgent struggle for justice may be of some use as ecological theologians strive to reverse the destruction of the earth.

Although a plethora of these insights might well be germane to ecological theology, I merely wish to explore briefly two of these: "theology as a second act" and "the evangelizing power of the poor."

Theology as a Second Act

For Gutiérrez and other liberation theologians, theology is primarily a "second act." The first act, he declares, is solidarity with the poor in their quest for liberation and involves commitment to a liberation or justice struggle; only after such a commitment is made, Gutiérrez claims, can theology be effectively done. Theology, therefore, must "take sides"; it cannot remain neutral when confronted with injustice:

> The first stage or phase of theological work is the lived faith that finds expression in prayer and commitment. To live the faith means to put into practice, in light of the demands of the reign of God, these fundamental elements of Christian existence. Faith is here lived "in the church" and geared to the communication of the Lord's message. The second act of theology, that of reflection in the proper sense of the term, has for its purpose to read this complex praxis in the light of God's word. There is need of discernment in regard to concrete forms that Christian commitment takes, and this discernment is accomplished through recourse to the sources of revelation. (Gutiérrez 1988: xxxiv)

What might the "first act" of a politically engaged ecological theology be? It might include, first of all, "listening" to nature, to a "groaning creation." Both John Carmody and Thomas Berry, I have argued, incorporate this moment of "listening" into their work. How might such a practice be pragmatically instituted in our churches? Our seminaries? Our religious education? Berry

181

and Carmody have spoken of listening not only to the earth in its awesome mystery but also to scientists, ecologists, and, in the case of Berry, environmental activists who are involved in the "justice struggle" of nature.

Social analysis is also a central part of Gutiérrez's "first act" and of liberation theologies in general. By exploring the social, economic, political, and cultural conditions that have led to devastating oppression and destruction in Latin America, Gutiérrez, in his "second act," was able to build on a solidarity with the poor to fashion a transformative theology.

As ecological theologians have begun to explore seriously the social, political, economic, and cultural conditions that have despoiled the earth, they are discerning that the forces that lead to the oppression of people in the Third World are often the same forces that have led to the oppression of nature throughout the world. If this is so, how might we develop a strategy of social action to counter those perhaps sometimes well-intentioned, but nevertheless ecologically horrific, forces?

The Evangelizing Power of the Poor

Gutiérrez and other liberation theologians have spoken of how, in attempting to evangelize the poor, they themselves have become evangelized. Working in solidarity with oppressed communities striving for liberation, Gutiérrez was led to a deeper appreciation of Christ's liberating message. Often bereft of food and basic human rights, the poor represent a painful signal that something is wrong, dreadfully wrong, with political and religious structures that do not address their indigence. The poor are "signs" that the promised utopia of God's reign has yet to be actualized. It was through his encounter with the poor that Gutiérrez achieved a *metanoia* in his ministry (Gutiérrez 1980: 112).

The source of Gutiérrez's conversion, and the conversion of many other Christians who have entered into "solidarity" with the dispossessed, might hold a useful key for ecological theologians. What is the source of ecological *metanoia*? Perhaps immersion into the dizzying extent of ecological destruction, as well as actual engagement with groups seeking a sustainable future, would be a source of such conversion. Might there not well be an "evangelizing power of the earth," in both its glory and despoliation, that could help drive the social transformation necessary to save our "home"? Listening to the voices of scientists and ecologists exploring the profundity of the crisis, visiting areas that have been scorched by conscienceless development, working with environmental advocacy groups (such as the growing number of North American women religious involved in "eco-ministry," as well as native peoples), and developing a valid social analysis might indeed be initial steps in fashioning a politically engaged ecological faith. As the "signs of the times" — acid rain, global warming, ozone depletion, and fouled air — reveal, we have little time to waste in continuing this journey.

Overall, liberation theology demonstrates dynamically that ecological concerns run along the fault lines of society — economic disparity, political oppression, systemic racism. Ecological destruction follows these fault lines and must be understood, liberation theologians argue, within the social structures of oppression and liberation that social analysis has illuminated. Moreover, in their reading of the gospel, liberation theologians argue that the church, when confronted with economic, social, political, or racial oppression, cannot remain neutral; it must take sides on behalf of the vulnerable, weak, and threatened. When these vulnerable elements turn out to be plants, nonhuman animals, and ecosystems, the church must also rise to their defense. Though the nuances of solidarity with the poor and solidarity with the earth and the rights of humans and those of nonhuman nature are not finely sketched by Boff or Gebara, their advocacy of a church that "takes sides" when confronted with injustice and threats to life is a cogent appeal to *metanoia* for the Christian churches in their relationship to the poor, the destitute, and our threatened nonhuman cohabitants of the planet.

Chapter 7

Contouring a Political Theology of the Environment

―――――――――――――

The economic logic behind dumping a load of toxic waste in the lowest-wage country is impeccable.... I've always thought that under-populated countries in Africa are vastly underpolluted.

— LAWRENCE SUMMERS, former chief economist for the World Bank, 1992

In his sobering book *Amazing Grace: The Lives of Children and the Conscience of a Nation* (1995), social critic Jonathan Kozol interviews children and adults in the Mott Haven section of the South Bronx, the poorest congressional district in the United States and an area with alarmingly high incidences of murder, drug abuse, and poverty. Unfortunately, this section of New York City also has one of the highest rates of asthma in the nation, and children with inhalers are commonplace. One of the main reasons for the high incidences of asthma, according to Kozol, is the medical-waste incinerator in this depressed district. Referring to a conversation with "Cliffe," a seven-year-old resident of Mott Haven, Kozol writes:

We head north for a block or two, then turn right and walk a long block to a rutted street called Cypress Avenue. After crossing Cypress, he hesitates again.

"Do you want to go down there?" he asks.

"They're burning bodies there," he says.

"What kind of bodies?"

"The bodies of people!" he says in a spooky voice, as if he enjoys the opportunity to terrify a grown-up.

"Is it the truth?"

He acts as if he doesn't hear my question and begins to hum. The place that Cliffe is referring to turns out to be a waste incinerator that was put in operation recently over the objections of the parents in the neighborhood. The incinerator, I am later reassured by Reverend Overall, does not burn entire "bodies." What it burns are so-called "redbag products," such as amputated limbs, fetal tissue, bedding, bandages, and syringes that are transported here from fourteen New York hospitals. The waste products of some of these hospitals, she says, were initially going to be burned at an incinerator scheduled to be built along the East Side of Manhattan, but the siting of a burner there had been successfully resisted by the parents of the area because of fear of cancer risks to children. (Kozol 1995: 7)

It is of course no accident that this medical-waste incinerator operates in one of poorest segments of U.S. society, having been successfully opposed by one of New York City's wealthiest communities. The asthma-afflicted children of the South Bronx as well as the environmental racism of the quote from Lawrence Summers reproduced at the opening of this chapter are testaments to the fact that the environmental crisis moves along the fault lines of social, economic, political, gendered, and racial oppression.[1] These children, like the thirty-five thousand children of Southern nations who die daily owing to environmental causes (as the UN report cited at the beginning of this work reveals [see p. 11, above]), point out that we cannot think of ecological destruction and human oppression of poor persons as separate and distinct phenomena. Both are inextricably intertwined in a structure of sin. It is this systemic, structural evil that a political theology of the environment must address if it is to speak credibly and constructively to our contemporary situation.

In this concluding chapter, I sketch out briefly the parameters of a political theology of the environment. I do this, first, by looking at the need for a new theological anthropology in light of social justice and environmental concerns. Second, I examine the need for a new ontology, a new way of being human, especially in our interrelationships with the nonhuman world, within the context of contemporary social and environmental concerns. Finally, I discuss the need for a new praxis, an integrated program of liberation and sustainability that seeks to make more concrete these anthropological and ontological considerations.

A New Theological Anthropology

The focus of our perspective on these various paradigms of ecological Christian literature has been the role of the human. In looking at the Gaia theory, process theology, ecofeminism, the new cosmology, and liberation theology, I have surfaced a variety of metaphors for the human role in relationship to nonhuman nature. Among these images are that of "trustee" (Thomas Seiger Derr), "steward" (Douglas John Hall), "person-in-community" (John B. Cobb Jr.), "gardener" (Rosemary Radford Ruether), "caretaker" and "citizens of the earth" (Sallie McFague), "the self-consciousness of the universe" (Thomas Berry and Brian Swimme), and "angels/Satan" of the earth (Leonardo Boff). All of these metaphors are placed as buoys, as it were, helping Christian theologians to navigate between the Scylla of a theological anthropology that perceives the human as lord, master, and *telos* of creation and the Charybdis of viewing the human as an inconsequential inhabitant in the overall functioning of the planet, as Gaia and deep ecology suggest.

All of the paradigms surveyed are striving to avoid a dangerous anthropocentrism without falsely underplaying the power of the human to both destroy and restore God's creation. A political theology of the environment acknowledges the tremendous human power to wreck and redeem the nonhuman world. It too is concerned with a theological anthropology and a fitting metaphor for humanity's engagement with the human and nonhuman world.

186

Realizing that an anthropocentric approach has been and continues to be deleterious and inappropriate for articulating the human relationship with planetary ecosystems, a political theology of the environment must construct a different model.

The problem with an anthropocentric approach as advocated by Thomas Seiger Derr and Richard John Neuhaus is not with the "anthro," as it were, but with the "centrism." Any theological discourse that is to remain true to the Judeo-Christian heritage must, of course, involve in a profound way the human voice and experience. Difficulty emerges, however, when that voice and that experience become the central focus of theological discourse, particularly when that voice is seen as radically distinct from nonhuman nature and the larger planetary system. Adumbrations of this view also cloud the trustee, gardener, caretaker, and stewardship models, which suggest that the human is in some sense a land-manager, who will report back to the "chief," that is, God, when his/her tenure as manager is over. While this model is certainly a crucial and important improvement over traditional understandings of the human as overlord, it is still in part grounded in an anthropocentric notion of the human as somehow separate from and superior to the rest of creation.

The notion of "citizens of the earth" also retains ties to an anthropocentric viewpoint by utilizing post-Enlightenment language of individual rights and responsibilities. Extending rights-language to nonhumans, however, seems both inappropriate and undesirable, for an emerging understanding of our relationship with the nonhuman world must transcend an Enlightenment understanding of justice as a set of "properties" inherent to and contained by the self. Consequently, the concept of "citizen" simply expands the context and responsibilities of human action to the nonhuman world but does not fundamentally question or change our basic self-understanding. Finally, the notion of "self-consciousness of the universe" similarly does not alter or critique the modern understanding of the human as a sentient self-reflective being who makes sense out of reality and therefore remains at the center of all thought and action as a self-contained, self-reflective entity. What is different in this model is simply the context: the ambit of human consciousness has been expanded to include the universe itself. All of these images, then, leave intact elements of an anthropocentric framework.

The notion of "person-in-community," however, does begin to push at the borders of an anthropocentric worldview. Process theology's understanding of the human as a participant in a process of growth that entails both human and nonhuman agents critically points to a radical interrelationship of the human and nonhuman. Part of this insight comes from the notion that the human agent is fundamentally both individual and collective, not only in human terms but in terms of the human interrelationship with the environment.

Building on this notion of a person-in-community paradigm that integrates concepts of the individual and collective, a political theology of the environment offers not an "anthropocentric" approach but rather an "anthro-harmonic" understanding of the human-nonhuman relationship. Harmonic in this case implies "of an integrated nature." An anthro-harmonic perspective acknowledges the importance of the human and makes the human fundamental but not exclusively focal. This metaphor also, building upon the insights of process theology, notes that the human self is simultaneously individual and communal, that "no subject is an island," as it were, because intersubjectivity is a fundamental reality of all human existence. Furthermore, one can only be fully human when the individual and communal elements of being human are integrated in such a way that they sustain all creation. The achievement of this integration is "harmony" not only among humans but also between humans and the rest of the biotic community.

The Anthro-harmonic Approach: A New Ontology

What the warning signs of the "eco-catastrophe" signal, and the probing of the various paradigms reviewed here also manifest, is that we are collectively groping for a new way to be human in light of social and environmental dilemmas. As mentioned, it is evident that our new behavior regarding the nonhuman world has to be rooted in new values, a novel understanding of the self, and a foundationally restructured understanding of our relationship with our environment. This is not only a social, economic, cultural, and political crisis; it is also, as Al Gore has pointed out, a spiritual crisis.

A political theology of the environment has to grasp the moral dimension of this new ontology. A preferential option for the poor and the oppressed, for this theological approach, becomes a moral anchor for locating the human agent. Political theology maintains that this new human-nonhuman relationship is fundamentally moral, not simply biological, and acknowledges, like process theology, a primal interrelationship between the human and nonhuman realms. It recognizes that humans and the larger environment are mutually constitutive, that a "dialectical contingency" exists between humanity and the rest of creation. This dialectical contingency suggests that the natural world is dependent upon humanity and that humanity is dependent upon the natural world. It thus avoids the false dichotomy of certain pre- and post-Enlightenment understandings of humans as transcending this world and deep ecology's understandings of the human as being irrelevant. It also steers clear of the anthropocentric dimension of many of the paradigms previously reviewed because although the human, the "anthro," remains *fundamental* in a political theology of the environment, the human is not "centric" because it is in relationship with the biotic realm.

This is not to deny, however, the many crucial and valuable contributions of these paradigms for an anthro-harmonic ontology. New cosmology, for example, has awakened activists around the world to a sense of awe of and reverence for the universe, a remarkably galvanizing idea that has permeated Third World theologians and ecofeminists as well as First World environmentalists. This awe and reverence must be a central part of this new ontology. However, while they may "incline" us toward an anthro-harmonic approach, awe and reverence do not in and of themselves lead to sustainable integration between humans and nonhumans. Here the contributions of ecofeminism and liberation theology, in particular, are directly helpful. With their

189

emphasis on justice, their notion of solidarity with victims of structural oppression, and their sense of the need for not only understanding but also transforming society, they help root the human-nonhuman relationship within a specific moral universe. The anthro-harmonic approach being proposed here as the basis of a political theology of the environment strives to unite the sense of awe and wonder at the graced-grandeur of the universe with a sense of compassion and indignation at the suffering and unjust victimization of many of creation's inhabitants.

A Praxis of Integration

The novel theological anthropology and ontology being suggested here can seem exceedingly abstract. What makes them concrete, however, is a praxis, a program of action and reflection as developed in liberation theology. This notion of praxis suggests two things for a political theology of the environment: the importance of identifying a context and the importance of adopting a distinctive vantage point. As liberation theology has attempted to show, all theology is contextual, arising from the wellsprings of a particular people, place, and moment in history. In addition, liberation theology, emanating initially from oppressed communities of Latin America, has adopted the perspective of the poor and downtrodden as the basis of the explication and transformation of human evil and suffering.

Arguing that a fundamental feature of theological discourse must be the experience of the poor, liberation theologians have said that the church, like the God of the prophets, must take the side of the poor. It cannot remain neutral in the face of systemic injustice and oppression. Utilizing the social justice perspective of liberation theology and ecofeminism, a political theology of the environment examines structural systems of oppression in both sociopolitical and ecological terms. When one looks at environmental destruction from a political-theological perspective, one witnesses a dual oppression, both of the poor and of vulnerable natural ecosystems.

The scope of a political theology of the environment, then, can encompass the awe-inspiring grandeur of a star-strewn sky on a still summer evening. But it cannot stop there. It must also embrace the asthma-ridden children of the South Bronx as fundamental members of that same universe. This gaze suggests that the universe will not be fully grace-filled until our interrelationships are governed by justice rather than simply mutuality. Until all can gaze upon the compelling beauty of the cosmos from positions of dignity and empowerment, the anthro-harmonic hope of a political theology will not have been achieved.

A Continuing Journey

This study, as suggested at the outset, is part of a larger journey. We have, as people of faith, been moving from creation — God's opening gambit in the covenant between divine and nondivine, the creator and the created — to our present environmental state, with its perforated ozone layer, contaminated water and land, shrinking biodiversity, overpopulation, and uncertain future. A principal question of this journey, which this work has sought to explore, is the role or vocation of the human and its importance in dealing with our environmental crisis. This has been waged through a critical examination of various paradigms in Christian ecological literature and the role they ascribe to the human. This has also entailed a quest for new metaphors that convey a new theological anthropology, ontology, and praxis. Finally, this has included an attempt to outline a political theology of the environment that anchors the human agent within a schema of justice.

As we stand on the edge of the twentieth century and peer toward a new millennium, the prospect of creating a just and sustainable future seems daunting at best. We are, in a sense, in the midst of a storm, adrift and struggling to get our bearings. We nevertheless must let drop our anchor, acknowledging the prospect of death and yet grasping for the possibility of life.

191

Notes

Introduction: Knowing Our Place

1. For an up-to-date and comprehensive overview of environmental issues, see the annual report of the Worldwatch Institute, *State of the World*, edited by Lester Brown. See also Ruether 1992, esp. chap. 4.

2. For a fascinating study of how these conflicting models of nature were adopted by competing biology departments in different U.S. universities earlier in this century, see McIntosh 1985.

3. When the *New Yorker* magazine ran a prepublication excerpt of Carson's manuscript, it received threatening legal letters from Velsicol, a U.S. chemical firm, as did Houghton Mifflin. For a compelling overview of U.S. corporate attempts to muzzle Carson's work, see the 1993 PBS video, "Rachel Carson's Silent Spring," part of *The American Experience* documentary series.

4. Karl Polanyi, in his influential critique of industrial capitalism, *The Great Transformation* (1944), was among the first social theorists to discern the deleterious effects of the self-regulating market on the natural world. See Baum 1996: 15–19.

5. The concept was originally referred to as the "Gaia hypothesis." After the Chapman conference in March 1988, at which leading scientists from around the world debated the concept, it has been increasingly referred to as the "Gaia theory" (see p. 60, above). I use the terms interchangeably throughout this work.

Chapter One: Christian Theological Responses to the Ecological Crisis

1. Lynn White Jr. (1907–87), former president of Mills College, was a specialist in medieval history and technology. He taught at Princeton, Stanford, and the University of California at Los Angeles, where he established the Center for Medieval and Renaissance Studies.

2. Peter W. Bakken, Joan Gibb Engel, and J. Ronald Engel, in their assiduously researched survey of Christian ecojustice literature (1995), suggest that theologian Joseph Sittler's 1961 address — entitled "Called

to Unity" — to the Third Assembly of the World Council of Churches in New Delhi marks the outset of post–World War II attempts to interweave environmental concerns, justice, and Christian faith (Bakken, Engel, and Engel 1995: 7). Sittler's address (published as Sittler 1962) declares that Christology becomes irrelevant when not enmeshed in the critical concerns of violence, poverty, and protection of the earth; Sittler also holds up elements of Scripture and tradition that point to such an integrative Christological framework. For in-depth treatments of Sittler's pioneering contributions to ecological theology, see Bouma-Prediger 1995: 61–102 and Heggen 1995.

3. As historian Elspeth Whitney observes in her creative assessment of the White debate (1993), White's thesis has been reiterated and critiqued in over two hundred books and articles by environmentalists, historians, theologians, and philosophers since its initial publication in 1967. Among the more salient anthologies and volumes in this legacy are Barbour, ed., 1973; Spring and Spring, eds., 1974; Mitcham and Grote, eds., 1984; Attfield 1983; and Hargrove, ed., 1986. Moreover, several religion journals, including *Faith and Thought, Zygon, Epiphany,* and the *Christian Century,* ran article series focusing on White's argument. Whitney argues that White's contention that medieval Christianity is culpable for our current ecological destruction does not stand up to the latest scholarship in medieval technology, which suggests that medieval religious values were far more complex than White proffers. In addition, Whitney contends that White, along with many theologians responding to him, sees religious values as the principal locomotive of European history, when actually the rise of capitalism, the rise of the nation-state, and other political and economic factors were probably far more pivotal in fomenting environmental degradation than was Christianity (Whitney 1993). For a helpful examination of this point, see Boutin 1991.

4. For a lucid presentation of the biblical limitations of White's thesis, see Blenkinsopp forthcoming.

5. For a consideration of White's location within the historiography of medieval technology, see Whitney 1990: 1–21.

6. In a letter to Thomas Sieger Derr, Lynn White Jr., half in jest, refers to himself as the "founder" of ecological theology. See Derr 1975.

7. Others who might be placed in this camp include biblical scholar and Anglican bishop John Austin-Baker and poet and farmer Wendell Berry. See especially Baker 1979 and Berry 1981.

8. William Coleman, in his article "Providence, Capitalism, and Environmental Degradation" (1976), argues that Christianity's role in ecological decimation lies not so much in nurturing destructive medieval technology but in fashioning a notion of divine providence at work in

nature and society. This doctrine, Coleman argues, helped foster the rise of economic individualism, political liberalism, and growth-orientation, which became hallmarks of industrial capitalism in Europe (see also Bakken, Engel, and Engel 1995: 42).

9. Attfield, at least in one case, proved prescient. Secular environmentalist and philosopher Max Oelschlaeger, for example, observes how White's article concretized his sense that religion was the primary cause of environmental degradation and nurtured his prejudicial view against religion. And he was not alone in this supposition. "Environmentalists themselves," he writes, "trailing in the wake of such scholars as Lynn White Jr., characteristically believe that Judeo-Christianity — its values, metaphysics, and institutions — is the cause of ecocrisis" (Oelschlaeger 1994: 20). (The fact that the White article was reprinted in a wide range of environmental publications, including the *Sierra Club Bulletin, The Whole Earth Catalogue, The Environmental Handbook,* and the *Oracle,* attests to its familiarity among secular environmental activists [Whitney 1993: 157–58].) More recently, however, Oelschlaeger has undergone a self-described "conversion experience" and now views religion not simply as an environmentalist's ally but as perhaps "the last, best chance" at stemming ecocatastrophe. For him, "there are no solutions for the systemic causes of ecocrisis, at least in democratic societies, apart from religious narrative" (Oelschlaeger 1994: 1–7). In light of his focus, one possible title for Oelschlaeger's work, in the spirit of Friedrich Schleiermacher, could have been "Religious Environmentalism: Speeches to Its Ecologically Cultured Despisers," for he attempts to address environmentalists, like himself, who have traditionally been skeptical of or downright hostile toward religion in an attempt to show religion's usefulness in their struggle.

10. In this analysis, and elsewhere, Attfield relies heavily on Glacken 1967. Passmore, according to Attfield, overlooks the fact that traditions of stewardship and cooperation with nature are "mainstream," rather than ancillary, Christian concerns (Attfield 1983a: 377).

11. Richard John Neuhaus, former Lutheran pastor who later became a Roman Catholic priest, in his early and controverted book, *In Defense of People: Ecology and the Seduction of Radicalism* (1971), argues that the environmental movement emanating from the 1960s is actually based on the protection of a quality environment for the elite against the poor. He thus calls for a "covenant with the poor" that accents the importance of humanity's societal role and the poor as the main guidepost of justice demands (for a précis of the book, see Bakken, Engel, and Engel 1995: 134).

12. According to Peter Bakken, Joan Engel, and Ronald Engel (1995), there are three major stages in the attempt to interweave justice, ecology,

and Christian faith in North American and international ecumenical circles. The first is the ecojustice movement in the mid-1960s, with its initial theological, ethical, biblical, historical, and public policy studies published in the early 1970s. The second is the attempt to initiate the WCC's program "Just, Participatory, and Sustainable Society" during the 1970s, which met, they claim, with mixed success. The third stage, marked by the WCC's initiative "Justice, Peace, and the Integrity of Creation," signified an expansion of the ecojustice project into a global and cross-cultural endeavor (1995: 7).

13. H. Paul Santmire, pastor at Grace Lutheran Church in West Hartford, Connecticut, was one of the early leaders of the Faith-Man-Nature group, an ecumenical collection of theologians, scientists, and church leaders emerging in the mid-1960s. He is also the author of one of the first full-length Christian treatments of ecological issues: *Brother Earth: Nature, God, and Ecology in Time of Crisis* (1970). Santmire concurs with White that the primary solution to the ecological crisis must entail a religious consciousness, which the church must spearhead in a self-critical fashion (Santmire 1970: 6–8). For an overview of both this movement and Santmire's contributions, see Bakken, Engel, and Engel 1995: 4–15 and passim. Here, I focus primarily on *The Travail of Nature,* owing to its significance as one of the first and still most comprehensive attempts to survey the long Christian historical legacy from an ecological vantage.

14. In contrast to Santmire, subsequent scholarship has focused on the equally fertile and varied thought of Saint Thomas Aquinas in light of ecological concerns. See especially the engaging analysis of William French (see French 1993, 1994). See also Thomas Berry's favorable use of Aquinas in Berry 1991: 17 and passim.

15. I would consider also ecofeminist and process ecological theology to be a part of this constructive approach, each of which will be considered in separate chapters.

16. Hall also treats the *imago Dei* in Hall 1993: 213–18.

17. Catholic theologian Elizabeth A. Johnson also brings this sense of immanence along with a Trinitarian focus to theological reflection on environmental concerns. See Johnson 1993a and 1993b.

18. It might seem surprising at first to associate the thought of Thomas Berry with that of John Carmody. Berry is, after all, a self-described "geologian" and Carmody, a "traditional" theologian. Yet Berry and Carmody reflect more than shared sensibilities in their respective works. Like Berry, Carmody has studied Eastern religions extensively and offers some elements of these Eastern faiths that are closely identified with nature as useful for a Christian theology of nature (Carmody 1983: 50–52). Similarly, like Berry, Carmody also focuses

on spirituality and the new spiritual implications of the ecological crisis, touching briefly on the themes of interrelatedness, naturalist prayer, nonviolence, reconciliation, hope, and witness (148–63). Moreover, both Berry and Carmody are more directly involved, in their books, with dialogues involving secular ecologists. Berry makes myriad references in *The Dream of the Earth* to the efforts of Greenpeace, Earth First! and the writings of a wide array of nonreligious environmental thinkers, from Rachel Carson to Brian Swimme (the U.S. mathematical cosmologist who contributed the book's foreword). Similarly, Carmody, explicitly in the first half of his book, provides his readers with "the recent dialogue between ecology and religion," providing reflections from energy specialist and ecologist Amory Lovins and from technology critic Jacques Ellul, among others. Finally, both Berry and Carmody write of the awesome speechlessness engendered by creation and of the need for silence in the presence of creation's divinely infused mystery. They both round out their volumes with a "dream." Berry's, of course, is the dream of the earth, to which we must somehow listen if we are going to survive into the future. Carmody (as will be discussed in the text below) concludes his work with the dream of an ecologically sustainable future, involving a child who, raised in this environment filled with natural sciences and lore of the earth's dynamic mystery, would develop a habit-of-being that treated the earth and other humans with respect (166–69).

19. Like Thomas Berry, Carmody views the emerging findings of science to be particularly germane to the emerging ecological consciousness, not only because they relate in statistical terms the character and extent of ecological destruction but also because they increasingly point to the mystery of nature and the cosmos.

20. Fritsch has been an active participant in the North American Conference on Christianity and Ecology.

21. Others who might be included in the listening camp include Irish Greenpeace co-director Sean McDonagh. See McDonagh 1986, 1994; as well as the work of Miriam Therese McGillis and Paula Gonzalez.

22. For a more popular attempt to respond to these queries within an expanded Christian framework, see Scharper and Cunningham 1993.

Chapter Two: The Gaia Hypothesis

1. Lovelock describes the provenance of the Gaia hypothesis in Lovelock 1979, 1–24. Though Lovelock first presented the Gaia hypothesis at a 1969 scientific conference at Princeton, he did not publish his idea until 1972, in a letter to *Atmospheric Environment.*

2. Interestingly, subsequent NASA findings suggest that microbes may have at one time existed on Mars.

3. The story of Earth's climate, for Lovelock, provides some of the most compelling evidence for the Gaia hypothesis. For the past 3.5 billion years, the climate has never been non-life-sustaining. Oceans have never frozen nor boiled, and the Ice Ages only affected 30 percent of Earth's surface (Lovelock 1979: 19).

4. Margulis and her son Dorion Sagan provide a terse, scientific description of Gaia: "Gaia is a theory of the atmosphere and surface sediments of the planet Earth taken as a whole. The Gaia hypothesis in its most general form states that the temperature and composition of the Earth's atmosphere are actively regulated by the sum of life on the planet — the biota. This regulation of the Earth's surface by the biota has been in continuous existence since the earliest appearance of widespread life. The assurance of continued global habitability according to the Gaian hypothesis is not a matter merely of chance. The Gaian view of the atmosphere is a radical departure from the former scientific concept that life on Earth is surrounded by and adapts to an essentially static environment. That life interacts with and eventually becomes its own environment; that the atmosphere is an extension of the biosphere in nearly the same sense that the human mind is an extension of DNA; that life interacts with and controls physical attributes of the Earth on a global scale — all these things resonate strongly with the ancient magico-religious sentiment that all is one" (Margulis and Sagan 1984: 60).

5. Peter Bunyard and Edward Goldsmith, in their edited collection *Gaia and Evolution: Proceedings of the Second Annual Camelford Conference on the Implications of the Gaia Thesis* (1989), illustrate how the Gaia hypothesis is being used as a foil against the advocates of neo-Darwinism who maintain that natural selection, competition, and survival of the fittest are the norms of biological life. Gaia gives those challenging neo-Darwinism a new tool, perhaps, to whittle away at a theory with which they have been uncomfortable for some time. For these scientists, neo-Darwinism is only part of the story. For them, evolution must be seen as an interactive process whose overall objective is stability within ever-changing life-processes.

6. Lovelock countered his Darwinian critics by constructing a computer model that he calls "Daisy World." The Daisy World model attempts to portray how surface temperature might be regulated. It postulates that the world's surface consists entirely of only light and dark daisies. The lower the temperatures, the more the dark daisies absorb heat; the higher the temperatures, the more the lighter daisies reflect heat. The model appears to demonstrate that light and dark daisies can

influence the temperature of Earth's surface on a planetary scale (Margulis and Sagan 1984: 65). For more detailed discussion of the Daisy World model, see Lovelock 1983.

7. Ironically, it was Lovelock's own research in the Arctic using his important invention, the electron capture detector, that made the discovery of the first "ozone hole" possible. With the ability to detect freon and other halogenated compounds in the air, this device helped trigger ecological concerns over ozone depletion and ultraviolet-radiation-engendered cancers (Margulis and Sagan 1984: 74).

8. In further distancing himself from ecologists, Lovelock advocates geophysiology rather than ecology, claiming that ecologists look at a single organ (or ecosystem) while geophysiologists look at the whole body (Gaia). As noted above, though Lovelock claims that Earth has special "organs" that, if destroyed, could lead to Gaia's malfunctioning (e.g., tropical rain forests, the Continental Shelf, wetlands), his perspective evokes few environmental values (Weston 1987: 221).

9. Lovelock also speaks of planetary colonization. In his book *The Greening of Mars* (1984), coauthored with Michael Allaby, Lovelock proposes someday to export Gaia's mechanism to Mars, thus making it habitable for humans. The disturbing environmental ethical questions surrounding such a proposal are explored by Anthony Weston (1987).

10. Interestingly, such volumes don't engage or challenge the Gaia hypothesis per se; they in effect use it as a springboard to show how humans must tread more respectfully on the planet. For a delineation of some of these Gaia-inspired religious and New Age developments, see Joseph 1990: 66–71.

11. Rosemary Radford Ruether provides a helpful overview of such goddess-centered musings in her work *Gaia and God* (1992: 247–53 and passim).

12. Often impractical and unsophisticated, Pedler's work is a personal, intriguing, outrageous, and compelling book of an individual Gaian eccentric, whose ideas have now come more and more into the mainstream since they were first published. Perhaps what seemed like quackery then appears to be in some ways more acceptable now in light of our environmental situation.

13. See also chapter 5 for Rosemary Radford Ruether's response to Gaian theory within an ecofeminism framework.

14. Revealingly, none of the principal commentators mentioned above, with the possible exception of Ruether, has delved into the Christian theological challenges raised by Gaia. What does the notion of the Earth as a living organism do to the notion of the incarnation? How does it affect the Judeo-Christian understanding of creation? How does it square with the traditional distinction in Christian tradition between

the creator and the created, a distinction of particular concern to the Reformers? What are the potential hazards of building an ethical or theological framework upon a scientific theory that may be altered or discredited with new scientific insights in the next few years or decades?

Chapter Three: Process Theology

1. Broadly understood, therefore, Heraclitus, Hegel, Spencer, Bergson, Peirce, James, Dewey, Mead, and Teilhard de Chardin can all be viewed as having some connection to process thought. See Ford 1974. Such an understanding underlies Ewert Cousins's eclectic collection, *Process Theology* (1971), which incorporates selections ranging from Bernard Loomer to Pierre Teilhard de Chardin. This stance, broadly speaking, argues that the principal realities of life are "events" or actual occasions rather than substances, as articulated in Whitehead's published Gifford Lectures, *Process and Reality.*

2. For a critique of this position, see Burrell 1982.

3. Cobb's book *Is It Too Late? A Theology of Ecology* (1972) was a result of his conversion experience, in conjunction with the influence of a plethora of conferences and papers. In the book, Cobb faced squarely the challenges of the environmental crisis from a process perspective. Subsequent titles that deal with environmental despoliation include *The Liberation of Life* (1981; with biologist Charles Birch), *For the Common Good* (1989; with economist Herman Daly), *Sustainability* (1992), as well as a spate of articles.

4. Some of these queries will be saved for the general conclusion to this chapter.

5. This insight is reflective to a certain degree of George Herbert Mead's social behaviorism, which also features interrelation as a core of the human self. This is most clearly articulated in his *Mind, Self, and Society.*

6. Such compartmentalization and abstraction of ideas has led Cobb to critique the specialization of the academy. See *For the Common Good,* chapter 6, "From Academic Discipline to Thought in Service of Community," 121–37.

7. By not placing absolute value on human life and, hence, moving beyond Kantian ethics, Cobb is able to speak approvingly of population control programs and abortion in conjunction with other initiatives to promote sustainability. He sees China as a template of a sustainable society. As he observes, "One model . . . , though admittedly an ambiguous one, is contemporary China. China seems to have learned to do more with less, to waste almost nothing, to give most of its people a sense of

meaningful participation in the corporate life, and to abolish degrading poverty" (Cobb 1992: 32). How Cobb can reconcile the student massacre at Tianamen Square, the forced sterilization of women and high rate of aborted female fetuses owing to government population control programs, the use of political prisoners in the labor force, and the support of ecologically hazardous projects such as Three Gorges Dam with the above sanguine portrait of China is difficult to ascertain.

8. Significantly, decentralization was the policy of the U.S. Republican Party in the 1994 elections. Heralded as the "Republican Revolution," this policy by many accounts does not augur well for the poor, who henceforth, if the Republican agenda is pursued, will not be protected by federal programs. (The limitations of such weakening of the federal government were highlighted during the U.S. civil rights movement of the 1950s and 1960s, when southern states argued that the federal government had no right to desegregate their society and disrupt their culture.)

9. McDaniel completed his doctoral work in religion under the direction of John B. Cobb Jr. at Claremont Graduate School in 1978. A professor of religion at Hendrix College in Conway, Arkansas, he also serves as director of the Steel Center for the Study of Religion and Philosophy. Moreover, in his environmental work, he has served as chairperson of Meadowcreek Project, an environmental education organization, and is a member of the Church and Society Working Committee of the World Council of Churches, in which capacity he has helped shape the WCC project on Justice, Peace, and the Integrity of Creation.

10. In rather involved fashion, McDaniel, quoting Whitehead's phrase that "God is a fellow sufferer who understands," asserts that God is somehow present in the suffering of individual pelican chicks. In this way, McDaniel argues that one can speak of redemption for this neglected pelican, who has a richness of experience of suffering that remains a mystery that we may not be able to grasp. The chick, for McDaniel, does make a contribution beyond itself by contributing to the empathetic life of God (1989: 43). McDaniel intimates that, for process theologians, God has empathy for each and every creature. The creature's ephemeral experiences are felt and blended with the felt needs and experiences of all other creatures. Consequently, the receptive aspect of God is "an ultimate, ongoing, intense harmony" that is best characterized by the word "beauty," what Whitehead refers to as the adventure of the universe as One (McDaniel 1989: 43).

11. Albert J. Fritsch, S.J., an engineer combining environmental concerns with a quest for social justice in Appalachia, assails McDaniel for his lack of practical steps to heal the earth, for his neglect of

Franciscan, Benedictine, Quaker, Carmelite, and other potentially fertile spiritualities, and for "distracting" Christians from the urgent vocation of environmental activism. "Where is a spirituality leading to profound change and service to and with the poor?" Fritsch wonders. See Fritsch 1991.

12. McDaniel describes in greater detail the manner in which animals are raised, and slaughtered, for food: "In the United States alone, tens of millions of animals are killed each year to provide meat for human consumption. Like us, they die individually, one-by-one. Most of them are reared indoors in factory-style farms by means of 'close-confinement' or 'intensive-rearing' methods. The animals enjoy no sunlight, no fresh air, and, often, no room to turn around. If they are laying hens, they are sometimes packed in groups of six to eight in wire-mesh metal cages the size of a page of daily newspaper; if they are pigs, they are often confined for up to five years in stalls just larger than their own bodies; if they are veal cows, they are taken from their mothers at birth and raised in permanent, restrained isolation.... They are slaughtered in different ways. Chickens are hung upside down on conveyor belts and cut with a knife; pigs and cows are stunned by an electric current or captive-bolt pistol, after which, while unconscious, their throats are cut" (1990a: 63–64).

13. For an example of McDaniel's incorporation of a Buddhist perspective, see especially McDaniel 1990b. To see his adaptation of Hindu thought, see McDaniel 1995, chapter 9. For his creative use of feminist analysis, see McDaniel 1989: 111–46. He also provides a sensitive critique of ecofeminism as outlined by Rosemary Radford Ruether. See McDaniel 1994b.

14. Significantly, the original subtitle of McDaniel's *Earth, Sky, Gods, and Mortals* is *Developing an Ecological Spirituality*. His schema for an ecological spirituality is also unfurled in *Of God and Pelicans,* chapter 3, "A Life-Centered Spirituality."

15. McDaniel quotes with favor Walter Brueggemann to help situate this notion of "shalom." Brueggemann writes, "The central vision of world history in the Bible is that all of creation is one, every creature in community with every other, living in harmony and security toward the joy and well-being of every other creature" (quoted in McDaniel 1990a: 18). Shalom is that concord that would mark a community that has embraced such a vision.

16. For more on the perspective of rabbits about to be consumed, and hence the impossibility of shalom within the "fallenness" of creation, see McDaniel 1994b.

17. Jay McDaniel, author information form, Twenty-Third Publications, unpublished.

18. For a terse synopsis of Keller's thesis, see McDaniel 1989: 132–37. I am here indebted to McDaniel's reading of Keller.

19. Keller talks of the possibilities of Whitehead's thought serving as a healing element for our culture and about his correspondence with a feminist perspective: "Of course, Whitehead works as a diagnostician more than as a problem-solver. But is such an alternative vision capable of exercising healing effects upon its culture? It depends. Without continuously and explicitly antipatriarchal work on itself and its real worlds, process thought will not and cannot advance the realization of its own vision. . . . I nowhere claim that feminism needs Whitehead — or any favored male thinker. We can appropriate these thoughts because of their affinity with values important for other reasons than the ones he would acknowledge, reasons more urgent than abstract. The urgency, as urge to make a difference, to perpetuate something other than the same old structures of my self, my world, my views, does not dictate any feminist purism (a form of separatism) in the choice of resources. We can only ask what, in the face of global history hurtling itself toward imminent disaster, helps something new to emerge" (1986: 211).

20. This is not to suggest that Keller is insensitive to suffering and structural injustice. Indeed, her feminist analysis is built upon a critique of the oppressive contours of patriarchal systems, and she challenges consumptive patterns of middle-class North Americans, as well as patterns of environmental racism, whereby impoverished minority areas are targeted for toxic waste sites and excessive pollution release (see Keller 1995b: 49, n. 1).

21. Keller recalls a *Life* magazine feature (May 1992) that depicts NASA's project to "terraform Mars," also known as the "greening of the red planet." Claiming that it is foolhardy not to look for another place to live (after destroying our own planet?), NASA's "young Turks" are exploring the possibility of making Mars a life-supporting planet (Keller 1995b: 39).

22. This is not to in any way diminish the deep-seated concern process ecological theologians have demonstrated for social justice. Cobb's practical dialogues, for example, in economics (Daly and Cobb 1989) and science (Cobb and Birch 1981) have yielded constructive and crucial pragmatic alternatives for economic forecasting that take into account depletion of Earth's resources, and his notion of the "person-in-community" has tremendous economic as well as ecological resonance. Moreover, the critique of the atomistic self brings freshness to a political theology's notion of human agency, which must be in dialogue with the individualistic aspects of Western thought and the pernicious dimensions of the atomistic self.

Chapter Four: The New Cosmology

1. Many theologians dispute that this fundamental imbalance between creation and redemption exists in Christian theology, arguing that the notion of grace and God's "indwelling" in matter, as expressed through the Trinity, belie such a diremption. Among those arguing such a position are David Burrell, CSC, Gregory Baum, and Catherine LaCugna.

2. Though partially informed by recent scientific discoveries of the universe, the "new story" contends that many contemporary scientists, locked in a mechanistic and knowledge-bound rather than wisdom-based paradigm, have, in the words of T. S. Eliot, "had the experience but missed the meaning." As Thomas Berry surmises, "To the scientists, the story is not in itself meaningful; it's ... an essentially random process going nowhere. If scientists only understood their own data, they would have a most remarkable story, because the emergent evolutionary process is a truly grand way of experiencing the universe" (Berry 1995b: 36). What advocates of the new cosmology are attempting to do, in a sense, is elevate science to a wisdom tradition, imbued not only with empirical data but also with a sense of the sacred and psychic dimensions of the unfolding of the universe (personal interview with Thomas Berry, July 6, 1996).

3. Berry speaks of being asked to address a group of Native Americans and not knowing what to say. As he stood outside pondering his topic, he recalls, the waves of the nearby lake said, "Tell them the story," and the wind said, "Tell them the story." After his talk, one of those attending said to Berry that he must have Native American blood in order for him to be able to relate the story of the earth and universe as he had. Berry cites this anecdote as an example of listening to nature.

4. I am indebted here to Mary Evelyn Tucker's terse but comprehensive biographical studies of Thomas Berry. See especially Tucker 1988.

5. Berry's dissertation, "The Historical Theory of Giambattista Vico," was published by the Catholic University Press of America, Washington, D.C, in 1949. Vico's categorization of history into ages of the gods, heroes, and humans was instrumental for Berry's proclivity for interpreting the great ages of human and earth history. For a fuller depiction of the influence of Vico on Berry's work, see Tucker 1988; see also Dalton 1994.

6. Berry notes that when Henry Airfield Osborne claimed in his work *Our Plundered Planet* (1947) that the earth was experiencing severe ecological destruction, Teilhard rejected his thesis, buoyed by an abundant optimism that Teilhard, Berry claims, imbibed in part from French spiritual writer Jean de Caussade's *Abandonment to Divine*

Providence, which advocated a sublimation of human will to God's will, thereby deemphasizing human responsibility for certain actions (Berry 1991: 25).

7. While appreciative of James Lovelock and Lynn Margulis's Gaia theory, Berry argues that it must be placed in a larger cosmological context. See Berry 1994.

8. Thomas Berry during the 1990s has become increasingly critical in his lectures and workshops of the role of transnational corporations in environmental destruction. Building upon the work of David C. Korten (see Korten 1995) and other corporation critics, Berry claims that with the globalization of the economy, and lack of diversity owing to corporate monoliths, we are now living in what can be called a "global company store" (personal interview, University of Notre Dame, February 10, 1996).

9. While Swimme's religious sensitivity may seem outlandish in the hard-nosed world of scientific empiricism, his cosmological reflections have received a hearing even within mainstream scientific circles. He has addressed the American Association for the Advancement of Science on the topic "Scientific Resources for a Global Religious Myth" (1994), for example, and continues to get invitations from traditional scientific societies.

10. Interestingly, the great African-American actor and singer Paul Robeson, for whom "Old Man River" became a signature song, changed the wording to have more political resonance as he became more deeply involved in the civil rights movement and socialist struggles.

11. This is suggested in part by the title of Brian Swimme and Matthew Fox's *Manifesto for a Global Civilization* (1982).

Chapter Five: Ecofeminism

1. *Theology Today* editor Patrick D. Miller insightfully depicts this quest in feminist theology. Claiming that a deeply felt resistance to aspects of divine sovereignty within feminist theology is not surprising, Miller continues: "The Bible itself sets forth notions of husbandly rule over wives and male rule over women and then tells us stories about such rule that curl the hair. Perpetuation of ecclesial male domination in hierarchical modes in the church and elsewhere simply reinforces the conviction of women that notions of sovereignty carry with them patterns of domination that suppress full and mutual responsibility, opportunity, and reward. It is to be expected that out of such encounter with human sovereignty, theologians, female and male, would seek to discover or construct a kind of theology that reveals a God in whose na-

ture and activity mutuality or some other kind of relationship replaces hierarchical control of the world and its creatures and whose imaging is appropriately set by images that are more open, gentle, vulnerable to others, and preserving of freedom in the creation in all its forms" (Miller 1996, 2).

2. For theologian Lois K. Daly, there are four main tenets of eco-feminism: (1) oppression of women and oppression of nature are interrelated; (2) this interrelationship must be probed to overcome these dual oppressions; (3) feminist analysis must include ecological insights; and (4) any suggested ecological solutions must entail a feminist perspective (Daly 1990: 88–89).

3. Rosemary Radford Ruether is Georgia Harkness Professor of Applied Theology at Garrett-Evangelical Theological Seminary, Northwestern University, in Evanston, Illinois. She is one of the most prolific and significant contributors to religious and theological feminism in both North America and, arguably, the world.

4. According to Steven Bouma-Prediger, Ruether was one of the first theologians to link liberation theology and a theology of nature and has consistently done so since the late 1960s. See Bouma-Prediger 1995, 12–14. To date, Bouma-Prediger's revised dissertation is the only sustained scholarly treatment of Ruether's ecological theology available in English. See also Hessel, ed., 1996, 5–7.

5. Elsewhere Ruether pithily writes: "We cannot criticize the hierarchy of male over female without ultimately criticizing and overcoming the hierarchy of humans over nature" (1983: 73).

6. Ruether critiques Lynn White's collapse of Hebraic and Christian views in "The Historical Roots of Our Ecologic Crisis" (see Ruether 1975a: 187).

7. This idea is also expressed in secular terms by Bill McKibben, who claims that "pristine" nature, unsmudged by humanity, is now gone, as traces of pollution are found even in polar regions. See McKibben 1989. It must be acknowledged, however, that grains, flowers, trees, and many types of animals have been cultivated and bred for centuries, representing a distinctive interaction between "nature" and humans.

8. Ruether's notion of "making friends" with the earth closely resembles the work of Passionist cultural historian Thomas Berry. See especially his book *Befriending the Earth* (1991). (Thomas Berry takes pains to point out that the title actually originated with environmental philosopher Albert LaChance of the University of New Hampshire.) Such a construction of a new order is consistent with Ruether's understanding of the prophetic, liberative tradition. As she claims: "Liberation theology today consists not only in a discovery of this prophetic, transformative side of the tradition but also its recontextualization or

restatement for today. Speaking a prophetic word of God is not simply an exegesis of past texts but the midrashic retelling of the story of liberation in the contemporary context. The Holy Spirit is a present, not simply a past, revelatory power. Thus liberation theologies are not simply confined to what they can 'find' in past tradition. They are empowered to restate the vision in new dimensions, not imagined or only hinted at and undeveloped in the past" (Ruether 1989b: 3).

9. This colloquy, which has also nurtured intra–Third World dialogue, is manifest most tangibly in Ruether, ed., 1996. Edited in collaboration with the ecofeminist Con-spirando Collective in Santiago, Chile, the volume includes contributions from Asia, Africa, and Latin America, including an article by Vandana Shiva, whose work is considered later in this chapter.

10. Sallie McFague is the E. Rhodes and Leona B. Carpenter Professor of Theology at the Divinity School of Vanderbilt University in Nashville, Tennessee. She served as dean of the Vanderbilt Divinity School from 1975 to 1979 and has taught at Smith College, Yale Divinity School, and Harvard Divinity School.

11. McFague further clarifies her theological agenda: "I propose that one theological task is an experimental one with metaphors and models for the relationship between God and the world that will help bring about a theocentric, life-centered, cosmocentric sensibility in place of our anthropocentric one" (1990: 202–3).

12. For a very accessible discussion of these models, see the interview with Sallie McFague in the video hosted by Bill Moyers entitled "Spirit and Nature," based on a 1990 symposium at Middlebury College in Middlebury, Vermont.

13. A Greenpeace television commercial graphically illustrates the future scenario McFague describes. In the ad, well-dressed businesspeople are walking, briefcases in hand, and all are wearing gas masks to screen out the brown, toxified air that surrounds them. A street person, *sans* gas mask, begs for and receives a token, which he then inserts into a public oxygen machine for some respiratory relief. The message is clear: in the future only the wealthy will be able to afford clean air. This trend is presently seen in the purchase of bottled water — many wealthy people, distrustful of the public water supply, increasingly procure water filters and bottled water, something that poor people cannot easily afford. This message, too, is becoming clear in North America (as it has been in the Third World for some time): only the affluent can afford safe drinking water.

14. Brazilian liberation theologian Leonardo Boff also attempts to link oppression of the earth with oppression of poor persons, particularly indigenous peoples. See his *Ecology and Liberation* (1995).

Influenced by contemporary science and process thought, McFague strives to show a compatibility between scientific theories of evolution and Christian solidarity with the poor. Contending that evolution is not entirely biological but also cultural and historical, McFague invokes Jesus' call to choose to be on the side of the oppressed and marginalized. We can now see that cultural evolution is of greater importance than natural selection, and we can have some say in the way we wish our culture to evolve on this planet. Cultural evolution is thus consistent with biological evolution in that both assert there is a next phase of evolution, one that involves a sharing of the resources of the planet. It contradicts evolutionary science, however (and here McFague helpfully parts company with process theology), in that the principle for this new evolutionary step to occur relies not on natural selection but on human solidarity with all, especially the outcasts and oppressed (1993: 171–74).

15. For an examination of the ecological implications of this notion of "household," see Scharper and Cunningham 1993.

16. Vandana Shiva is founder of the Research Foundation of Science, Technology, and Natural Resource Policy near Delhi. After receiving a doctorate in theoretical physics, she worked for the Indian Institute for Management in Bangalore and continues to devote time to the Chipko movement, a women's "tree-hugger" initiative in India. As Rosemary Radford Ruether writes, "The person who has taken the lead in shaping...social feminism, for Indians in particular and for Asian women generally, is Vandana Shiva" (Ruether, ed., 1996: 61).

17. For a fine case study of SAPs and their effect on Third World ecology, agriculture, and people, see Mihevc 1996. What Shiva describes as the "monoculture" of such developmentalist programs Mihevc describes as a "fundamentalist theology," especially in terms of the World Bank.

18. An example of such "maldevelopment," according to Shiva, is the Mahaweli Development Program in Sri Lanka. Adopting a short-term vantage, the project built dams across Sri Lanka's longest river, which led to deforestation and an altered landscape, as well as the displacement of thousands of peasant families, who were then resettled. In addition to ecological destruction, the project led to social unrest, for the resettlement resulted in a majority Sinhalese community in the Eastern Province of Sri Lanka, an area that had a heretofore balanced ethnic composition (1996: 72).

19. Shiva further elucidates this connection between science and sexism: "Modern science was a consciously gendered patriarchal activity. As nature came to be seen more like a woman to be raped, gender too was recreated. Science as a male venture, based on the subjugation of female nature and female sex, provided support for the polarization of gender. Patriarchy as the new scientific and technological power was

a political need of emerging industrial capitalism. While, on the one hand, the ideology of science sanctioned the denudation of nature, on the other, it legitimized the dependency of women and the authority of men. Science and masculinity were associated in domination over nature and all that is seen as feminine" (1996: 69).

20. Women's ecological movements are not simply found in the Third World. In North America, for example, Roman Catholic women religious are becoming deeply involved in ecological ministry. Many congregations are devoting money and members to ecological projects. Among the most prominent of these are Sr. Mirian Therese McGillis and Sr. Paula Gonzalez, both of whom help coordinate sustainable, ecologically sensitive communities. Others include Sr. Janis Yeakel, ASC, of Earthworks in Plymouth, Indiana, and Sr. Virginia Jones of the Nazareth Center for Ecological Spirituality in Kalamazoo, Michigan. Just as women religious were the first to take the teachings of Vatican II seriously, allowing the conciliar documents to permeate their chapters and help restructure their organizations, so too are they taking the lead in the Catholic religious environmental movement. In addition to establishing full- and part-time "eco-ministries," many orders have had environmental audits done of their properties, leading to energy-saving measures, recycling, organic farming, and the creation of wildlife sanctuaries.

21. The Chipko movement's inaugural action occurred in March 1973 in Gopeshwar village, where thirty ash trees in the region had been granted to a sporting goods producer by forest authorities. Gaura Devi, a widow in her fifties, with most of the men out of town collecting land compensation, allegedly stood before a gun-wielding tree "harvester": claiming that the forest is her people's *maika* (mother's home) and saying that if the trees were taken, landslides would devastate their fields and homes. She and her companions forced the enraged loggers to leave without their timber. See Philipose 1989.

22. A starting for this polyvalent relationship with nature is perhaps taking a look at concrete historical examples of women's ecological activity. Shiva does this admirably with the Chipko movement. Ruether and McFague, in contrast, along with some other ecofeminists, tend to be less concrete in their analysis, avoiding or neglecting such critical North American environmental advocates as author Susan Fenimore Cooper, artist Deborah Passmore, and biologist Rachel Carson (Norwood 1993: 275–84; I am indebted to Max Oelschlaeger for suggesting this source). Moreover, as suggested, the transformative work presently being done by Roman Catholic sisters to promote ecological sustainability goes apparently unmentioned in their analysis.

Chapter Six: Liberation Theology

1. A compelling, well-researched, and heartrending account of the suffering of Christians in Latin America who have embraced a liberationist perspective is provided in Lernoux 1980.

2. For an examination of liberation theologians' use of dependency theory, see McGovern 1989; Garcia 1987; Boff and Boff 1986; and Witvliet 1985. It is intriguing to note that these overviews of liberation theology have no reference to ecological concerns among liberation theologians, indicating that such an emphasis is of very recent vintage.

3. See Boff and Boff 1987; Ferm 1986a and 1986b; and Hennelly 1995.

4. Surveys of liberation theology, as the above notes attest, abound. Though first brought to the attention of North American readers by Orbis Books, founded in 1970 by Philip J. Scharper and Rev. Miguel D'Escoto, M.M., under the sponsorship of the Maryknoll Fathers and Brothers, liberation theologians are now published by major presses around the world, as are commentaries upon their work.

5. For an incisive examination of this rich symbol of liberation, see Haight 1985.

6. See Boff and Elizondo, eds., 1995, for articles linking Latin American liberation theology and the environment.

7. For an important overview of Latin American environmentalism, see Price 1994.

8. For a brief biographical sketch of Boff, see Ferm 1988, 124–28.

9. Other advisory board members of the Ecology and Justice series include scholars Mary Evelyn Tucker and John A. Grim of Bucknell University and Sean McDonagh, author and former missionary in the Philippines affiliated with Greenpeace Ireland. The establishment of such a series, which attempts to bridge social justice, religious, and environmental issues, by the world's foremost publisher of liberation theology, Orbis Books, is itself a manifestation of the growing nexus between liberationist and ecological concerns.

10. For a trenchant overview of how these global economic patterns negatively impact the environment, see McDonagh 1994, 1–102, as well as Mihevc 1995.

11. As exemplified by the 1992 conference of Latin American bishops in Santo Domingo (CELAM IV), the role of the church in the subjugation of Latin America's First Peoples has become a significant issue for liberation theology and the Latin American church. Boff shares this concern, linking it with liberation theology's notion of a preferential option for the marginalized. He also forges a link between the logic of domination of ranching, mining, and state interests exploiting the Latin

American rain forest as they simultaneously shred the integrity of the indigenous communities within the Amazon rain forest (Boff 1995a, 1995b). For a gripping account of this process, see Cowell 1990.

12. On the relationship of political ecology and socialism, or the "Red-Green Debate," see Ryle 1988.

13. Boff delineates further this rights-based discourse for nonhuman nature when he discusses a "socio-cosmic democracy," with the elements of nature "such as mountains, plants, rivers, animals, and the atmosphere" being considered new citizens who share in the human banquet, while humans share in the cosmic banquet" (1995b: 74). This reflects Aldo Leopold's notion of humanity becoming "just plain citizen" in relationship to the biotic community in his *A Sand County Almanac: Sketches Here and There* (1949).

14. Gebara's embrace of panentheism and the metaphor of earth as God's body is in keeping with the perspective of process theologians John B. Cobb Jr. and Jay McDaniel, as well as the work of Sallie McFague, as we have seen.

Chapter Seven: Contouring a Political Theology of the Environment

1. See Westra 1994 on environmental racism.

Bibliography

Introduction: Knowing Our Place

Baum, Gregory. 1996. *Karl Polanyi on Ethics and Economics*. Montreal: McGill-Queens University Press.

Carson, Rachel. 1951. *The Sea around Us*. New York: Oxford University Press.

————. 1962. *Silent Spring*. New York: Houghton Mifflin.

Commoner, Barry. 1971. *The Closing Circle: Nature, Man, and Technology*. New York: Alfred A. Knopf.

De Steiguer, J. E. 1997. *The Age of Environmentalism*. New York: McGraw-Hill.

Dunlap, Riley E. 1991. "Trends in Public Opinion toward Environmental Issues: 1965–1990." *Society and Natural Resources* 4:285–312.

Ehrlich, Paul. 1968. *The Population Bomb*. New York: Sierra Club and Ballantine Books.

Gore, Al. 1992. *Earth in the Balance*. Boston: Houghton Mifflin.

Hall, Douglas John. 1993. *Professing the Faith: Christian Theology in a North American Context*. Minneapolis: Augsburg Fortress.

Hessel, Dieter T. 1995. Preface to *Ecology, Justice, and Christian Faith: A Critical Guide to the Literature*, ed. Peter W. Bakken, Joan Gibb Engel, and J. Ronald Engel. Westport, Conn.: Greenwood Press.

The Limits to Growth: A Report for the Club of Rome's Project on the Predicament of Mankind. 1972. New York: Universe Books.

McIntosh, Robert P. 1985. *The Background of Ecology: Concept and Theory*. Cambridge: Cambridge University Press.

Ruether, Rosemary Radford. 1992. *Gaia and God: An Ecofeminist Theology of Earth-Healing*. San Francisco: HarperCollins.

White, Lynn, Jr. 1967. "The Historical Roots of Our Ecologic Crisis." *Science* 155:1203–7.

Chapter One: Christian Theological Responses to the Ecological Crisis

Attfield, Robin. 1983a. "Christian Attitudes to Nature." *Journal of the History of Ideas* 44:369–86.

———. 1983b. *The Ethics of Environmental Concern.* New York: Columbia University Press.

Baker, John Austin. 1979. "Biblical Views of Nature." *Anticipation* 25 (January): 40–46. Reprinted in Charles Birch et al., eds., *Liberating Life: Contemporary Approaches to Ecological Theology,* 9–26. Maryknoll, N.Y.: Orbis Books, 1991.

Bakken, Peter W., Joan Gibb Engel, and J. Ronald Engel. 1995. *Ecology, Justice, and Christian Faith: A Critical Guide to the Literature.* Westport, Conn.: Greenwood Press.

Barbour, Ian G., ed. 1973. *Western Man and Environmental Ethics.* Reading, Mass.: Addison-Wesley.

Baum, Gregory. 1996. *Karl Polanyi: On Ethics and Economics.* Montreal: McGill-Queens University Press.

Berry, Thomas. 1988. *The Dream of the Earth.* San Francisco: Sierra Club Books.

———. 1991. *Befriending the Earth: A Theology of Reconciliation between Humans and the Earth.* Mystic, Conn.: Twenty-Third Publications.

Berry, Wendell. 1981. *The Gift of Good Land.* Berkeley, Calif.: North Point.

Birch, Charles, William Eakin, and Jay B. McDaniel. 1988. *Liberating Life: Contemporary Approaches to Ecological Theology.* Maryknoll, N.Y.: Orbis Books.

Blenkinsopp, Joseph. 1997. "Global Stewardship: Toward an Ethic of Limitation." In *The Challenge of Global Stewardship: Roman Catholic Responses,* ed. Todd Whitmore and Maura Ryan. South Bend, Ind.: University of Notre Dame Press.

Bouma-Prediger, Steven. 1995. *The Greening of Theology: The Ecological Models of Rosemary Radford Ruether, Joseph Sittler, and Jürgen Moltmann.* Atlanta: Scholars Press.

Boutin, Maurice. 1991. "La lecture écologique de la Bible." In *Environnement et développement: Questions éthiques et problemes socio-politiques,* ed. José A. Prades, Jean-Guy Vaillancourt, and Robert Tessier, 209–29. Montreal: Fides.

Brueggemann, Walter. 1977. *The Land.* Philadelphia: Fortress.

———. 1996. "The Loss and Recovery of Creation in Old Testament Theology." *Theology Today* 53, no. 2 (July): 177–90.

Callicott, J. Baird. 1990. "Genesis Revisited: Muirian Musings on the Lynn White Jr., Debate." *Environmental History Review* 14:65–92.

Carmody, John. 1983. *Ecology and Religion: Toward a New Christian Theology of Nature.* New York: Paulist.

Christiansen, Drew, S.J. 1994. "Nature's God and the God of Love: Response to Daniel Cowdin." In *Preserving the Creation: Environmental Theology and Ethics,* ed. Kevin W. Irwin and Edmund D. Pellegrino. Washington, D.C.: Georgetown University Press.

Christiansen, Drew, S.J., and Walter Grazer, eds. 1996. *"And God Saw That It Was Good": Catholic Theology and the Environment.* Washington, D.C.: United States Catholic Conference.

Coleman, William. 1976. "Providence, Capitalism, and Environmental Degradation." *Journal of the History of Ideas* 37:27–44.

Derr, Thomas Sieger. 1975. "Religion's Responsibility for the Ecological Crisis: An Argument Run Amok." *Worldview* 18 (January): 39–45.

———. 1995. "The Challenge of Biocentrism." In *Creation at Risk: Religion, Science, and Environmentalism,* ed. Michael Cromartie, 85–104. Grand Rapids, Mich.: Eerdmans.

Dunlap, Riley E. 1991. "Trends in Public Opinion toward Environmental Issues: 1965–1990." *Society and Natural Resources* 4:285–312.

Dunlap, Riley E., and Angela G. Mertig. 1991. "The Evolution of the U.S. Environmental Movement from 1970 to 1990: An Overview." *Society and Natural Resources* 4:208–19.

Episcopal Commission for Social Affairs of the Canadian Conference of Catholic Bishops. 1993. *The Environmental Crisis: The Place of the Human Being in the Cosmos.* Ottawa: CCCB.

French, William. 1993. "Beast-Machines and the Technocratic Reduction of Life: A Creation-Centered Perspective." In *Good News for Animals? Christian Approaches to Animal Well-Being,* ed. Charles Pinches and Jay B. McDaniel, 24–43. Maryknoll, N.Y.: Orbis Books.

———. 1994. "Catholicism and the Common Good of the Biosphere." In *An Ecology of the Spirit: Religious Reflection and Environmental Consciousness,* ed. Michael Barnes, 177–94. Lanham, Md.: University Press of America.

Freudenberg, Nicholas, and Carol Steinsapir. "Not in Our Backyards: The Grassroots Environmental Movement." *Society and Natural Resources* 4:235–45.

Fritsch, Albert J., S.J. 1987. *Renew the Face of the Earth.* Chicago: Loyola University Press.

———. 1992. *Down to Earth Spirituality.* Kansas City: Sheed and Ward.

———. 1994. "Appropriate Technology and Healing the Earth." In *Embracing Earth: Catholic Approaches to Ecology,* ed. Albert La-Chance and John E. Carroll, 96–114. Maryknoll, N.Y.: Orbis Books.

Fritsch, Albert J., S.J., and Warren E. Brunner. 1986. *Appalachia: A Meditation.* Chicago: Loyola University Press.

Fritsch, Albert J., S.J., and the Science Action Coalition. 1980. *Environmental Ethics: Choices for Concerned Citizens.* Garden City, N.Y.: Doubleday.

Glacken, C. J. 1967. *Traces on the Rhodian Shore: Nature and Culture in Western Thought from Ancient Times to the End of the Eighteenth Century.* Berkeley: University of California Press.

Granberg-Michaelson, Wesley. 1989. "Preserving the Earth." *One World* (November): 11–15.

———. 1991. "An Ethics for Sustainability." *Ecumenical Review* 43 (January): 120–30.

———. 1994. "Creation in Ecumenical Theology." In *Ecotheology: Voices from South and North,* ed. David G. Hallman, 96–106. Maryknoll, N.Y.: Orbis Books.

Hall, Douglas John. 1986. *Imaging God: Dominion as Stewardship.* Grand Rapids, Mich.: Eerdmans.

———. 1989. *Thinking the Faith: Christian Theology in a North American Context.* Minneapolis: Fortress.

———. 1990. *The Steward: A Biblical Symbol Come of Age.* Grand Rapids, Mich.: Eerdmans.

———. 1993. *Professing the Faith: Christian Theology in a North American Context.* Minneapolis: Fortress.

Hargrove, Eugene C., ed. 1986. *Religion and the Environmental Crisis.* Athens: University of Georgia Press.

Haught, John F. 1993. *The Promise of Nature.* Mahwah, N.J.: Paulist.

———. 1994. "Religion and the Origins of the Environmental Crisis." In *An Ecology of Spirit: Religious Reflection and Environmental Consciousness,* ed. Michael Barnes, 27–41. Annual Publication of the College Theology Society, vol. 36. Lanham, Md.: University Press of America.

Heggen, Bruce. 1995. "A Theology for Earth: Nature and Grace in the Thought of Joseph Sittler." Ph.D. diss. Montreal: McGill University.

Hessel, Dieter T. 1995. Preface to *Ecology, Justice, and Christian Faith: A Critical Guide to the Literature,* ed. Peter W. Bakken, Joan Gibb Engel, and J. Ronald Engel. Westport, Conn.: Greenwood Press.

———., ed. 1992. *After Nature's Revolt: Eco-Justice and Theology.* Minneapolis: Fortress.

Himes, Michael J., and Kenneth R. Himes. 1990. "The Sacrament of Creation: Toward an Environmental Theology." *Commonweal* 117 (26 January): 42–49.

Hobsbawm, Eric, and Terrence Ranger, eds. 1983. *The Invention of Tradition*. Cambridge: Cambridge University Press.

Irwin, Kevin W., and Edmund D. Pellegrino, eds. 1994. *Preserving the Creation: Environmental Theology and Ethics*. Washington, D.C.: Georgetown University Press.

Johnson, Elizabeth A. 1993a. *She Who Is: The Mystery of God in Feminist Theological Discourse*. New York: Crossroad.

———. 1993b. *Women, Earth, and Creator Spirit*. Mahwah, N.J.: Paulist.

———. 1994. "Powerful Icons and Missing Pieces: Response to Gabriel Daly." In *Preserving the Creation: Environmental Theology and Ethics,* ed. Kevin W. Irwin and Edmund D. Pellegrino, 60–66. Washington, D.C.: Georgetown University Press.

Leopold, Aldo. 1949. *A Sand County Almanac and Sketches Here and There*. New York: Oxford University Press.

McDonagh, Sean. 1986. *To Care for the Earth: A Call to a New Theology*. London: Geoffrey Chapman.

———. 1994. *Passion for the Earth: The Christian Vocation to Promote Justice, Peace, and the Integrity of Creation*. Maryknoll, N.Y.: Orbis Books.

McIntosh, Robert P. 1985. *The Background of Ecology: Concept and Theory*. Cambridge: Cambridge University Press.

McMullin, Ernan. 1981. "How Should Cosmology Relate to Theology?" In *The Sciences and Theology in the Twentieth Century,* ed. A. R. Peacocke. Stocksfield, England: Oriel.

Milbank, John. "Out of the Greenhouse." Unpublished.

Mitcham, Carl, and Jim Grote, eds. 1984. *Theology and Technology: Essays in Christian Analysis and Exegesis*. Lanham, Md.: University Press of America.

Moltmann, Jürgen. 1985. *God in Creation: A New Theology of Creation and the Spirit of God*. San Francisco: Harper and Row.

———. 1991. *History and the Triune God: Contributions to Trinitarian Theology*. London: SCM.

Moncrief, Lewis W. 1970. "The Cultural Basis for Our Environmental Crisis." *Science* 170:508–12.

Nash, James A. 1991. *Loving Nature: Ecological Integrity and Christian Responsibility*. Nashville: Abingdon.

Nash, Roderick Frazier. 1989. *The Rights of Nature: A History of Environmental Ethics*. Madison: University of Wisconsin Press.

Neuhaus, Richard John. 1971. *In Defense of People: Ecology and the Seduction of Radicalism.* New York: Macmillan.

Oelschlaeger, Max. 1994. *Caring for Creation: An Ecumenical Approach to the Environmental Crisis.* New Haven: Yale University Press.

Passmore, John. 1974. *Man's Responsibility for Nature.* New York: Scribner.

Santmire, H. Paul. 1970. *Brother Earth: Nature, God, and Ecology in Time of Crisis.* New York: Thomas Nelson.

———. 1975. "Reflections on the Alleged Ecological Bankruptcy of Western Theology." *Anglican Theological Review* 57 (April): 131–52.

———. 1985. *The Travail of Nature: The Ambiguous Ecological Promise of Christian Theology.* Philadelphia: Fortress.

———. 1992. "Healing the Protestant Mind: Beyond the Theology of Human Dominion." In *After Nature's Revolt: Eco-Justice and Theology,* ed. Dieter T. Hessel, 57–78. Minneapolis: Fortress.

———. 1994. "Is Christianity Ecologically Bankrupt? The View from Asylum Hill." In *An Ecology of Spirit: Religious Reflection and Environmental Consciousness,* ed. Michael Barnes, 11–26. Annual Publication of the College Theology Society, vol. 36. Lanham, Md.: University Press of America.

Scharper, Stephen B., and Hilary Cunningham. 1993. *The Green Bible.* Maryknoll, N.Y.: Orbis Books.

Sittler, Joseph. 1962. "Called to Unity." *Ecumenical Review* 14 (January): 177–87.

Spring, David, and Eileen Spring, eds. 1974. *Ecology and Religion in History.* New York: Harper and Row.

White, Lynn, Jr. 1967. "The Historical Roots of Our Ecologic Crisis." *Science* 155 (1967): 1203–07.

———. 1971. *Dynamo and Virgin Reconsidered: Essays in the Dynamism of Western Culture.* Cambridge, Mass.: MIT Press.

———. 1973. "Continuing the Conversation." In *Western Man and Environmental Ethics: Attitudes toward Nature and Technology,* ed. Ian G. Barbour, 55–64. Reading, Mass.: Addison-Wesley.

———. 1978. *Medieval Religion and Technology: Collected Essays.* Berkeley: University of California Press.

Whitney, Elspeth. 1990. *Paradise Restored: The Mechanical Arts from Antiquity through the Thirteenth Century.* Philadelphia: American Philosophical Society.

———. 1993. "Lynn White, Ecotheology, and History." *Environmental Ethics* 15 (Summer): 151–69.

Chapter Two: The Gaia Hypothesis

Barlow, Connie. 1991. *From Gaia to Selfish Genes: Selected Writings in the Life Sciences.* Cambridge, Mass.: MIT Press.

Barnaby, Frank, ed. 1988. *The Gaia Peace Atlas: Survival into the Third Millennium.* New York: Doubleday.

Berry, Thomas. 1994. "The Gaia Theory: Its Religious Implications." *ARC: The Journal of the Faculty of Religious Studies* (McGill University) 22:7–19.

Berry, Thomas, and Brian Swimme. 1992. *The Universe Story: From the Primordial Flaring Forth to the Ecozoic Era; A Celebration of the Unfolding of the Cosmos.* San Francisco: HarperCollins.

Bunyard, Peter, and Edward Goldsmith, eds. 1989. *Gaia and Evolution: Proceedings of the Second Annual Camelford Conference on the Implications of the Gaia Thesis.* Cornwall, England: Wadebridge Ecological Centre.

Dawkins, Richard. 1982. *The Extended Phenotype: The Gene as the Unit of Selection.* San Francisco: Freeman.

Doolittle, W. Ford. 1981. "Is Nature Really Motherly?" *CoEvolution Quarterly* 29:58–63.

Hall, Douglas John. 1987. "The Integrity of Creation: Biblical and Theological Background of the Term." In *Reintegrating God's Creation: A Paper for Discussion.* Church and Society Documents, no. 3 (September 1987), 25–36. Geneva: World Council of Churches, Programme Unit on Faith and Witness, Subunit on Church and Society.

Joseph, Lawrence E. 1990. *Gaia: The Growth of an Idea.* New York: St. Martin's Press.

Lovelock, James E. 1979. *Gaia: A New Look at Life on Earth.* New York: Oxford University Press.

———. 1983. "Daisy World: A Cybernetic Proof of the Gaia Hypothesis." *CoEvolution Quarterly* 31:66–72.

———. 1987. "The Reintegration of Creation." In *Reintegrating God's Creation: A Paper for Discussion.* Church and Society Documents, no. 3 (September 1987). Geneva: World Council of Churches, Programme Unit on Faith and Witness, Subunit on Church and Society.

———. 1990. *The Ages of Gaia: A Biography of Our Living Earth.* New York: Bantam Books. Originally published by W. W. Norton, 1988.

———. 1991. "Gaia: A Way of Knowing." In *The Age of Ecology: The Environment on CBC Radio's Ideas,* ed. David Cayley, 163–68. Toronto: James Lorimer.

Lovelock, James E., and Michael Allaby. 1984. *The Greening of Mars.* New York: Warner Books.

Margulis, Lynn, and Dorion Sagan. 1984. "Gaia and Philosophy." In *On Nature,* ed. Leroy S. Rouner, 60–78. South Bend, Ind.: University of Notre Dame Press.

———. 1986. *Microcosmos: Four Billion Years of Evolution from Our Microbial Ancestors.* New York: Summit Books.

Miller, Alan S. 1991. *Gaia Connections: An Introduction to Ecology, Ecoethics and Economics.* Lanham, Md.: Rowman and Littlefield.

Pedler, Kit. 1991. *The Quest for Gaia.* London: Paladin.

Rouner, Leroy S. *On Nature.* South Bend, Ind.: University of Notre Dame Press.

Ruether, Rosemary Radford. 1992. *Gaia and God: Toward an Eco-feminist Theology of Earth Healing.* San Francisco: HarperCollins.

Sagan, Dorion, and Lynn Margulis. 1983. "What Gaia Means to the Ecologist." *The Ecologist: Journal of the Post-industrial Age 15.*

———. 1994. "Gaia and Philosophy." In *On Nature,* ed. Leroy S. Rouner, 60–78. South Bend, Ind.: University of Notre Dame Press.

Sahtouris, Elisabet. 1989a. *Gaia: The Human Journey from Chaos to Cosmos.* New York: Pocket Books.

———. 1989b. "The Gaia Controversy: A Case for the Earth as a Living Planet." In *Gaia and Evolution: Proceedings of the Second Annual Camelford Conference on the Implications of the Gaia Thesis,* ed. Peter Bunyard and Edward Goldsmith, 55–65. Cornwall, England: Wadebridge Ecological Centre.

Saunders, Peter. 1989. "The Evolution of a Complex Dynamical System." In *Gaia and Evolution: Proceedings of the Second Annual Camelford Conference on the Implications of the Gaia Thesis,* ed. Peter Bunyard and Edward Goldsmith, 83–89. Cornwall, England: Wadebridge Ecological Centre.

Scheler, Max. 1961. *Man's Place in Nature.* Trans. Hans Meyerhoff. Boston: Beacon Press. Originally published 1928.

Schneider, Stephen H., and Penelope Boston. 1991. *Scientists on Gaia.* Cambridge, Mass.: MIT Press.

Swimme, Brian, and Matthew Fox. 1982. *Manifesto for a Global Civilization.* Sante Fe: Bear and Co.

Thompson, William Irwin. 1987. *Gaia: A Way of Knowing: Political Implications of the New Biology.* Great Barrington, Mass.: Inner Traditions/Lindisfarne Press.

———. 1991. "Gaia: A Way of Knowing." In *The Age of Ecology: The Environment on CBC Radio's Ideas,* ed. David Cayley, 168–82. Toronto: James Lorimer.

Turner, Frederick. 1991. *Rebirth of Value: Meditations on Beauty, Ecology, Religion, and Education.* Albany: State University of New York Press.

Weston, Anthony. 1987. "Forms of Gaian Ethics." *Environmental Ethics* 9 (fall): 217–30.

Chapter Three: Process Theology

Angeles, Peter A. 1981. *Dictionary of Philosophy.* New York: Harper and Row.

Bracken, Joseph A. 1987. "The Triune Symbol: Persons, Process, and Community." *Gregorianum* 68, nos. 1–2:413:14.

Brock, Rita Nakashima. 1988. *Journeys by Heart: A Christology of Erotic Power.* New York: Crossroad.

Brown, Delwin. 1981. *To Set at Liberty: Christian Faith and Human Freedom.* Maryknoll, N.Y.: Orbis Books.

Brown, Delwin, Ralph E. James Jr., and Gene Reeves, eds. 1971. *Process Philosophy and Christian Thought.* Indianapolis: Bobbs-Merrill.

Burrell, David B. 1982. "Does Process Theology Rest on a Mistake?" *Theological Studies* 43, no. 1 (March): 125–35.

Chodorow, Nancy. 1978. *The Reproduction of Mothering: Psychoanalysis and the Sociology of Gender.* Berkeley: University of California Press.

Clarke, Norris. 1979. *The Philosophical Approach to God.* Winston-Salem, N.C.: Wake Forest University Press.

Cobb, John B., Jr. 1972. *Is It Too Late? A Theology of Ecology.* Beverly Hills, Calif.: Bruce.

———. 1975. *Christ in a Pluralistic Age.* Philadelphia: Westminster.

———. 1980. "Process Theology and Environmental Issues." *Journal of Religion* 60, no. 4 (October): 441–58.

———. 1982a. *Beyond Dialogue: Toward a Mutual Transformation of Christianity and Buddhism.* Philadelphia: Fortress.

———. 1982b. *Process Theology as Political Theology.* Philadelphia: Westminster.

———. 1985. "Points of Contact between Process Theology and Liberation Theology in Matters of Faith and Justice." *Process Studies* 14, no. 2 (Summer): 124–41.

———. 1988a. "Ecology, Science, and Religion: Toward a Postmodern Worldview." In *The Reenchantment of Science: Postmodern Proposals,* ed. David Ray Griffin, 99–113. Albany: State University of New York Press.

————. 1988b. "Minjung Theology and Process Theology." In *An Emerging Theology in World Perspective: Commentary on Korean Minjung Theology,* ed. Jung Young Lee, 51–56. Mystic, Conn.: Twenty-Third Publications.

————. 1990. "Afterword: The Role of Theology of Nature in the Church." In *Liberating Life: Contemporary Approaches to Ecological Theology,* ed. Charles Birch, William Eakin, and Jay B. McDaniel, 261–72. Maryknoll, N.Y.: Orbis Books.

————. 1992. *Sustainability.* Maryknoll, N.Y.: Orbis Books.

————. 1993a. "Intellectual Autobiography." *Religious Studies Review* 19, no. 1 (January): 9–11.

————. 1993b. "Process Theism." In *Process Theology: A Basic Introduction,* ed. Robert C. Mesle, 134–47. St. Louis: Chalice Press.

————. 1994. "Ecology and Process Theology." In *Ecology: Key Concepts in Critical Theory,* ed. Carolyn Merchant, 322–26. Atlantic Highlands, N.J.: Humanities Press.

Cobb, John B., Jr., and Charles Birch. 1981. *The Liberation of Life: From the Cell to the Community.* Cambridge: Cambridge University Press.

Cobb, John B., Jr., and David Ray Griffin. 1976. *Process Theology: An Introductory Exposition.* Philadelphia: Westminster.

Cousins, Ewert, ed. 1971. *Process Theology: Basic Writings by the Key Thinkers of a Major Modern Movement.* New York: Newman Press.

Daly, Herman, and John B. Cobb Jr. 1989. *For the Common Good: Redirecting the Economy toward Community, the Environment, and a Sustainable Future.* Boston: Beacon.

Davaney, Sheila Greeve, ed. 1981. *Feminism and Process Thought: The Harvard Divinity School/Claremont Center for Process Studies Symposium Papers.* Lewiston, N.Y.: Edwin Mellen.

Ford, Lewis. 1974. "Process Philosophy." In *The New Catholic Encyclopedia.* Vol. 16. New York: Publishers Guild and McGraw Hill.

Fritsch, Albert. 1991. Review of *Earth, Sky, Gods and Mortals,* by Jay B. McDaniel. In *Spirituality Today* (Spring): 87–88.

Gilligan, Carol. 1982. *In a Different Voice: Psychological Theory and Women's Development.* Cambridge, Mass.: Harvard University Press.

Griffin, David Ray. 1984. "John B. Cobb, Jr." *A Handbook of Christian Theologians,* ed. Martin E. Marty and Dean G. Peerman, 691–709. Nashville: Abingdon.

————. 1989. *God and Religion in the Postmodern World.* Albany: State University of New York Press.

———. 1992. "Process Theology." In *A New Handbook of Christian Theology*, ed. D. W. Musser and J. L. Price, 383–88. Nashville: Abingdon.

———. 1994. "Whitehead's Deeply Ecological Worldview." *Worldviews and Ecology: Religion, Philosophy, and the Environment*, ed. Mary Evelyn Tucker and John A. Grim, 190–206. Maryknoll, N.Y.: Orbis Books.

———, ed. 1988. *The Reenchantment of Science*. Albany: State University of New York Press.

———, ed. 1989. *Varieties of Postmodern Theology*. Albany: State University of New York Press.

———, ed. 1990. *Sacred Interconnections: Postmodern Art, Spirituality, and Political Economy*. Albany: State University of New York Press.

Hartshorne, Charles. 1968. *Beyond Humanism*. Lincoln: University of Nebraska Press.

Hill, William. 1976. "Two Gods of Love: Aquinas and Whitehead." *Listening* 4 (1976): 249–64.

Keller, Catherine. 1986. *From a Broken Web: Separation, Sexism, and Self*. Boston: Beacon.

———. 1994. "Chosen Persons and the Green Ecumenacy: A Possible Christian Response to the Population Apocalypse." In *Ecotheology: Voices from South and North*, ed. David G. Hallman, 300–311. Maryknoll, N.Y.: Orbis Books.

———. 1995a. "Catherine Keller" (interview). In *Listening to the Land: Conversations about Nature, Culture, and Eros*, ed. Derrick Jensen, 273–81. San Francisco: Sierra Club Books.

———. 1995b. "Talk about the Weather: The Greening of Eschatology." In *Ecofeminism and the Sacred*, ed. Carol J. Adams, 30–49. New York: Continuum.

———. 1996. *Apocalypse Now and Then: A Feminist Guide to the End of the World*. Boston: Beacon Press.

McDaniel, Jay B. 1988. "Land Ethics, Animal Rights, and Process Theology." *Process Studies* 17, no. 2 (summer): 88–102.

———. 1989. *Of God and Pelicans: A Theology of Reverence for Life*. Philadelphia: Westminster.

———. 1990a. *Earth, Sky, Gods, Mortals: Developing an Ecological Spirituality*. Mystic, Conn.: Twenty-Third Publications.

———. 1990b. "Revisioning God and the Self: Lessons from Buddhism." In *Liberating Life: Contemporary Approaches to Ecological Theology*, ed. Charles Birch, William Eakin, and Jay B. McDaniel, 228–58. Maryknoll, N.Y.: Orbis Books.

———. 1994a. "Chosen Persons and the Green Ecumenacy: A Possible Christian Response to the Population Apocalypse." In *Ecotheology:*

Voices from South and North, ed. David G. Hallman, 300–311. Maryknoll, N.Y.: Orbis Books.

———. 1994b. "Four Questions in Response to Rosemary Radford Ruether." In *An Ecology of the Spirit: Religious Reflection and Environmental Consciousness,* ed. Michael Barnes, 57–60. Lanham, Md.: University Press of America and the College Theology Society.

———. 1994c. "The Garden of Eden, the Fall, and Life in Christ." In *Worldviews and Ecology: Religion, Philosophy, and the Environment,* ed. Mary Evelyn Tucker and John A. Grim, 71–82. Maryknoll, N.Y.: Orbis Books.

———. 1994d. "A God Who Loves Animals and a Church That Does the Same." In *Good News for Animals? Christian Approaches to Animal Well-Being,* ed. Charles Pinches and Jay B. McDaniel, 75–102. Maryknoll, N.Y.: Orbis Books.

———. 1995a. "Catherine Keller" (interview). In *Listening to the Land: Conversations about Nature, Culture, and Eros,* ed. Derrick Jensen, 273–81. San Francisco: Sierra Club Books.

———. 1995b. "Talk about the Weather: The Greening of Eschatology." In *Ecofeminism and the Sacred,* ed. Carol J. Adams, 30–49. New York: Continuum.

———. 1995c. *With Roots and Wings: Christianity in an Age of Ecology and Dialogue.* Maryknoll, N.Y.: Orbis Books.

McKibben, Bill. 1989. *The End of Nature.* New York: Random House.

Mellert, Robert B. 1975. *What Is Process Theology?* New York: Paulist.

Mesle, C. Robert. 1993. *Process Theology: A Basic Introduction.* St. Louis: Chalice Press.

Murray, Leslie A. 1988. *An Introduction to the Process Understanding of Science, Society, and the Self: A Philosophy for Modern Humanity.* Lewiston, N.Y.: Edwin Mellen.

Pailin, David A. 1983. "Process Theology." In *The Westminster Dictionary of Christian Theology,* ed. A. Richardson and J. Bowden, 467–70. Philadelphia: Westminster.

Pixley, George V. 1974. "Justice and Class Struggle: A Challenge for Process Theology." *Process Studies* 4, no. 3 (fall): 159–75.

Pregeant, Russell. 1988. *Mystery without Magic.* Oak Park, Ill.: Meyer-Stone Books.

Shepard, Paul. 1982. *Nature and Madness.* San Francisco: Sierra Club Books.

Smith, Archie, Jr. 1987. "Black Liberation and Process Theologies." *Process Studies* 16, no. 3 (fall): 174–90.

Suchocki, Marjorie Hewitt. 1982. *God-Christ-Church: A Practical Guide to Process Theology.* New York: Crossroad.

Trethowan, Illtyd. 1985. *Process Theology and the Christian Tradition: An Essay in Post-Vatican II Thinking*. Still River, Mass.: St. Bede's Publications.

Whitehead, Alfred North. 1929. *Process and Reality: An Essay in Cosmology*. New York: Macmillan.

Whitney, Barry. 1980. "Divine Immutability in Process Philosophy and Contemporary Thomism." *Horizons* 7:49–68.

Chapter Four: The New Cosmology

Baum, Gregory. 1987. "The Grand Vision: It Needs Social Action." In *Thomas Berry and the New Cosmology*, ed. Anne Lonergan and Caroline Richards. Mystic, Conn.: Twenty-Third Publications.

Berry, Thomas. 1949. *The Historical Theory of Giambattista Vico*. Washington, D.C.: Catholic University of America Press.

———. 1978. *The New Story*. Chambersburg, Pa.: Anima Books.

———. 1980. *Management: The Managerial Ethos and the Future of Planet Earth*. Chambersburg, Pa.: Anima Books.

———. 1982. *Teilhard in the Ecological Age*. Chambersburg, Pa.: Anima Books.

———. 1986. *Technology and the Healing of the Earth*. Chambersburg, Pa.: Anima Books.

———. 1987. "Twelve Principles for Understanding the Universe and the Role of the Human in the Universe Process." In *Thomas Berry and the New Cosmology*, ed. Anne Lonergan and Caroline Richards. Mystic, Conn.: Twenty-Third Publications.

———. 1988. *The Dream of the Earth*. San Francisco: Sierra Club Books.

———. 1990a. *Befriending the Earth: A Theology of Reconciliation between Humans and the Earth* (audiovisual). Mystic, Conn.: Twenty-Third Publications.

———. 1990b. Foreword to *Earth, Sky, Gods, and Mortals: Developing an Ecological Spirituality*, by Jay B. McDaniel, v–viii. Mystic, Conn.: Twenty-Third Publications.

———. 1991. *Befriending the Earth: A Theology of Reconciliation between Humans and the Earth*. Mystic, Conn.: Twenty-Third Publications.

———. 1992. *Religions of India: Hinduism, Yoga, Buddhism*. Chambersburg, Pa.: Anima Books.

———. 1993. "Ecological Geography." In *Worldviews and Ecology*, ed. Mary Evelyn Tucker and John A. Grim. Lewisburg, Pa.: Bucknell University Press.

————. 1994. "Ecology and the Future of Catholicism: A Statement of the Problem." In *Embracing Earth: Catholic Approaches to Ecology,* ed. Albert J. Lachance and John E. Carroll, xi–xii. Maryknoll, N.Y.: Orbis Books.

————. 1995a. "The University." Unpublished.

————. 1995b. "Thomas Berry." In *Listening to the Land: Conversations about Nature, Culture, and Eros,* ed. Derrick Jansen, 35–43. San Francisco: Sierra Club Books.

Berry, Thomas, and Brian Swimme. 1992. *The Universe Story: From the Primordial Flaring Forth to the Ecozoic Era; a Celebration of the Unfolding of the Cosmos.* San Francisco: HarperCollins.

French, William C. 1990. "Subject-Centered and Creation-Centered Paradigms in Recent Catholic Thought." *Journal of Religion* 70 (January): 48–72.

Grassie, William John. 1994. "Reinventing Nature: Science Narratives as Myths for an Endangered Planet." Ph.D. diss. Philadelphia: Temple University.

Grimm, John. 1987. "Time, History, Vision." *Cross Currents* 37, nos. 2–3: 225–39.

Hardy, Sarah. 1981. *The Woman That Never Evolved.* Cambridge, Mass.: Harvard University Press.

Hessel, Dieter T., ed. 1996. *Theology for Earth Community: A Field Guide.* Maryknoll, N.Y.: Orbis Books.

Hope, Marjorie, and James Young. 1994. "Islam and Ecology." *Cross Currents* 44, no. 2 (summer): 180–92.

Keller, Evelyn Fox. 1990. *Body/Politics: Women and the Discourses of Science.* New York: Routledge.

Korten, David C. 1995. *When Corporations Rule the World.* West Hartford, Conn.: Kumarian Press.

Lonergan, Anne, and Caroline Richards, eds.. 1987. *Thomas Berry and the New Cosmology.* Mystic, Conn.: Twenty-Third Publications.

McFague, Sallie. 1992. "A Square in the Quilt: One Theologians' Contribution to the Planetary Agenda." In *Spirit and Nature: Why the Environment Is a Religious Issue,* ed. Steven C. Rockefeller and John C. Elder, 39–58. Boston: Beacon.

Muratore, Stephen. 1988. "The 'New' Teilhard at the NACCE: Thomas Berry, the 'New Story,' and the Battle for the Christian Mind." *Epiphany* 8 (winter): 6–14.

Ortolani, Valerio. 1984. *Personalidad Ecologica.* Puebla, Mexico: Universidad Iberoamericana.

Schiebinger, Londa. 1993. *Nature's Body: Gender in the Making of Modern Science.* Boston: Beacon.

Swimme, Brian. 1984. *The Universe Is a Green Dragon: A Cosmic Creation Story.* Santa Fe: Bear and Company.

———. 1987a. "Berry's Cosmology." *Cross Currents* 37, nos. 2–3: 218–24.

———. 1987b. "Science: A Partner in Creating the Vision." In *Thomas Berry and the New Cosmology,* ed. Anne Lonergan and Caroline Richards. Mystic, Conn.: Twenty-Third Publications.

———. 1993. "Cosmogenesis." In *Worldviews and Ecology,* ed. Mary Evelyn Tucker and John A. Grim. Lewisburg, Pa.: Bucknell University Press.

———. 1996. *The Hidden Heart of the Cosmos: Humanity and the New Story.* Maryknoll, N.Y.: Orbis Books.

Swimme, Brian, and Matthew Fox. 1982. *Manifesto for a Global Civilization.* Sante Fe: Bear and Company.

Tucker, Mary Evelyn, and John A. Grim, eds. 1993. *Worldviews and Ecology.* Lewisburg, Pa.: Bucknell University Press.

Tucker, Mary Evelyn. 1988. "Thomas Berry: A Brief Biography." *Religion and Intellectual Life* 5 (summer): 107–14.

———. 1993. "Thomas Berry and the New Story." *Journal of Theology* (United Theological Seminary) 98:74–95.

Chapter Five: Ecofeminism

Adams, Carol J., ed. 1995. *Ecofeminism and the Sacred.* New York: Continuum.

Berry, Thomas. 1991. *Befriending the Earth: A Theology of Reconciliation between Humans and the Earth.* Mystic, Conn.: Twenty-Third Publications.

Betcher, Sharon V. 1994. "Watery Depths: Ecofeminism and 'Redemptive' Wetlands." *ARC: The Journal of the Faculty of Religious Studies* (McGill University) 22:51–59.

Biehl, Janet. 1990. *Rethinking Ecofeminist Politics.* Boston: South End.

Boff, Leonardo. 1995. *Ecology and Liberation: A New Paradigm.* Trans. John Cumming. Maryknoll, N.Y.: Orbis Books.

Bouma-Prediger, Steven. 1995. *The Greening of Theology: The Ecological Models of Rosemary Radford Ruether, Joseph Sittler, and Jürgen Moltmann.* Atlanta: Scholars Press.

Chopp, Rebecca. 1989. "Seeing and Naming the World Anew: The Works of Rosemary Radford Ruether." *Religious Studies Review* 15 (January): 8–11.

Daly, Lois K. 1990. "Ecofeminism, Reverence for Life, and Feminist Theological Ethics." In *Liberating Life: Contemporary Approaches* to *Ecological Theology,* ed. Charles Birch, William Eakin, and Jay B. McDaniel, 88–108. Maryknoll, N.Y.: Orbis Books.

Diamond, Irene, and Gloria Orenstein, eds. 1990. *Reweaving the World: The Emergence of Ecofeminism.* San Francisco: Sierra Club Books.

Frome, Michael. 1974. *Battle for the Wilderness.* New York: Praeger.

Griffin, Susan. 1978. *Woman and Nature: The Roaring inside Her.* New York: Harper and Row.

Hartshorne, Charles. 1941. "The Theological Analogies and the Cosmic Organism." In *Man's Vision of God and the Logic of Theism,* 171–211. New York: Willett, Clark, and Co.

Hennelly, Alfred T. 1995. *Liberation Theologies: The Global Pursuit of Justice.* Mystic, Conn.: Twenty-Third Publications.

Hessel, Dieter T., ed. 1996. *Theology for Earth Community: A Field Guide.* Maryknoll, N.Y.: Orbis Books.

Hinsdale, Mary Ann. 1991. "Ecology, Feminism, and Theology." *Word and World* 11 (spring): 156–64.

Kinsley, David. 1995. *Ecology and Religion: Ecological Spirituality in Cross-Cultural Perspective.* Englewood Cliffs, N.J.: Prentice-Hall.

Kloppenburg, J. R. 1988. *First the Seed: The Political Economy of Plant Biotechnology.* Cambridge: Cambridge University Press.

MacKinnon, Mary Heather, and Moni McIntyre, eds. 1995. *Readings in Ecology and Feminist Theology.* Kansas City: Sheed and Ward.

McCoy, Marjorie Casebier. 1984. "Feminist Consciousness in Creation: 'Tell Them the World Was Made for Woman, Too.'" In *Cry of the Environment: Rebuilding the Christian Creation Tradition,* ed. Philip N. Joranson and Ken Butigan, 132–47. Santa Fe: Bear and Co.

McFague, Sallie. 1982. *Metaphorical Language: Models of God in Religious Language.* Philadelphia: Fortress.

———. 1987. *Models of God: Theology for an Ecological, Nuclear Age.* Philadelphia: Fortress.

———. 1990. "Imaging a Theology of Nature: The World as God's Body." In *Liberating Life: Contemporary Approaches to Ecological Theology,* ed. Charles Birch, William Eakin, and Jay B. McDaniel, 201–27. Maryknoll, N.Y.: Orbis Books.

———. 1992. "A Square in the Quilt: One Theologian's Contribution to the Planetary Agenda." In *Spirit and Nature: Why the Environment Is a Religious Issue,* ed. Steven C. Rockefeller and John C. Elder, 39–58. Boston: Beacon.

———. 1993. *The Body of God: An Ecological Theology.* Minneapolis: Fortress.

———. 1995. "An Earthly Theological Agenda." In *Ecofeminism and the Sacred,* ed. Carol J. Adams, 84–98. New York: Continuum.

McKibben, Bill. 1989. *The End of Nature.* New York: Random House.

Merchant, Carolyn. 1980. *Death of Nature: Women, Ecology, and the Revolution.* San Francisco: Harper and Row.

———. 1989. *Ecological Revolutions: Nature, Gender, and Science in New England.* Chapel Hill: University of North Carolina Press.

———. 1992. *Radical Ecology: The Search for a Livable World.* New York: Routledge.

———, ed. 1994. *Ecology: Key Concepts in Critical Theory.* Atlantic Highlands, N.J.: Humanities Press International.

Mihevc, John. 1995. *The Market Tells Them So: The World Bank and Economic Fundamentalism in Africa.* Penang, Malaysia: Third World Network.

Miller, Patrick D. 1996. "Editorial." *Theology Today* 53, no. 1 (April): 1–4.

Norwood, Vera. 1993. *Made from This Earth: American Women and Nature.* Chapel Hill: University of North Carolina Press.

Philipose, Pamela. 1989. "Women Act: Women and Environmental Protection in India." In *Healing the Wounds: The Promise of Ecofeminism,* ed. Judith Plant, 67–75. Philadelphia: New Society.

Plant, Judith, ed. 1989. *Healing the Wounds: The Promise of Ecofeminism.* Philadelphia: New Society.

Rabuzzi, Kathryn Allen. 1989. "The Socialist Feminist Vision of Rosemary Radford Ruether: A Challenge to Liberal Feminism." *Religious Studies Review* 15 (January): 4–8.

Ramsey, William. 1986. *Four Modern Prophets: Walter Rauschenbusch, Martin Luther King, Jr., Gustavo Gutiérrez, and Rosemary Radford Ruether.* Atlanta: John Knox.

Ruether, Rosemary Radford. 1971. "Mother Earth and the Megamachine." *Christianity and Crisis* (December 13): 267–72. Reprinted in Carol P. Christ and Judith Plaskow, eds., *Womanspirit Rising: A Feminist Reader in Religion.* San Francisco: Harper and Row, 1979.

———. 1972. *Liberation Theology.* New York: Paulist Press.

———. 1974. "Rich Nations/Poor Nations and the Exploitation of the Earth." *Dialog* 13 (summer): 201–7.

———. 1975a. *New Woman/New Earth: Sexist Ideologies and Human Liberation.* New York: Seabury.

———. 1975b. "Women, Ecology, and the Domination of Nature." *The Ecumenist* 14 (November–December): 1–5.

———. 1978. "The Biblical Vision of the Ecological Crisis." *Christian Century* (November 22): 1129–32.

———. 1981. "Ecology and Human Liberation: A Conflict between the Theology of History and the Theology of Nature." In *To Change the World.* New York: Crossroad.

———. 1983. *Sexism and God-Talk: Toward a Feminist Theology.* Boston: Beacon.

———. 1985. "A Feminist Perspective." In *Doing Theology in a Divided World,* ed. Virginia Fabella and Sergio Torres, 65–71. Maryknoll, N.Y.: Orbis Books.

———. 1989a. *Disputed Questions: On Being a Christian.* Maryknoll, N.Y.: Orbis Books.

———. 1989b. "Rosemary Radford Ruether: Retrospective." *Religious Studies Review* 15 (January): 1–4.

———. 1989c. "Toward an Ecological-Feminist View of Nature." In *Healing the Wounds: The Promise of Ecofeminism,* ed. Judith Plant, 145–50. Philadelphia: New Society.

———. 1990. "Eschatology and Feminism." In *Lift Every Voice,* ed. Susan Thistlewaite and Mary Potter Engel. San Francisco: Harper-SanFrancisco.

———. 1992. *Gaia and God: Toward an Ecofeminist Theology of Earth Healing.* San Francisco: HarperCollins.

———. 1994a. "Ecofeminism: Symbolic and Social Connections of the Oppression of Women and the Domination of Nature." In *An Ecology of the Spirit: Religious Reflection and Environmental Consciousness,* ed. Michael Barnes, 45–56. Lanham, Md.: University Press of America.

———. 1994b. "Ecofeminism and Theology." In *Ecotheology: Voices from South and North,* ed. David G. Hallman, 199–204. Maryknoll, N.Y.: Orbis Books.

———, ed. 1996. *Women Healing Earth: Third World Women on Ecology, Feminism, and Religion.* Maryknoll, N.Y.: Orbis Books.

Scharper, Stephen B., and Hilary Cunningham. 1993. *The Green Bible.* Maryknoll, N.Y.: Orbis Books.

Shiva, Vandana. 1989. *Staying Alive: Women, Ecology, and Development.* London: Zed Books.

———. 1991a. *Ecology and the Politics of Survival: Conflicts over Natural Resources in India.* Tokyo: United Nations University Press.

———. 1991b. *The Violence of the Green Revolution: Third World Agriculture, Ecology, and Politics.* London: Zed Books.

———. 1993. *Monocultures of the Mind: Perspectives on Biodiversity and Biotechnology.* London: Zed Books.

———. 1996. "Let Us Survive: Women, Ecology, and Development." In *Women Healing Earth: Third World Women on Ecology, Feminism, and Religion,* ed. Rosemary Radford Ruether, 65–73. Maryknoll, N.Y.: Orbis Books.

Shiva, Vandana, and Maria Miles. 1993. *Ecofeminism.* London: Zed Books.

Snyder, Mary Hembrow. 1988. *The Christology of Rosemary Radford Ruether: A Critical Introduction.* Mystic, Conn.: Twenty-Third Publications.

Spretnak, Charlene. 1993. "Critical and Constructive Contributions of Ecofeminism." In *Worldviews and Ecology: Religion, Philosophy, and the Environment,* ed. Mary Evelyn Tucker and John A. Grim. Maryknoll, N.Y.: Orbis Books.

Warren, Karen. 1990. "The Power and Promise of Ecological Feminism." *Environmental Ethics* 12, no. 3 (summer): 125–46.

Chapter Six: Liberation Theology

Anderson, Terry L., and Donald R. Leal. 1991. *Free Market Environmentalism.* Boulder, Colo.: Westview Press.

Birch, Charles, William Eakin, and Jay B. McDaniel, eds. 1990. *Liberating Life: Contemporary Approaches to Ecological Theology.* Maryknoll, N.Y.: Orbis Books.

Boff, Leonardo. 1994. "Social Ecology: Poverty and Misery." In *Ecotheology: Voices from South and North,* ed. David G. Hallman, 235–47. Maryknoll, N.Y.: Orbis Books.

———. 1995a. *Ecology and Liberation: A New Paradigm.* Trans. John Cumming. Maryknoll, N.Y.: Orbis Books.

———. 1995b. "Liberation Theology and Ecology: Alternative, Confrontation, or Complementarity?" In *Ecology and Poverty: Cry of the Earth, Cry of the Poor.* Vol. 5 of *Concilium,* ed. Leonardo Boff and Virgil Elizondo, 67–77. Maryknoll, N.Y.: Orbis Books.

Boff, Leonardo, and Clodovis Boff. 1986. *Liberation Theology: From Confrontation to Dialogue.* Trans. Robert R. Barr. San Francisco: Harper and Row.

———. 1987. *Introducing Liberation Theology.* Trans. Paul Burns. Maryknoll, N.Y.: Orbis Books.

Boff, Leonardo, and Virgil Elizondo, eds. 1995. *Ecology and Poverty: Cry of the Earth, Cry of the Poor.* Vol. 5 of *Concilium.* Maryknoll, N.Y.: Orbis Books.

Braidotti, Rosi, et al. 1994. *Women, the Environment and Sustainable Development: Towards a Theoretical Synthesis.* London: Zed Books.

Bullard, Robert D. 1992. "Environmental Blackmail in Minority Communities." In *Race and the Incidence of Environmental Hazards,* ed. B. Bryant and P. Mohai, 82–94. Boulder, Colo.: Westview Press.

Cowell, Adrian. 1990. *Decade of Destruction: The Crusade to Save the Amazon Rainforest.* New York: Henry Holt.

Dankelman, Irene, and Joan Davidson. 1988. *Women and Environment in the Third World: Alliance for the Future.* London: Earthscan Publications.

Ferm, Deane William. 1986a. *Third World Liberation Theologies: A Reader.* Maryknoll, N.Y.: Orbis Books.

――――. 1986b. *Third World Liberation Theologies: An Introductory Survey.* Maryknoll, N.Y.: Orbis Books.

――――. 1988. *Profiles in Liberation: 36 Portraits of Third World Theologians.* Mystic, Conn.: Twenty-Third Publications.

Galer, Nora, Virginia Guzmán, and María Gabriela, eds. 1985. *Mujer y desarrollo.* Lima: Flora Tristán.

Garcia, Ismael. 1987. *Justice in Latin American Theology of Liberation.* Atlanta: John Knox.

Gebara, Ivone. 1989. *Mary, Mother of God, Mother of the Poor.* Maryknoll, N.Y.: Orbis Books.

――――. 1995. "Cosmic Theology: Ecofeminism and Panentheism." In *Readings in Ecology and Feminist Theology,* ed. Mary Heather MacKinnon and Moni McIntyre, 208–13. Kansas City: Sheed and Ward.

――――. 1996. "The Trinity and Human Experience." In *Women Healing Earth: Third World Women on Ecology, Feminism, and Religion,* ed. Rosemary Radford Ruether, 13–23. Maryknoll, N.Y.: Orbis Books.

Gibellini, Rosino. 1995. "The Theological Debate on Ecology." In *Ecology and Poverty: Cry of the Earth, Cry of the Poor.* Vol. 5 of *Concilium,* ed. Leonardo Boff and Virgil Elizondo, 125–34. Maryknoll, N.Y.: Orbis Books.

Gruen, Lori, and Dale Jamieson, eds. 1994. *Reflecting on Nature: Readings in Environmental Philosophy.* Oxford: Oxford University Press.

Gudynas, Eduardo. 1995. "Ecology from the Viewpoint of the Poor." In *Ecology and Poverty: Cry of the Earth, Cry of the Poor.* Vol. 5 of *Concilium,* ed. Leonardo Boff and Virgil Elizondo, 106–14. Maryknoll, N.Y.: Orbis Books.

Guha, Ramachandra. 1989. "Radical American Environmentalism and Wilderness Preservation: A Third World Critique." *Environmental Ethics* 11 (spring): 71–83.

Gutiérrez, Gustavo. 1980. "The Irruption of the Poor in Latin America and the Christian Communities of the Common People." In *The Challenge of Basic Christian Communities,* ed. Sergio Torres and John Eagleson, trans. John Drury, 107–23. Maryknoll, N.Y.: Orbis Books.

————. 1988. *A Theology of Liberation: History, Politics, and Salvation*. Trans. and ed. Sister Caridad Inda and John Eagleson. Rev. ed. Maryknoll, N.Y.: Orbis Books. Originally published 1973.

————. 1994. "Option for the Poor: Assessment and Implications." *ARC: The Journal of the Faculty of Religious Studies* 22 (McGill University): 61–71.

Haight, Roger. 1985. *An Alternative Vision: An Interpretation of Liberation Theology*. New York: Paulist.

Hallman, David G., ed. 1994. *Ecotheology: Voices from South and North*. Maryknoll, N.Y.: Orbis Books.

Hedström, Ingemar. 1990. "Latin America and the Need for a Life-Liberating Theology." In *Liberating Life: Contemporary Approaches to Ecological Theology*, ed. Charles Birch, William Eakin, and Jay B. McDaniel, 111–24. Maryknoll, N.Y.: Orbis Books.

Hennelly, Alfred T., S.J. 1995. *Liberation Theologies: The Global Pursuit of Justice*. Mystic, Conn.: Twenty-Third Publications.

Jakowska, Sophie. 1986. "Roman Catholic Teaching and Environmental Ethics in Latin America." In *Religion and Environmental Crisis*, ed. Eugene C. Hargrove, 127–53. Athens: University of Georgia Press.

Leopold, Aldo. 1949. *A Sand County Almanac and Sketches Here and There*. New York: Oxford University Press.

Lernoux, Penny. 1980. *Cry of the People: United States' Involvement in the Rise of Fascism, Torture, and Murder and the Persecution of the Catholic Church in Latin America*. Garden City, N.Y.: Doubleday.

McDonagh, Sean. 1986. *To Care for the Earth: A Call to a New Theology*. London: Geoffrey Chapman.

————. 1994. *Passion for the Earth: The Christian Vocation to Promote Justice, Peace, and the Integrity of Creation*. Maryknoll, N.Y.: Orbis Books.

McGovern, Arthur F. 1989. *Liberation Theology and Its Critics: Toward an Assessment*. Maryknoll, N.Y.: Orbis Books.

Mihevc, John. 1995. *The Market Tells Them So: The World Bank and Economic Fundamentalism in Africa*. Penang, Malaysia: Third World Network.

Oelschlaeger, Max. 1994. *Caring for Creation: An Ecumenical Approach to the Environmental Crisis*. New Haven: Yale University Press.

Price, Marie. 1994. "Ecopolitics and Environmental Nongovernmental Organizations in Latin America." *The Geographical Review* 84, no. 1 (January): 42–58.

Przewozny, Bernard. 1988. "Integrity of Creation: A Missionary Imperative." *SEDOS Bulletin* 11 (December 15): 363–74.

Rezende, Ricardo. 1994. *Rio Maria: Song of the Earth.* Trans. and ed. Madeleine Adriance. Maryknoll, N.Y.: Orbis Books.

Rio Declaration on Environment and Development. 1992.

Ryle, Martin. 1988. *Ecology and Socialism.* London: Century Hutchinson.

Sachs, Aaron. 1995. *Eco-Justice: Linking Human Rights and the Environment.* Worldwatch Paper 127 (December). Washington, D.C.: Worldwatch Institute.

Scharper, Stephen B. 1988. "Transcendence and Transformation: Gustavo Gutiérrez's Notion of Liberation and the Reductionist Critique." M.A. thesis. University of St. Michael's College, Toronto School of Theology.

Stinson, Douglass. 1993. "Sustainable Accords? Free Trade and the Environment." *Latinamerica Press* 25, no. 24 (1 July): 1.

Tinker, George E. "The Full Circle of Liberation: An American Indian Theology of Place." *Ecotheology: Voices from South and North,* ed. David Hallman, 218–24. Maryknoll, N.Y.: Orbis Books.

Vitale, Luis. 1983. *Hacia una historia del ambiente en América Latin: De las culturals aborígenes a la crisis ecológica actual.* Mexico City: Editorial Nueva Imagen.

Westra, Laura, and Peter S. Wentz. 1995. *Faces of Environmental Racism: Confronting Issues of Global Justice.* Lanham, Md.: Rowan and Littlefield.

Willis, E. David. 1985. "Proclaiming Liberation for the Earth's Sake." In *For Creation's Sake: Preaching, Ecology, and Justice,* ed. Dieter T. Hessel, 55–70. Philadelphia: Geneva Press.

Witvliet, Theo. 1985. *A Place in the Sun: An Introduction to Liberation Theology in the Third World.* Maryknoll, N.Y.: Orbis Books.

Chapter Seven: Contouring a Political Theology of the Environment

Kozol, Jonathan. 1995. *Amazing Grace: The Lives of Children and the Conscience of a Nation.* New York: Crown Publishers.

Westra, Laura. 1994. *An Environmental Proposal for Ethics: The Principle of Integrity.* Boston: Rowman and Littlefield.

Index